THE ORGANIC MASCULINE

The Organic Masculine

Lore Book I: The Magician

MATT STURM

Living Kosmos

COPYRIGHT

Published by Living Kosmos, LLC
30 N Gould St | Suite R | Sheridan, WY 82801 | USA www.livingkosmos.com
Printed in the United States of America. ISBN-13: 979-8-9904819-0-9

ADVANCED PRAISE

"This book presents a comprehensive understanding of what it means to be an upstanding man today. More importantly, it offers a methodology for men to step into their unique life-affirming masculinity. Matt Sturm is the single most efficient teacher that I have ever known. Read this book to get the foundation. And then reach out to Matt to be held accountable to the implementation. You will never regret it."

—Matt Mochary, author of *The Great CEO Within*

"The Organic Masculine deftly organizes the best consciousness maps we have today into a genuine inner workbook for genuine men serious about the sacred opportunity they've been given to evolve Human Masculinity itself. Using the forge of masculine sexuality, Sturm has created an accelerant for men to get painfully, blissfully honest with ourselves about how much of our bodies-hearts-minds-spirits we are actually bringing into our vital play power that is our life. The immense coordinating of so many tiers, stages, archetypes, lines, polarities and evolutionary processes he uses as the field of his focus shows Sturm's particular genius. But the indelible presence of the sacred and how he holds our species and all of life as precious and invaluable is his particular Blessing to us."

—Adam Gainsburg, Founder of SoulSign Astrology

"In our current zeitgeist of deep confusion contrasted by pure potential, Matt Sturm offers a much-needed way-finder in a world of uncertainty and unknowns. The Organic Masculine invites us into a love for nuance, the courage to play and the desire to thrive, all in service to awakening our inner archetypal Magician. With our Wizard Within we learn to alchemize our antiquated aspects of masculinity to activate our primordial ancestral aliveness. Realizing our creative power to do so, with confidence we can engage the friction and tension of these times to reforge our masculine identities on our own terms thus making way for whatever responsive and relevant actions urge to emerge through the depths of our individual and collective being."

—Justin Hartery, Founder of Source Embodiment Process

"Finally, a smart book of substance about men and masculinity, for anyone looking for an integral road-map that brings together wisdom from the world's leading minds. Matt deftly weaves together the mythic, spiritual, philosophical, historical and practical - while adding his own helpful critiques and personal vulnerability - into a systematic approach to understanding consciousness, the universe, and paradigms of masculinity. An ambitious book that is also deeply satisfying."

—Dr. Jessica Gold, The Thinking Man's Intimacy Coach

"Matt's exploration of masculinity is as bold and comprehensive as I've had the pleasure to explore. Who are we as humans? Where are we going? What role does masculinity play in that evolutionary process? These questions set the foundation for the important personal exploration of what does it mean to be masculine in this world at this time. Be ready to have the way you look at yourself and the world forever changed."

—Dane Holewinski, Transformational CEO coach & Founder of Decode

CONTENTS

FORWARD

I remember the moment of inception that produced *The Organic Masculine.*

Matt and I were in my kitchen in early February 2022. We had just spent a week on pilgrimage in Northern Spain and Southern France. It was a week of playing detective, piecing together bits of data on the sacred sites from medieval Jewish and Christian mysticism. This particular pilgrimage is known for its capacity to bring about the manifestation of soul purpose. At that point, it had felt like nothing more than a long road trip with good bonding time between friends, and some nice sightseeing. The morning after we returned, Matt slept in. Very unusual for him. When he finally emerged, I knew it had been a long night.

"How was your night?" I asked.

"Well, I got an insight to write a book on men's sexuality. It wouldn't let me go. I was up all night with it."

I smiled. I could see from his (rarely) disheveled appearance that this 'insight' really had gotten under his skin. It was stalking him.

For the next year and a half, I witnessed my friend and colleague devote every aspect of his life to the earnest stewardship of this Divinely inspired seed. He nurtured it across oceans, courted it through multiple relationships, and poured the totality of his life-force, time, and love into making tangible the vision that claimed him that February. Perhaps I am one of only a few that knows the excruciating intimacy with which he metabolizes his direct experience of all that was coming through his channel. Matt's courage to surrender home, work, identity, tribe, and personal belongings to stay clear as a conduit for this next-level vision is rare in today's world. As I witnessed the manuscript come into form, I watched my friend emerge into a deeper embodied expression of his gifts, a clear and articulate channel of wisdom, and a deeply available human being for life and love. What he has brought into form is a modern-day map of authentic masculinity.

At the heart of this map is Ken Wilbur's integral model which lends helpful understanding of the phases of consciousness. Yet Matt is bold enough to challenge some of Wilbur's limiting ideas around archetype as well as expound beyond the lens of consciousness into the expression of masculinity through sexuality and relationship in each of the phases. This new and accurate perspective makes the integral map applicable in a way that addresses many limitations to current day masculinity.

In my experience working with men over the last decade through eastern tantric and western shadow work modalities, sexuality is either deeply suppressed or overtly controlling their expression of power integrated with love. *The Organic Masculine* embraces eros as an essential expression of the evolution of consciousness. This invites an engagement with sexuality not as a prescribed equation to create desired results (being a better lover, feeling empowered with your woman), but as an innate expression of the soul in its own evolutionary journey. This relaxation of tension around what should be, into an affirmation of what is naturally frees up a man's vitality allowing sexuality to move into its next authentic phase of expression. Here, even the shadow aspects of sexuality when consciously embraced are part of a man's recognition of his wholeness, not his lack. Matt's wisdom offers a compassionate context for being honest about sexuality, while offering a steady handrail to help men claim more of what is possible in relation to his sexuality (and consciousness).

This book includes all aspects of masculinity in a loving totality. It acknowledges the inherent necessity of what has been, what is, and what is possible. Patriarchy, the Woke Movement, and all expressions in between are revealed as parts of a constituent 'whole masculine' that is continually evolving. What is outlined here is not a redefinition of outdated masculinity; it is the very groundwork for a *total masculinity*. Not one man will embody its entirety, but each man in his own authentic meeting of his unique expression will inhabit his essential part.

Most men's books today speak to specific growth edges in the male experience, which are helpful on an individual front. This book's scope makes it applicable and inclusive of all men regardless of where they stand on the spectrum of embodied masculinity. Matt synthesizes multiple streams of wisdom - the psyche, consciousness, sexuality, mundane life, relationships, spirituality and purpose - and skillfully relates them to now times. From his embodied experience, Matt shares personal anecdotes and stories bringing poignant meaning to his thesis. His compassionate guidance invites a personalized entry into this vast material opening the doors for intimate transformation in addition to context and understanding. This workbook is a journey through one's personal healing into the inherent participation within a whole, coherent system. It carves out a path for a new paradigm, not just a new man.

As a woman reading this book it spoke to me on multiple levels. I came into deeper recognition of my own inner masculine and the driving influences informing my experience of eros and transcendence. Perhaps most enlightening to me was the original explication of masculinity through sexuality and relationship through the integral paradigms. This lent profound understanding to my intuitive sense of my own relationship journey with 'other,' as well as a deep-felt recognition of how to support others in the paradigm of relationship they are currently available for.

Matt's qualitative road map looks through the lens of the core needs in each paradigm and the expression of sexuality and relationship that emerges from this. This answers profound questions of why men do what they do. As a mother, a daughter, a partner and lover I find even more compassion and choice in my engagement with the men in my life. This is profoundly empowering.

Matt has offered men and women a great service with this book. If you are on a quest for deeper embodiment, and if you are on the path of evolution into an integrated whole, *The Organic Masculine* offers the best map to date for masculinity and challenges you to engage completely in your process of becoming.

Katherine Zorensky
August 2023
beingkatherinez.com
Axioms of Grace Podcast

ACKNOWLEDGEMENTS AND DEDICATION

Begin by acknowledging the source of the teachings to dispel all confusion.

—Tibetan proverb

I owe my thanks to the many people who have served as teachers and guides for me on my path. Adam Gainsburg's Open Heart modality informs much of my approach to living this human life. Agama Yoga, Daniella Cotreau, and Eagle all shaped me through yoga. In addition to Agama, I owe thanks to Charles Muir for teaching me energetic and sexual practices. The somatic, therapeutic, and meditative aspects described here are inspired by my study of Hakomi psychotherapy and Reggie Ray's somatic meditation. Thank you to Pamela Eakins for opening the door to the Western Mystery tradition to me. I'd like to share my deepest gratitude to Asha Eden Rose and my teachers of expanded states of consciousness—you know who you are. Thank you to Anani Rose for editing the first version of this manuscript, for your whole-hearted commitment and dedication to what this work could become. Thank you to Katherine Zorensky for your unwavering support and enthusiasm. Thank you to all awakened beings who are speaking through these pages.

Whatever new synthesis this work presents is built upon original theses of many courageous pioneers who've come before. Most notably, these include Alfred North Whitehead, Carl Jung, Robert Moore & Douglas Gillette, Jon Eisman, Ken Wilber, and Susan Cook-Greuter.

May these teachings be of benefit to all who encounter them. May the healing and awakening that is catalyzed here ripple outward to all beings everywhere to support our journeys of realizing wholeness.

INVOCATION

by Anani Rose, editor

For your courage, I honor you.
For your work and introspection,
For your willingness to look at what is
And who you are deep in your shadows
And to say yes to change,
I honor you.

For following the call that I could be *MORE*, do *MORE*,
That WE have been called here for a higher purpose, men
For your willingness to burn what was and no longer serves in the pyres of yesterday—
To look at the world calling for more authentic you,
Next to your brothers saying *YES* That WE can do so much more—
For ourselves
For each other
For our families and the planet,
We say YES to our greatness.

Thank you—
For hearing the call of the wild and reclaimed Divine Masculine.
This is transformation
Steeped in centuries-long battles
This is ability to affect global change
This is radical freedom within self
As what it means to be a man is reborn—

Welcome
To the revolution, my brothers,
It begins now, within you.

INTRODUCTION

What does it mean to be a man? Each generation of men is challenged to answer this question. But intellectual definitions pale in comparison with our actions. The poetry of our lives provides the truest definition of manhood. How do I want to live as a man? For men today, this question demands a scope and immediacy that is far beyond what was asked of our fathers and grandfathers. The very core of masculinity is being questioned in the collective dialogue. Is it still a good thing to be a man? Does masculinity even mean anything? Do we need a return to traditional values, or shall we deconstruct the masculine gender altogether?

In these pages, you'll find my answers to the question of manhood. I recognize both the good and the shadow of traditional values of masculinity. Similarly, deconstructing the social conditioning of gender has both benefits and limits. These approaches will only take us so far. Neither tradition nor poststructuralism will suffice to meet the challenges of our generation. What is being called for today is a new masculinity, and each one of us, across all genders, has a part to play in shaping it.

By my reckoning, now is the most exciting time in the past ten thousand years to be a man. Today's cultural changes around masculinity are historically unprecedented. With the beginning of agriculture, the farming villages that would become Western civilization developed a mythology for what it means to be a man. It's a man's job to *fight, rule*, and *provide*. This mythology has been with us in various forms all throughout Western history. Now in the twenty-first century, our culture has largely deconstructed this myth about men and will continue to do so. Today, it is no longer true that it is a man's job to fight, rule, and provide. Let's consider each of these three roles.

In our globalized village, who is there left to fight? The wars the West has engaged in over the last fifty years have neither been noble nor just. In past centuries, men would be summoned to battlefields to band together with their brothers and fight to the death to protect what they held most precious in life. Very few battlefields today offer a rite of passage into warriorship. Nor is physical combat even a relevant skillset for the average man today. We no longer live in a world where it is a man's job to fight.

Nor is it a man's job to rule. We have no evidence that our society is best served by political and economic power being held primarily by men. In fact, we have compelling data to suggest that societies that share power and authority equally between genders are more resilient, more cooperative, and invest more in future generations.

It is no longer true that we need men to provide for their wives because women are not strong enough or smart enough to provide for themselves. If this argument was ever true, it was tenuous at best. But today, there can be no doubt that it is not men's role in society to provide for women.

That said, we still need both men and women to provide for children, for the elderly, and for their communities.

However, the ways we've been providing are fundamentally broken. Our economic system is chopping, mining, and polluting ecosystems and calling that value creation. Over the last two hundred years, modernization has begun the sixth mass-extinction event in the history of this planet. It is the great *Anthropocene extinction*. We are threatening to annihilate our civilization and most of the complex life on this planet along with us. Consider this: if you are investing your savings and retirement in the stock market, you are voting with your dollars to maximize profit at the expense of the earth. The result is that we're handing the next generation a dying planet.

So if it is no longer our role as men to fight, rule, and provide, where does that leave us? Masculinity is having an identity crisis. Today, the mythology that informs our social structures is being recognized for what it is—a collective belief system. Incredible pressures are arising both internally and externally for our culture to change the meaning of masculinity. The voices of those who've been marginalized and oppressed by *hegemonic masculinity* are now being centered in our social dialogue. This is the internal pressure. Our global degradation of ecosystems and biodiversity will dismantle our civilization within a matter of decades on our current trajectory. This is the external pressure. Change is happening, and masculinity is ground zero.

I want to share more about this term *hegemonic masculinity* and why I think we should be using it over other terms like *patriarchy* or *toxic masculinity*. *Hegemony* is a word that means "dominant power." So *hegemonic masculinity* describes a social system where a small group of men wield power and authority over other groups. This dominating force is exploiting and oppressive toward subordinated groups, which include women, other genders, minority races and classes, other sexual preferences, other religions, and even other men. I use this term because it is precise. *Toxic masculinity* can mean just about anything. The term *patriarchy* tends to include all men in a social system. But there are many groups of men, for example, gay men, who face oppression in our system. Hegemonic masculinity illuminates the core distortion, which is men dominating and wielding power over others.

I've been engaging in men's work for over a decade now. Most men I meet have experienced the violence and exploitation of other men throughout their lives. At the same time, most men also benefit from this power structure in subtle, sometimes invisible ways. At least, my privilege was invisible to me before I started studying it.

When I was growing up, I saw the cruelty and greed of men in power, and I said to myself, "I'll never be one of *those men*." I made a judgment and then a promise to myself. I variously felt anger, resentment, despair, grief, fear, and self-righteousness toward the ways I saw men acting in the world. All of this stemmed from an even deeper feeling of helplessness. At core, I had a sense that being a man *could* and *should* feel right, but I absolutely could not align myself with the horrors being carried out by men in power in the world or our culture's pictures of what it means to be a "real man." What I chose instead was *disaffected masculinity*. I labeled *men* as the problem and disowned my own masculinity. My working hypothesis was that I could choose to live a non-masculine life.

Fast-forward a few decades and I now understand that disaffected masculinity enables and empowers hegemonic masculinity. By refusing to stand up and advocate for what is true, I am allowing those who are abusing power to go right ahead and continue. In addition, by disowning my masculinity, I was disconnected from my potency, fertility, presence, and, in general, the incredibly creative gifts that masculinity can bestow.

Reaction against violent men who disrespect and hoard has led to the rise of the sensitive nice guy. This version of masculinity is emotional, empathetic, and values cooperation. This type of man represents a significant and much-needed step forward for our planet. And yet, something is missing from this picture. In a word, it's the *killer*. The sensitive nice guy is unable to integrate the inner killer, and incapable of dealing with the outer killers making a muck of the world. Insofar as the sensitive guy is a reaction *against* something or someone, he will always be partial, never whole. This disownership brings with it masculine disempowerment. On my journey, I came to recognize the sensitive nice guy as a step on the path but not the realized picture of manhood that I was seeking.

Another example of what I see: I know men who have been violent or abusive. They have caused serious harm with their unchecked aggression. And I have seen them internalize the judgment that *men are the problem*. On my path, I pointed the finger outside and said, "You are the problem." For these men, the finger points back inside. Their judgment is "I am the problem." And this brings a crippling amount of shame along with it.

What we are lacking today is a vision of masculinity that we can uphold as honorable and true. Today, the old mythos of masculinity is burning in the fires of transformation. What we've inherited from the past is falling apart—massively, catastrophically, existentially. Like the forest that utilizes the wildfire to go to seed, the destruction of old masculine structures presents us with the opportunity to plant seeds for a new vision of what it means to be a man and, ultimately, what it means to be human. This is why it's such an exciting time to be exploring masculinity. What we envision and embody in the coming decades will set a new imprint for the next ten thousand years to come. This will be remembered as the turning point.

This book series presents my forays into a contemporary vision for masculinity, what I call *the organic masculine*. Here in *Lore Book I: The Magician*, we'll explore the archetype of the Magician and understand masculinity within the context of our evolving consciousness. This first book lays the foundation for the following three books in the series, *The Warrior, The Lover,* and *The Monarch*. As a whole, these books will present a cutting-edge immersion into manhood across consciousness, sexuality, embodiment, and sovereignty. I don't hold my perspectives as the universal new truth. Rather, I am offering my insights and field notes as your brother walking a parallel path of growth and discovery.

Your answer to the question of manhood is what really matters. This next vision of masculinity cannot come through any top-down, proscriptive mode. Rather, each of us will discover our truths by looking within. Therefore, this material is presented as a series of *workbooks*. I'll be inviting you to actively engage with these concepts to find your authentic masculinity. What I am presenting here is my map of the terrain. It is up to you to make the journey. I don't expect that you'll agree with everything I have to say—I make unapologetically radical claims about manhood and reality. Nor do I presume to have everything figured out. Please read with discernment. I offer these workbooks as the raw material for you to craft your own masterpiece. My hope is that the inspiration sparked here will take you deep into your exploration.

Given that context, I'd like to share some of my story with you.

I was raised as a white, cisgendered, hetero-passing guy in a Catholic, upper-middle-class family in middle America. I grew up within the privileged in-group of society across pretty much all categories. I don't hold my upbringing as better or worse than anyone else's, but it's important for me to acknowledge the social privileges I've benefited from, and the blind-spots that I hold as a result.

Within this upbringing, the messaging that I internalized was that I need to hide my sexuality and save it until marriage; the erotic impulses that I do feel are sinful and worthy of shame; being a man means repressing my emotions and not being weak; my worth as a man is measured by my performance in academics and sports; and in order to safely exist as a man among women, I need to diminish my power and caretake women's feelings.

Meanwhile, I witnessed other men acting out in violence, abusing power and authority, disrespecting boundaries, and selfishly hoarding resources. So as I entered adulthood, I explored alternatives to the dominant masculine script. I delved into feminine expressions of myself. Wearing eyeliner and a dress, I gave myself permission to express my turn-on without shame.

I also explored my attraction to men. Though I'm primarily attracted to women, queer identification offered me an inroad into gay subculture. I was drawn to queer community, in part, because I could inhabit masculine roles outside of hegemonic masculinity. In gay culture, I felt free to flirt and express my desires without feeling like I was demeaning or oppressing anyone. I felt safe to be strongly sexual.

At the age of twenty-nine, my travels took me to a yoga school in Thailand where I discovered sexual neo-tantra. Here, I participated in rituals to name and release the sexual shame I'd been carrying my entire life. I discovered tools to have more connected sex—something that my partner at the time and I had been in deep struggle around. I encountered a wholly different worldview where sexuality and the body are held as inherently sacred. Unlike my Catholic upbringing, I discovered a spiritual tradition where women and men occupy spiritual leadership as equals. I was deeply moved by these ideas. More importantly, the practices that I began engaging in yielded massive changes in my life: I healed layers and layers of sexual wounding; I started learning how to be a safe, attuned lover while connecting to my power; and I discovered my spiritual path. With all of this transformation opening for me, I devoted myself to the yogic-sexual path with a passion.

I almost walked away from these teachings right at the beginning though. The school was teaching partners to embody opposite polarities (i.e., the masculine and feminine archetypes). As with a magnet, polarizing with a partner creates attraction in relationship, which becomes the fuel for ongoing growth and great sex, according to the teaching.

But as a person who didn't subscribe to the dominant expression of masculinity, this polarity model wasn't working for me. I could see the logic of the teaching, but in my mind, choosing to be a sexual man meant adhering to the broken social scripts of hegemonic masculinity. When I brought this up, I will never forget what my instructor said in response: "Is there an expression of masculinity that feels authentic for you?" My entire adult life I had been disowning hetero-masculine sexuality. I felt deeply uncomfortable with the question. Up to this point, I had been funneling my sexual desires through my queer and feminine sides.

From this prompt, I took it upon myself to choose my own path into masculinity. I had to find my version: one that honored my values and represented me. If I was going to wear this label of masculinity, including all its baggage, it was going to be something that I had digested and formulated all the way through, something I could stand behind and be proud of. Discovering my authentic masculinity would call me to release my blame toward "those kinds of men" and to forgive myself for being a man. It would open me to reclaim sexual masculinity within myself, to own my desires, and to take responsibility for the power that I hold. This exploration has grown into a primary passion in my life. To my amazement, I have been discovering that masculinity offers a vast treasure chest for empowerment, maturation, and self-realization.

The Organic Masculine

The Organic Masculine is my term for any form of masculinity that is life affirming. This essence of masculinity is alive, empowered, generative, and compassionate. It is wise, creative, and loving. The organic masculine is sacred in the way that all of life is sacred. The existence of such a masculinity is the core thesis of this book. Inviting you into the *direct embodied experience* of life-affirming masculinity is why it's a workbook not a philosophical treatise.

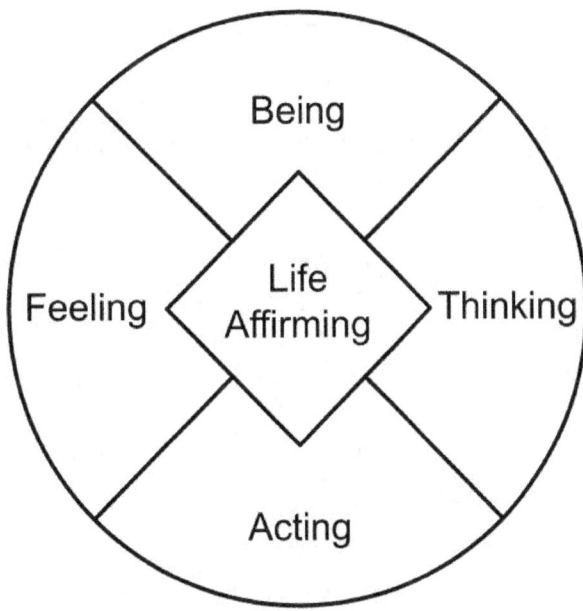

Figure i. The four quadrants of the organic psyche

This deeper experience of masculinity is available to each human, inclusive of sex, gender, and orientation. It is universal. The organic masculine does not represent one fixed picture of manhood. In fact, each individual's experience of the organic masculine is wholly unique and constantly evolving. How do we know the organic masculine when we see it? Janine Benyus famously observed, "Life creates the conditions conducive to life." When the masculine is thinking, feeling, acting, and being in ways that support the flourishing of life, that is the organic masculine. I illustrate the four quadrants of the psyche in fig i, above.

This essential nature of masculinity does not stand alone. The organic masculine forms a triad with the organic feminine and the organic androgyne, which I similarly define as *life-affirming* gender archetypes. I use the organic androgyne to be inclusive of gender expressions that are (a) both masculine and feminine, (b) neither masculine nor feminine, and (c) third genders.[1] Masculinity, femininity, and androgyny are high archetypes. Each holds archetypes within itself, for example, the wild woman within the organic feminine. At the same time, each can be accessed as an archetype fully itself. These high archetypes fit together with the four quadrants of the psyche to create a bi-cone shape (fig. ii). I'll go into detail on these three high-archetypes later on. Together, they form a symbolic tapestry that we can use to access our centers and the ordering and life-giving energies of the kosmos. Aligning with these archetypes connects us to the creative flow of life.

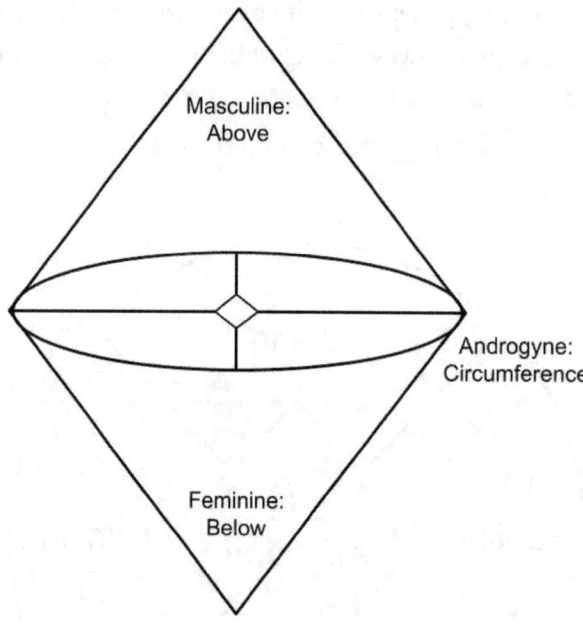

Figure ii. The three gendered high-archetypes

Sexuality

Throughout these pages, I utilize sexuality as a tool for exploration. For me, sex offers the most primary, direct access to understanding masculinity. How I have sex, why I have sex, and who

I get to be during sex have shown me the deepest truths about my masculinity. Sex reveals my primal motivations, beliefs, and wounds. In addition, sex opens me to my purest love, strongest passion, and inherent vitality. Sexual energy is the creative energy of life itself. For these reasons, I think of sex as a *magical window* into my core. Sure, sex feels great, and that's wonderful, but that's only part of the picture. As a tool for healing, personal growth, and self-realization, sexuality is unparalleled.

Desire is the motivating force for my journey in life. On a soul level, I came into human form to learn certain lessons, heal certain wounds, and shine my unique light back into the kosmos. The desires of my body and heart point me directly to my life path. So, by receiving my desires, I align to my truth. Once I open to my desires, they make a claim on me to be responsive to them. Enacting my desires is a fiercely courageous act because it always leads me from known safety into the new. As I engage with these attractions and aversions, triggers and ecstasies, I open myself to be touched by life. This is sexual alchemy. Opening to life without reservation is the ultimate sexual act in which my essence is re-created through naked contact with reality. In this sense, desire and sexuality go far beyond intercourse. The full measure of sexuality is an uninhibited *YES* to communion with the ever-new, present moment. It is the birthright of each and every one of us if we dare to choose it. Throughout this series of workbooks, I'll invite you to explore sex as a tool for healing, as a method of empowerment, and as a doorway into union with all that is.

To be honest, sex has generally been challenging for me. I've struggled with premature ejaculation and impotence. I grew up with a daily porn addiction. I've worked through layer after layer of performance pressure and shame. My deepest codependence, my core unworthiness, and my fear of not belonging all rise to the surface through sex. I've variously worn the hats of sexual victim, perpetrator, and savior. It's not because I'm an all-star of epic sex or a paragon of masculinity that I sat down to write this book. Rather, it's by embracing these deep struggles that I've entered the process of transforming my wounds into medicine. The wisdom I've gained through the depth of my journey is what I have to share here—no more and no less. For those who are called to this path of self-becoming, may this book be a resource.

Notes

[1] "The original human nature was not like the present, but different. The sexes were not two as they are now, but originally three in number; there was man, woman, and the union of the two, having a name corresponding to this double nature, which had once a real existence, but is now lost, and the word 'Androgynous' is only preserved as a term of reproach." *Symposium*, Plato.

WHAT IS MASCULINITY ANYWAY?

To begin, take a breath. Slow down with me. Feel into your body. Allow your awareness to center in the space of your heart. What I'd like you to do is: ask your heart to show you an experience you had of masculinity. When did you experience the masculine, either within yourself or through an interaction with another? The story of what happened and any judgments around it are less relevant. What you're going for is the recognition that *this* was an experience of masculinity. You may have to move through some layers of hurt, shame, or anger in this exploration. Take your time. You don't have to try to dig something up. Trust your heart to show you.

When your heart naturally and innately recognizes masculinity, that is the true masculine.

All other perspectives presented here are footnotes to this statement. There is no singular definition for masculine traits. Masculinities are as diverse as the colors of the rainbow. And yet, I know it when I feel it. Whatever it is for you, trust that. This is our foundation.

Masculinity is not solely found within. It is also relational, and indeed it spans all layers and levels of the kosmos. So in order to describe masculinity, let's take a very brief tour of the realms of consciousness (*fig. iii.*).

Realm	Description
High Causal	Primal differentiations of Spirit
Causal	Archetypes and symbols
Subtle	Identities and expressions
Gross	Physical bodies

Figure iii. Realms of consciousness

The gross realm is our physical three-dimensional reality. It includes our bodies and all physical matter. The subtle realm consists of biofield energy (i.e., prana, chi, eroticism), emotions, thoughtforms, and dream imagery. It holds human identities and expressions. The causal realm is the layer where the archetypes and symbols live. These are transpersonal patterns of meaning that are universally accessible by all humans. Above causal is the high causal realm, which is where the primal differentiations of Spirit exist. This realm includes polarities like subject/object and light/dark. The high causal realm can either be viewed as the first step down from unity consciousness or the last step up before pure awareness.

The masculine, feminine, and androgyne express through these states of consciousness: gross, subtle, causal, and high causal (*fig. iv.*).

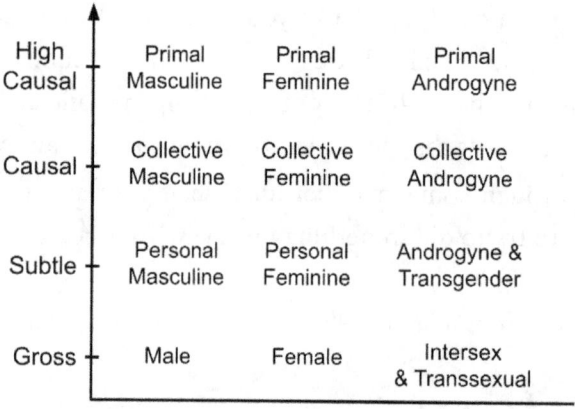

Figure iv. Sexual diversification through realms of consciousness

At the gross level, sex is determined by biology and physiology. These are the physical structures, functions, and hormones of bodies as male, female, and intersex.[1] Each of these categories exists on a spectrum of diverse embodiment and carries social conditioning along with it. We'll dive into these nuances in later chapters.

The subtle realm is the next level of refinement in consciousness. This level is composed of subtle-energies and thoughtforms. Here, we have masculinities, femininities, and androgynies as genders. These are not physical manifestations. Rather, they are the categories of meaning that we attribute to behavior and identity. At the subtle level, gender is held and experienced by each individual. My *gender identity* is how I experience a particular gender as a part of me. My *gender expression* is how my behavior and social signaling is interpreted by others about my gender.

Stepping up to the causal realm, this layer holds the archetypes. These symbols are transpersonal, and thus, they are larger than any single individual. Carl Jung asserted that these patterns exist in the collective unconscious where the myths and dream symbols across all cultures and ages are sourced from.[2] Archetypes are universal. Here, we have the various archetypes of masculinity, femininity, and androgyny. They have the quality of being *overdetermined*, which means multiple layers of interpretation are simultaneously valid. There is no singular definition for archetypes at the exclusion of other meanings.

Finally, in the high casual realm, we have the primal masculine, feminine, and androgyne. Here, the masculine defines itself in polarity and contrast with the feminine. It is through this polarity that the masculine and feminine know themselves and each other. As I will explore more, below, there is no singular or definitive way that the masculine and feminine polarize, which means there are no universal gender traits. It is always contextually dependent. The primal androgyne, in most spiritual traditions, is the precursor to the polarized masculine and feminine. This first blueprint for human possibility includes all genders and expressions.

Thus, in my view, there is a principle of masculinity and maleness that constellates through the physical, individual, and transpersonal layers of reality. Following Rupert Sheldrake, we can call this a *morphic field*: an organizing pattern of influence in consciousness.[3] Each of the masculine, feminine, and androgyne patterns exist as morphic fields.

The high-archetype of masculinity is held in the collective unconscious and thus is not fully knowable. It expresses through its morphic field in mythology, gender, and sex. The high-archetype is singular though unbounded. As the high-archetype of masculinity condenses downward through gender and sex, it becomes infinitely diverse. This means there is no singular, correct version of masculine gender.[4]

In addition, the morphic field of masculinity is constantly evolving. It remembers all past instances and, in each new moment, is growing, improvising, and mutating. Sheldrake calls the capacity of fields to evolve *morphic resonance*.[5] So masculinity, in addition to possessing an unbounded number of expressions, is continually changing.[6]

Morphic resonance is one aspect of the larger fundamental drive of the kosmos to evolve, which I call *Eros*.[7] We live in an evolving universe that has moved from an undifferentiated beginning through continuous evolution toward greater complexity, beauty, and wholeness. Eros is the universal drive of *becoming*. As the universe evolves, the masculine, feminine, and androgyne evolve along with it.

Given that the masculine is infinitely varied, ever changing, and can never be fully known, it becomes difficult to say anything definitive about it. But here is what we can affirm: the masculine is one half of a primal pair of opposites that define themselves through contrast with each other. The masculine is that which polarizes with the feminine.

In *figure v.*, below, I provide a few examples of masculine and feminine polarities from diverse traditions. Notice that each pair of polarities stands on its own. However, there is no correlative or logically indicative link between these pairs. For instance, the masculine role of *provider* has no particular claim on the traits of *structure, consciousness*, or *skillful means*. I could even make the argument that the masculine *provider* is more closely related to the feminine *flow* of resources, while the feminine *nurturer* creates the nest or masculine *structure*. Similarly, at first glance, *consciousness* would appear to be more aligned with *perfect insight*, and *form* with *skillful means*. So, even within related traditions (i.e., Buddhist and Hindu versions of tantra), there is not a uniform agreement on the masculine and feminine. The masculine is that which, in a given expression, polarizes with the feminine. They are contextually descriptive rather than universally definitive. The masculine defines itself through polarity, intercourse, and communion with the feminine.

Masculine	Feminine	Source
Provider	Nurturer	Western cultural norm[8]
Structure	Flow	David Deida[9]
Consciousness	Form	Sāṃkhya philosophy[10]
Skillful means	Perfect insight	Tibetan tantra[11]
Aggressive	Passive	Biological determinism[12]
Autonomy	Communion	Object relations theory[13]

Figure v. Examples of masculine/feminine polarities

If the masculine and feminine define themselves through differentiation from each other, then the androgyne is all of the blended, multiple, othered, trans, and queer permutations of gender that play in the spaces in between. The androgyne is not solely one pole and not solely the other pole. Queer and trans subcultures have been blossoming in current times, but the mythology of the androgyne reaches all the way back through recorded history. This signals the archetypal nature of the androgyne, which is timeless, universal, and collective.

The Divine Hermaphrodite may be the most universally recognized symbol of Spirit. Virtually every theistic religion starts with an Original Being who embodies both male and female.

—Jenny Wade[14]

Just two examples: in Jewish mythology, Adam Kadmon, the primal human, is depicted as a man-woman;[15] and in Hinduism, Ardhanārīśvara is the half-male, half-female god.[16] Both Eastern and Western myth access the high-archetype of the androgyne (see *figures vi. and vii.*, below).

More broadly, archetypes open a channel to tremendous amounts of raw life force. Freud and Jung called it *libido*. In these workbooks, I'll refer to it as *erotic energy*. By connecting to the archetypes we create a link for their unbounded energy to flow into our individual form.

Figure vi., left, Symbola Aureae Mensae (1617)
Figure vii., right, Ardhanārīśvara, sixth century. Rajasthan, India

Myth is the secret opening through which the inexhaustible energies of the cosmos pour into human cultural manifestation.

—Joseph Campbell[17]

Connecting to an archetypal energy can be so powerful that the ego can be consumed or shattered by it. Carl Jung describes the psychological journey of *individuation* primarily as a process of separating the ego from the unconscious rule of the archetypes. The goal of connecting to archetypal energy is to develop enough resilience in the self to integrate the energy. This is known as centering within the ego-archetype axis.[18] If I'm solely in the ego, there is no transpersonal life-force download. Entirely in the archetype means there is no way to guide the primal energies that hold equal potential for destruction and creation. Finding the healthy point of balance between ego and archetype is key.

In addition, we care about archetypes because they hold the transformational mechanism for maturation, known as initiation. By my count, the masculine grows through four developmental archetypes, or life-stages: the Golden Boy, the Hero, the Man, and the Elder. Initiation is the process that graduates us from one life stage to the next. Without initiation, we get stuck.

The Golden Boy is the masculine child archetype. He is carefree, innocent, playful, and precocious. He is protected and cared for by adults. When the Golden Boy separates from the safety of the Mother figure, he grows into the Hero. Also called the Prince, this archetype is about adventure, glory, conquest, building skills, romance, and brotherhood. When the Hero chooses to make *the willing sacrifice*, he initiates into Manhood. This stage also includes the Father archetype. The Man takes on responsibility, service, leadership, and fertility. As the Man matures, he opens to the mysteries of life and accrues wisdom. When the Man offers his active leadership to the next generation, he becomes the Elder. The role of the Elder is mentorship and guidance. He carries the wisdom traditions and acts as the bridge to the unseen realms. In the coming chapters, we'll explore these four archetypal life stages in more depth.

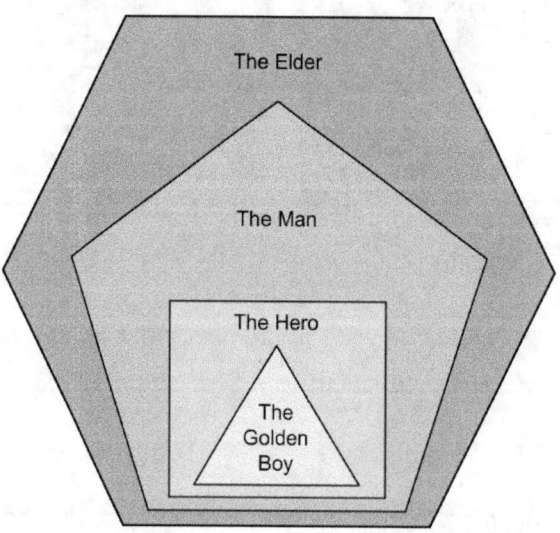

Figure viii. Archetypal progression of the masculine

In addition to the life stages, there are four masculine archetypes that describe the parts of the psyche.[19] These are the King, the Warrior, the Magician, and the Lover. Put forward by Moore and Gillette, these four archetypes have been a cornerstone of the men's movement since the

1990s. While my version of the four archetypes is inspired by Moore and Gillette, I incorporate some notable additions and changes.

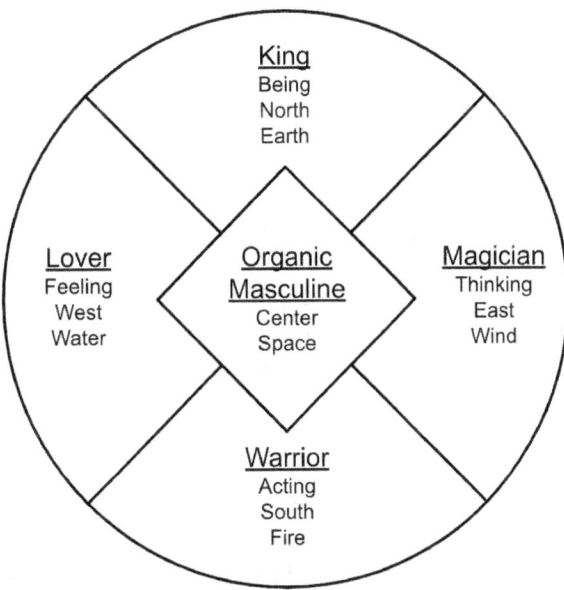

Figure ix. The archetypal masculine psyche

In the figure above, I illustrate the four archetypes of the masculine psyche. When I am operating as the masculine, I am connected to one of these four energies. The King, Warrior, Magician, and Lover each have a vast variety of sub-flavors that are both individually and culturally interpreted. Some of the flavors are wounded or immature. Other flavors are healthy and mature: organic. These four archetypes correspond to the four qualities of the organic psyche: being, thinking, acting, and feeling (see *fig. i.* in the introduction). In addition, I map them to the four cardinal directions and the four elements. Together they form a mandala, which is a universal symbol for wholeness.[20]

The mandala represents the outer universe as well as the inner psyche, the totality of which, I refer to as the *kosmos*. Whereas the term *cosmos* refers to the scientifically measurable universe, the ancient Greeks used the term *kosmos* (κόσμος) to be inclusive of the seen and unseen aspects of existence.[21]

At the center of the mandala is the element of space. Symbolically, the center is where the magic happens.[22] This is where we connect with the life-giving energies of the archetypes. At the center, we encounter the sacred, regenerative, and ordering qualities of life. Buddha nature, the atman, and the Divine all reside at the center.[23] This is where we access and integrate the organic masculine.

Each of the four quadrants touches the center and has its unique transcendent expression in the center. It is through the process of initiation that we, as individuals, develop our King, Warrior, Magician, and Lover, which in turn, provide access to the organic masculine at the center.

In all humans, masculinity is just one aspect of self, which will be integrated into waking consciousness to greater or lesser degrees. In addition, we each have the feminine and the androgyne. These three high-archetypes exist in the collective unconscious, making them universally accessible to all humans. Each one integrates and matures through initiation and each offers unique access to the center.

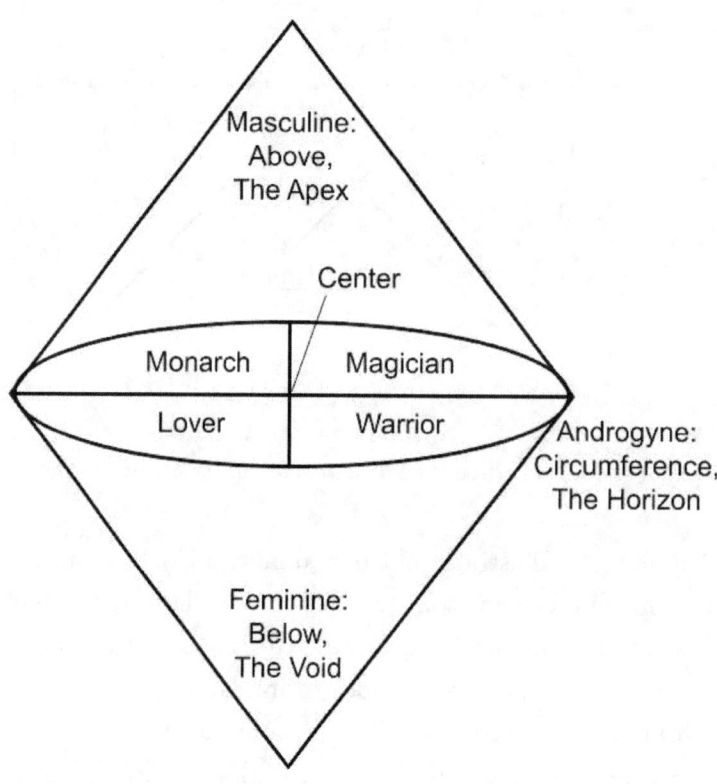

Figure x. Archetypal structure of the psyche

Putting it all together now, figure x. above illustrates the gender-archetypal structure of the psyche. This is an expansion on the simpler illustration, figure ii., in the introduction. Here, the gender-neutral archetype of the Monarch is listed instead of the King. The Monarch, Warrior, Magician, and Lover are accessible (indeed integral) to all humans spanning all sexes and genders. The symbolic shape of the psyche is mirrored in mythology, like the Babylonian shape of the universe (fig xi.), and in physics in the shapes of spiral galaxies (fig xii.).

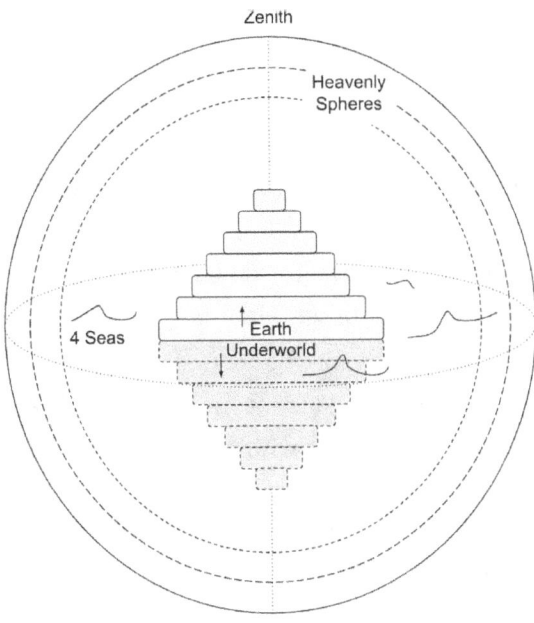

Figure xi. The Babylonian universe[24]

Figure xii. Spiral galaxies with relativistic jets[25]

Symbolically, masculine initiation happens through the journey to the apex. The *above* direction provides the masculine access into the center. The apex shows up mythically as the sacred mountain, the pyramid, the pillar, the phallus, the cross, the heavens, and the tree.

As the feminine and masculine define themselves through polarity with each other, the feminine's access to the center is opposite and counterbalancing to the masculine's apex. The feminine enters the sacred through a descent—her direction is below where she encounters the void. Symbolically, we see this as the cave, the underworld or the earth, the tomb, the womb, the yoni, and the temple.

The androgyne genders are *both* and *neither* and *something different altogether.* This multiplicity is how the androgyne enters the center. They move from the known toward the circumference: the periphery, the edge, the fringe. At a certain point, hir bearings are lost and through this disorientation, they reach the horizon. Paradoxically, the horizon is the center. Symbols include the mirror, the portal, the labyrinth, sexual union, marriage, and dismemberment.

The King and the Queen hold unique positions for the masculine and feminine. While this archetype is one of the four quadrants, it is also the fruition of them all. The masculine initiation at the apex *is* the King. Similarly, the feminine initiation into the void *is* the Queen. The King and Queen utilize the other three archetypes for foundation and support. In my view, the Monarch does not hold this unique position for the Androgyne. Mythologically, the Androgyne's reigning archetype is the Magician, which is consistent with hir role as the one who doesn't fit in and as the trickster. Please don't take this as dogma though. Feel into it for yourself.

Now, finally, I am ready to offer my full answer to the question posed in the title of this chapter: *What is masculinity anyway?* In my view, masculinity is experienced through the heart of each individual. This recognition is natural and innate. It provides the foundation for each of us to understand masculinity. The masculinity that we touch directly is one member of a primordial trinity of sexual diversification in the kosmos together with the feminine and the androgyne. Masculinity defines itself contextually through polarization with the feminine. It is a morphic field, a primal groove in consciousness, that constellates throughout archetype, gender, and sex.

The archetype holds the erotic potential of masculinity, which becomes actualized in gender and sex through the process of initiation. Masculinity evolves through and within each individual, each generation, each civilization, and humanity. Across every level and scale is a need to mature through the life cycle via initiation. When the maturation process stalls, then a wounded, unhealthy version of masculinity develops, which drives toward death and eventual renewal as part of the inherent intelligence of its life cycle.[26] The masculinity of Western civilization is currently in one such stall and drive toward death. In its healthy, mature state, masculinity is by his nature, life affirming. I call this *the Organic Masculine.*

Notes

[1] "Intersex refers to people with any of a multiplicity of configurations of chromosomes, genitals, and hormones that defy the simplicity of male and female distinctions." "Sexism, Hetero-sexism, and Trans* Oppression: An Integrated Perspective," Buggs, Catalano, and Wagner; quoted in *Teaching for Diversity and Social Justice*, Adams et al.

[2] "A more or less superficial layer of the unconscious is undoubtedly personal. I call it the personal unconscious. But this personal unconscious rests upon a deeper layer, which does not derive from personal experience and is not a personal acquisition but is inborn. This deeper layer I call the collective unconscious. I have chosen the term "collective" because this part of the un-conscious is not individual but universal; in contrast to the personal psyche, it has contents and modes of behaviour that are more or less the same everywhere and in all individuals. It is, in other words, identical in all men and thus constitutes a common psychic substrate of a suprapersonal nature which is present in every one of us." *Collected Works of C. G. Jung, Volume 9 (Part 1)*, Jung.

[3] "According to [my hypothesis of formative causation], the nature of things depends on fields, called morphic fields. Each kind of natural system has its own kind of field: there is an insulin field, a beech field, a swallow field, and so on. Such fields shape all the different kinds of atoms, molecules, crystals, living organisms, societies, customs, and habits of mind. Morphic fields, like the known fields of physics, are non-material regions of influence extending in space and continuing in time. They are localized within and around the system they organize. When any particular system ceases to exist, as when an atom splits, a snowflake melts, or an animal dies, its organizing field disappears from that place. But in another sense, morphic fields do not disappear: they are potential organizing patterns of influence, and can appear again physically in other times and places, wherever and whenever the physical conditions are appropriate. When they do so, they contain within themselves the memory of their previous physical existences." *The Presence of the Past*, Sheldrake.

[4] "It is clear from the new social research as a whole that there is no one pattern of masculinity that is found everywhere. We need to speak of 'masculinities', not masculinity. Different cultures, and different periods of history, construct gender differently." *The Men and the Boys*, Conell.

[5] "The process by which the past becomes present within morphic fields is called morphic resonance. Morphic resonance involves the transmission of formative causal influences through both space and time. The memory within the morphic fields is cumulative, and that is why all sorts of things become increasingly habitual through repetition. When the repetition has occurred on an astronomical scale over billions of years, as it has in the case of many kinds of atoms, molecules, and crystals, the nature of these things has become so deeply habitual that it is effectively change-less, or seemingly eternal." *The Presence of the Past*, Sheldrake.

[6] "There is abundant evidence that masculinities do change. Masculinities are created in specific historical circumstances and, as

those circumstances change, the gender practices can be contested and reconstructed." *The Men and the Boys*, Conell.

[7] "The fundamental, intrinsic, evolutionary drive of the Kosmos to evolve higher and higher wholes is the same force that produced mammals from dust and Integral from Archaic—a drive that Whitehead called 'the creative advance into novelty' and Integral calls 'Eros.'" *The Religion of Tomorrow*, Wilber.

[8] "The role of nurturer, throughout history has been frequently, and quite strictly coded as the mother's role, and with rhetoric entrenching mothers as the emotional centers of the family who formed sacred bonds with their children.... The ability to provide for children financially was a facet unique to fathers, and it justified them as 'protector[s] of children.' Also the right of the father to yield labor from his children in agrarian culture was another factor justifying paternal custody." "The Mother-Love Myth: The Effect of the Provider-Nurturer Dichotomy in Custody Cases," Caetano.

[9] "Like the ocean, the native state of the feminine is to flow with great power and no single direction. The masculine builds canals, dams, and boats to unite with the power of the feminine ocean and go from point A to point B. But the feminine moves in many directions at once. The masculine chooses a single goal and moves in that direction. Like a ship cutting through a vast ocean, the masculine decides on a course and navigates the direction: the feminine energy itself is undirected but immense, like the wind and deep currents of the ocean, ever changing, beautiful, destructive, and the source of life." *The Way of the Superior Man*, Deida.

[10] "In Sāṃkhya puruṣa signifies the observer, the 'witness'. Prakṛti includes all the cognitive, moral, psychological, emotional, sensorial and physical aspects of reality. It is often mistranslated as 'matter' or 'nature' - in non-Sāṃkhyan usage it does mean 'essential nature' - but that distracts from the heavy Sāṃkhyan stress on prakṛti's cognitive, mental, psychological and sensorial activities. Moreover, subtle and gross matter are its most derivative byproducts, not its core. Only prakṛti acts. Puruṣa and prakṛti are radically different from each other, though both are considered beginningless, eternal, and ultimately inseparable." Sāṃkhya, Lusthaus.

[11] "In a bodhisattva-yana context the ritual vajra may symbolize sunyata (emptiness) and the bell may symbolize constantly a form; or vajra will indicate skillful means (*thabs, upaya*) and bell perfect insight (*shes rab, prajna*). To the untutored layman, 'vajra' is a synonym of penis and 'padma' (lotus or bell) is a synonym of vagina....The yogin represents skillful means, his penis (vajra) is the wishfulfilling gem that enters the vagina (lotus) of the yogini whose nature is perfect insight." *Dzogchen: Sex*, Dowman.

[12] "We hypothesize that an ancestral history of frequent and violent intergroup conflict has shaped the social psychology and behavior of men in particular. Compared with women, men are more likely to engage in intergroup rivalry because for them the (reproductive) benefits, for example, in access to mates and prestige gains, sometimes outweigh the costs. Indeed, research on traditional societies shows that tribal warfare is almost exclusively the domain of men, and that male warriors have more sexual partners and greater status within their community than other men do... Thus, there is some theoretical and empirical support for the idea that men's behaviors

and cognitions are more intergroup oriented than women's. We refer to this idea as the male-warrior hypothesis." "Gender Differences in Cooperation and Competition: the Male-Warrior Hypothesis," Van Vugt et al.

[13] In this perspective, children begin life merged with their mothers, who are the sources of nourishment, love, and the primary attachment bond. As boys develop into individual, autonomous, sexual beings, they must differentiate themselves from their mothers. The masculine motivation is toward *autonomy*. Identity is defined in contrast and opposition to the feminine mother figure. Girls, in contrast, maintain their attachment bond and are able to identify with their mother figures as they mature into adolescence and adulthood. The feminine motivation is therefore *communion*.

[14] *Transcendent Sex: When Lovemaking Opens the Veil*.

[15] "And when Moses had called the genus 'man,' quite admirably did he distinguish its species, adding that it had been created 'male and female,' and this though its individual members had not yet taken shape." *Philo Vol 1*, Philo.

[16] "This is, in fact, the hermaphrodite form of a human being or animal combining characteristics of both sexes. In Indian iconography there are many examples of Ardhanārīśvara Siva in which the matted locks, half vertical eye, serpent, sacred thread, necklace of human skull, tiger's skin, and male organ are shown on the right side, and frizzled locks, normal eye, moon god, ear-pendant, one breast, beaded girdle, silken saree and anklet are shown on the left side." *SIVA Mahādeva, the Great God*, Agrawala.

[17] *The Hero with a Thousand Faces*, Campbell.

[18] "In this Ego-archetypal axis, the Ego is able to guide the archetype's enormous energies into creative expression in the world and to receive this life-giving Libido of the archetype without being overwhelmed or possessed by it." *The King Within: Accessing the King in the Male Psyche*, Gillette and Moore.

[19] "As you know, I believe, with Jung, that the four quarters of mythology show the world being quadrated, that there are four corners of the world, there are four elements. The Navajo said there are four winds. The Hindus said there are four faces of god. The early Christians said if you are going to have a complete gospel, there have to be four gospels. Jung said myths, mythic images, are the faces that instincts bring to the world. Humans quadrate the world in mythic images. There must be a four-fold instinctuality. He thought it was typology: intuition, thinking, sensation and feeling. I found out later that Tony Wolf, his lover and teacher, thought it was something else. I find that I am in her tradition. She thought that there were four structural forms of the female psyche, not four functions like Jung thought, but four structural forms. I believe there are four structural forms and that they correspond to four energies in the human soul." *The Archetype of Initiation*, Moore.

[20] Although "wholeness" seems at first sight to be nothing but an abstract idea (like anima and animus), it is nevertheless empirical in so far as it is anticipated by the psyche in the form of spontaneous or autonomous symbols. These are the quaternity or mandala symbols, which occur not only in the dreams of modern people who have never heard of them, but are widely disseminated

in the historical records of many peoples and many epochs. Their significance as symbols of unity and totality is amply confirmed by history as well as by empirical psychology. *The Collected Works of C. G. Jung, Volume 9 (Part 2)*, Jung.

[21] "Our word 'cosmos' generally refers to 'outer space.' But the word derives from the Greek kosmos (signifying 'embroidery'), which implied not a universe filled with disconnected noun-things but the orderliness and harmony of woven patterns with which the universe is embroidered and moves." *A Beginner's Guide to Constructing the Universe*, Schneider.

[22] "The navel of the world [is] the umbilical point through which the energies of eternity break into time. Thus the World Navel is the symbol of the continuous creation: the mystery of the maintenance of the world through that continuous miracle of vivification which wells within all things." *The Hero with a Thousand Faces*, Campbell.

[23] "The mandala, though only a symbol of the self as the psychic totality, is at the same time a God-image, for the central point, circle, and quaternity are well-known symbols for the deity. The impossibility of distinguishing empirically between 'self' and 'God' leads, in Indian theosophy, to the identity of the personal and supra-personal Purusha-Atman. In ecclesiastical as in alchemical literature the saying is often quoted: 'God is an infinite circle (or sphere) whose centre is everywhere and the circumference nowhere.' This idea can be found in full development as early as Parmenides." *The Collected Works of C. G. Jung, Volume 9 (Part 1)*, Jung.

[24] Derived from *The Earliest Cosmologies*, Warren.

[25] Image source: NASA/JPL-Caltech; Artist's concept of the two types of spiral galaxies that populate our universe.

[26] "Only birth can conquer death—the birth, not of the old thing again, but of something new. Within the soul, within the body social, there must be—if we are to experience long survival—a continuous 'recurrence of birth' (palingenesia) to nullify the unremitting recurrences of death." *The Hero with a Thousand Faces*, Campbell.

HOW TO USE THESE WORKBOOKS

I grew up playing all sorts of video games and board games. One of my favorite genres is the roleplaying game (RPG). In this type of game, players take on the role of characters who go on quests, explore worlds, fight monsters, and find treasure. Along the way, they level-up their stats to become more powerful. The player-characters form an adventuring party where they learn to work together. If all goes well, the player-characters advance into a state of immortal glory and fame by saving the world.

I'm here to invite you on a journey. In order to make the journey, you will need to form a party of characters. All the members of your party are internal parts of yourself. This party consists of the Magician, the Warrior, the Lover, the Queen, the androgynous Wizard (you can imagine David Bowie if you like), and the King. The Organic Masculine workbook series presents a Book of Lore for each of these members of your party. The Lore Book you are holding now is the first in this series and belongs to the Magician.

The narrator in roleplaying games is often referred to as the dungeon master (DM). My name is Matt, and I'll be your DM for this journey. I'm here to describe the world to you and to provide challenges so you can find your growth edges. As we move through the Lore Books, I'll be sharing quite a bit about my experiences. I don't expect that your experiences will be the same as mine, but hopefully it's close enough that you'll be able to translate this material into your terms when you need to.

These Lore Books describe the mythology and archetypes for each character. In addition, you will be presented with real-life quests in order to level-up. These quests will teach you how to find these characters in yourself and how to mature into healthy, powerful versions of them. Each character has a gift for you in the form of an initiation. The Magician will explain more about archetypes and initiations as we progress—after all, this is his realm of expertise.

In this first Lore Book, the Magician's gift is consciousness. This extensive section lays a metaphysical foundation, namely *Integral Theory,* which I'll be referencing throughout the subsequent workbooks. And as I mentioned above, the Magician describes how to work with archetypes and initiations so that you can most effectively engage with the inner characters that follow.

The second Lore Book is the Warrior's. In this book, we'll explore male aggression and violence. The Warrior's gift and initiation is sexual self-mastery leading to full-body nonejaculatory orgasms. True to the Warrior archetype, his initiation requires discipline, embodiment, and steadfastness. It's one that is earned through focused action and dedication.

The next Lore Book is the Lover, and it builds on the knowledge of the Magician and the action of Warrior. His gift and initiation is erotic awakening. The Lover takes us into the world of feeling, which includes facing and releasing trauma, attachment wounds, and strategic self-protective strategies. The Lover's path is one of embodiment and sensuality.

The final Lore Book is the Monarch's. This workbook covers the three gendered aspects of the Monarch: the Queen, the Androgyne, and the King. I refer to these as high-archetypes. They are distinct because they hold many archetypes within them and they are gendered, sexual typologies. These three emerge through the fruition of the Magician, Warrior, and Lover characters working together in the psyche. The Queen's gift is sacred marriage, the Androgyne's gift is breaking paradigms, and the King's gift is sovereignty. Their gifts are arranged this way because this workbook is tailored primarily toward the masculine perspective. If this was a women's workbook, the King's gift would be sacred marriage and the Queen's gift would be sovereignty. Meanwhile, if this was a transgender-focused workbook, we would break all the above paradigms, true to hir gift.

In addition to engaging with this workbook as an individual, I recommend that you explore it together with other humans. In his Lore Book, the Monarch explains everything you need to know about forming and running an effective men's group. I have found men's groups to be immensely valuable and rewarding. Each chapter in these workbooks could easily supply the topic for an evening men's gathering. If you are in a romantic or sexual partnership, there will be certain sections that will be very helpful—essential even—to read together with your partner. All of the sections would be useful to explore with your therapist, coach, or counselor. Each chapter contains prompts for journaling and discussion to invite you to engage with the material as we progress. I trust that you are starting to get a sense for the *real-world quests* that are about to come your way.

Take a nice deep breath with me.

Now, imagine a dingy pub on the outskirts of a small town in a faraway land. Inside the pub, you can overhear the bartender talking about a scourge that has beset the town—if only there were someone who could help. At a round table in the corner of the pub, we find six characters sitting down for a pint of ale.

THE MAGICIAN

The Archetype of the Magician

Figure 1.1 The Magician, Rider-Waite tarot

Tell me whence comes it that thou measurest the Universe and the limits of the Earth, thou who bearest a little body made of a little earth? Count thyself first and know thyself, and then shalt thou count this infinite Earth. And if thou canst not reckon thy body's little store of clay, how canst thou know the measures of the immeasurable?

—Palladas

The Magician is the part of my psyche that leads me into the mysteries of life. He is my curiosity about how everything works, within and without. He is my love of learning. As a seeker of truth, the Magician represents my insatiable desire to understand and to know. He inspires me to explore the universe and to answer the question "Who am I?" His magic appears both during playful fun and in deep concentration. Either way, his spells transform my world as well as my inner landscape. He inspires me to perfect my craft. The Magician accesses the esoteric powers of the kosmos. As a guide from the mundane into the sacred, he is the one who leads me into *wholeness.*

As an external agent, the Magician is a guru, mentor, or teacher. He is Merlin to King Arthur, Moses to the Israelites, and Virgil to Dante. The Magician is the steward of spiritual knowledge; he is the initiator into the mysteries; and he provides guidance for the arduous path of transformation.

By describing the qualities of the Magician in this chapter, I am opening my channel to enter into relationship with this archetype.

Figure 1.2 "Le Triomphe de Bacchus" with his wand, the thrysus[1]

The Magician's Wand

The tool of the Magician is the wand. This is how he conducts the creative life force of the kosmos into form. Consider the baton of the symphony conductor, which draws out the harmonious melodies from the orchestra. Consider a relay race where the baton is passed from runner to runner, gathering energy. The baton is the power object, and when it passes the finish line, the race is won.

Hermes/Mercury is the mythological messenger god and primordial Magician archetype within Western consciousness. He carries the caduceus, a winged staff entwined with two snakes. This staff is an alchemical symbol for the union of opposites: masculine solar energies uniting with feminine lunar energies to create a transcendent third. It can also be understood as the rise of kundalini through the central channel along the spine. The staff bestows the power to settle quarrels and bring order. It signifies that the wielder is speaking on behalf of divine powers.

Figure 1.3 Hermes[2]

The Rod of Asclepius, which is depicted as a single serpent entwining a staff, is a Greek symbol of healing and medicine. Moses carried a staff that he transformed into a snake and used to part the Red Sea. Like a lightning rod, the Magician's wand is the focal point that channels divine energies.

For men, our cock is the life-giving wand of power. It is the magical instrument we use to channel divine energies. How I treat my cock shows me how I'm relating to all of life. Am I using my cock to release stress and help me go to sleep? Am I disrespecting my cock's power in addictive patterns? Or am I honoring this magical wand as a gift from the gods?

In the chapter that follows, we will hear the story of Black Elk's vision where he is told, "They have given you the sacred stick and your nation's hoop, and the yellow day; and in the center of the hoop you shall set the stick and make it grow into a shielding tree, and bloom."[3] As men in the mature Magician archetype, we plant our sacred stick in the center of the hoop to give life. We do this sexually, energetically, symbolically, and archetypally.

Figure 1.4 Asclepius[4]

On a deeper level, the Magician makes himself into the wand. It is said that he becomes *transparent*, like a hollow reed.[5] He is the conduit between heaven and earth. It is the Magician's task to transmit creative life force from the unseen realms into form. In order to do so, his egoic personality must learn to work in service to the higher energies that he is accessing. This means establishing a healthy relationship between the personal ego and the transpersonal archetypes. Mythologically, Jesus on the cross becomes the wand that conducts Christ consciousness into humanity.

Magic

The Magician casts the spell to access the creative forces at the center of the mandala. Across many cultures, the Magician *casts a circle* to create sacred space.[6] According to British folklore, Merlin created the magic circle of Stonehenge.[7] Within the circle, the Magician balances the energies of the four alchemical elements: Fire, Water, Wind, and Earth. On the Tarot Magician pictured above,

his altar holds the four suits: Wands, Cups, Swords, and Pentacles. These four elements combine to produce the symbol for wholeness. At the center of the circle, the Magician accesses the magical, life-giving energies.

The Magician archetype includes the expert, the craftsman, the technician, and the occultist. Each of these trades utilizes specialized knowledge that is not available to outsiders.[8] Technical jargon, trade secrets, and esoteric techniques separate the mundane world from the sacred realm of the Magician. While the products of the Magician appear to be something magical to outsiders, from the Magician's perspective, it is a natural outcome of the manipulation of specialized forces. This is equally true of computer programming, woodworking, and spiritual practice. In his full expression, the Magician holds the lore and blueprints of creation. He accesses the unseen realms of the kosmos, the inner depths of the psyche, and the secrets of birth and death. Mythologically, Moses parts the Red Sea and transcribes the word of God for his people; and Jesus raises Lazarus from the dead.

Consciousness

The journey I am proposing that we take together is not to the moon or even to the stars. The distance to the stars is much less than the distance within ourselves. The discovery of ourselves is endless, and it requires constant inquiry, a perception which is total, an awareness in which there is no choice.

—J. Krishnamurti[9]

Thinking is the quality of the Magician, which properly includes all mental activity. In its broadest context, the Magician is an explorer and channeler of *consciousness.* Reasoning, the use of language, imagination, dreaming, intuition, meditation, prayer, and concentration are all functions of the Magician. Just as our thoughts are ephemeral like the clouds or swift like the wind, the action of the Magician is connected to the alchemical element of Air. Like the rising sun in the East, the Magician channels new light and new ideas into the world.

As an aside, native, pagan, and neo-shamanic traditions attribute different elements to different directions on the medicine wheel. Each system holds its own wisdom and inner coherence.[10] Here is the system I am presenting in this workbook. It is what feels intuitively right for me:

Direction	Archetype	Quality	Element
East	Magician	Thinking	Wind
South	Warrior	Acting	Fire
West	Lover	Feeling	Water
North	King	Being	Earth

Figure 1.5 Qualities of the four quadrants

Let's consider the mental tools of the Magician. In medieval alchemy, *meditation* was the act of inner-dialogue with the unseen realms. Jung interprets this as a process whereby the alchemist accesses the creative realms of the unconscious.[11] Alchemical meditation is an active, cognitive relationship with the objects of focus wherein the mystery unfolds.

The *logos*, or the word, is the ordering and structuring principle of the kosmos. Hermes/Mercury as messenger god delivers the *logos* into the world.[12] These can each be understood as higher order mental faculties of the Magician.

For Jung, dreams provide a direct communication channel to the unconscious realms and, thus, to our basic nature.[13] Dreams are an essential experiential realm for many spiritual traditions, providing initiations, connections with ancestors, and invaluable wisdom about the nature of the kosmos. As an example, the Aboriginal people of Australia hold dreaming as the central facet of reality:

Indeed, Aborigines had no conception of themselves as the 'crown' of God's creation in the way that world religions often deify man. Life per se was a web of interactive particles, of which mankind and nature were coequal partners. Therefore the role of mankind in the drama of life was to re-create through ritual and ceremony the eternal moment of the Dreaming by calling upon the assistance of all nature, whether it be organic or geological. Any dichotomy between man and nature was regarded as an accident, a product of the hiatus between mankind and his knowledge of the Dreaming, not an eternal severance as suggested by the time-lapse that separated mankind from the Primordial Event Itself.

—James Cowan[14]

Prayer, mantra, chanting, and singing have been used across all spiritual traditions as tools to access deities and expanded states of consciousness. The foundational element of prayer is the ego's recognition of a greater realm, ordering principle, or intelligence—a *transcendent other*. It is through this recognition, supplication, and receptivity that the Magician channels the transpersonal energies into the world.

Through his craft, the Magician learns how to navigate the vast realms of consciousness. These include the conceptual mind (i.e., ego consciousness), somatic experiences and personal unconscious, and the transpersonal realms of consciousness that include the archetypes.[15] The meditation protocols in the pages that follow focus on stepping out of the conceptual mind into the direct experience of reality, primarily through embodiment.

While the spells and feats of the Magician are exciting, it is important to hold them within the greater context of the Magician's mission, which is *wholeness*. Throughout cultures and history, the role of the Magician has been as a healer, guide, and tender of sacred space on behalf of the people in his community.[16] The Magician is a servant. In the internal landscape, the role of the Magician is to integrate egoic consciousness with the unconscious to unify the Self. Jung defines the *Self* as the totality of the psyche.[17] The Self has an innate drive toward wholeness, which can also be understood spiritually as the path to realization. The Magician is the archetypal energy that guides and impels us toward Self-hood, toward wholeness.

Prompts for Journaling and Discussion

How do you experience the Magician within?

Which people in your life have served as Magicians for you?

What famous Magicians from pop culture and mythology do you admire or identify with?

Draw a self-portrait of the Magician within you.

Notes

[1] Painting by Charles La Fosse, 1700.

[2] *Myths of Old Greece Vol II*, Pratt.

[3] *Black Elk Speaks*, Neihardt.

[4] From the Archaeological Museum of Epidaurus.

[5]"*Intelligence of Transparency* is the mode of consciousness. 'Transparency' means 'letting the light shine through.' Here we have the same idea of transmission that is suggested by Hermes as the transmitter of the messages of the higher divinity. Clearly the mode of consciousness called transparent must be one which affords a free channel of communication, which permits the free passage downward and outward of the superconscious Light which is above and within." *The Tarot, A Key to the Wisdom of the Ages*, Case.

[6] See *Chapter 13* for a deeper discussion of sacred space.

[7] "Stonehenge was said to be Merlin's project. A huge boundary of megaliths surrounds a sacred space, in whose center stands a stone altar. Another stone is situated in the perimeter so that, at dawn on the solstice, the sun's rays pass up along this stone and finally break over the top of it to illuminate the central altar." *The Magician Within: Accessing the Shaman in the Male Psyche*, Moore and Gillette.

[8] "The shaman was the guardian of esoteric knowledge and the technician of sacred power. His secret wisdom was of natural laws and psychological dynamics. The shaman knew, and could interpret, the cycles of nature, the workings of the heavens - the phases of the moon, the progress of the sun - and perhaps most important, the movements of the herds up which the lives of his people depended." *The Magician Within: Accessing the Shaman in the Male Psyche*, Moore and Gillette.

[9] *Choiceless Awareness*, Krishnamurti.

[10] In the following chapter on Black Elk, his people's system is presented in his vision. The cup (water) is west, the wing (air) is north, the pipe (fire) is east, and the stick and hoop (earth) is south.

[11] "Ruland's *Lexicon alchemiae* defines *meditatio* as follows: 'The word *meditatio* is used when a man has an inner dialogue with someone unseen. It may be with God, when He is invoked, or with himself, or with his good angel.' The psychologist is familiar with this 'inner dialogue'; it is an essential part of the technique for coming to terms with the unconscious. Ruland's definition proves beyond all doubt that when the alchemists speak of *meditari* they do not mean mere cogitation, but explicitly an inner dialogue and hence a living relationship to the answering voice of the 'other' in ourselves, i.e., of the unconscious. The use of the term 'meditation' in the Hermetic dictum 'And as all things proceed from the One through the meditation of the One' must therefore be understood in this alchemical sense as a creative dialogue, by means of which things pass from an unconscious potential state to a manifest one." *Collected Works of C. G. Jung, Volume 12*, Jung.

[12] "Human consciousness at its height is developed largely by the mastering of words. Arising from language, at the same time it gives rise to language, consciousness creates our experience as it defines creation. The words we use for things allow us to distinguish this from that. They also profoundly color how we think and feel about those things. What we cannot name is therefore not fully real or fully experienced for us. As far as our psyche is concerned, an unnamed thing is 'uncreated.' Thus the biblical image of Yahweh creating the world by naming it is true to human psychological processes." *The Magician Within: Accessing the Shaman in the Male Psyche*, Moore and Gillette.

[13] "Dreams are impartial, spontaneous products of the unconscious psyche, outside the control of the will. They are pure nature; they show us the unvarnished, natural truth, and are therefore fitted, as nothing else is, to give us back an attitude that accords with our basic human nature when our consciousness has strayed too far from its foundations and run into an impasse." *The Earth Has a Soul: The Nature Writings of C. G. Jung*, Jung.

[14] *Mysteries of the Dream-Time*, Cowan.

[15] "The shaman has access to the whole terrain of the human unconscious. He knows the passwords that can take the Ego in and out of these magical realms. He can voyage inside himself without getting lost, or falling under the enchantment of any one place or structure in sacred geography. It is the Magician who wrote the Tibetan and the Egyptian Books of the Dead, giving advice to departed Egos for the negotiation of the fearful inner landscapes of the afterworld. He wrestles with demons and power animals, and is on intimate terms with complexes; he uses his knowledge of these structures to keep himself free from them. With his mercurial agility, he can cross any particular unconscious boundary, and so it is he who keeps a man's immortal soul free and aids other members of the human community in both personal and social liberation and transformation." *The Magician Within: Accessing the Shaman in the Male Psyche*, Moore and Gillette.

[16] "These ritualistic marvels, amongst the most sensational on the magician's list, have therefore been severed from the lifeline and used for purposes of display. But the majority of the miracles derive from the practical functions of the medicine-man or wizard, whose paramount duty has always consisted in ensuring the prosperity of the tribe, clan or society to which he belonged, or of the patrons to whom he was attached." *The Myth of the Magus*, Butler.

[17] "I call this centre the 'self,' which should be understood as the totality of the psyche. The self is not only the centre, but also the whole circumference which embraces both conscious and unconscious; it is the centre of this totality, just as the ego is the centre of consciousness." *Collected Works of C. G. Jung, Volume 12*, Jung.

| 2 |

Mythos of the Magician—Black Elk

Figure 2.1 Black Elk, standing on Harney Peak, the highest point in the Black Hills of South Dakota, "the center of the earth."[1]

My friend, I am going to tell you the story of my life, as you wish; and if it were only the story of my life I think I would not tell it; for what is one man that he should make much of his winters, even when they bend him like a heavy snow? So many other men have lived and shall live that story, to be grass upon the hills. It is the story of all life that is holy and is good to tell, and of us two-leggeds sharing in it with the four-leggeds and the wings of the air and all green things; for these are children of one mother and their father is one Spirit.

—Black Elk[2]

Once there was a boy named Kahnigapi who sometimes heard voices. He wanted to be a warrior like the heroes of his people: riding horses, hunting with his bow, and fighting great battles. He dreamed of killing the wasichus, the invading white soldiers and settlers, to protect his people. The boy lived in a nomadic village with his family and kin near the Powder River Basin on land that is today called southern Montana and northern Wyoming.

One day, when he was five years old, he was riding his horse with a bow his grandfather had given him. He saw a bird that he might be able to shoot. But the bird spoke to him: "Listen! A voice is calling you!" Startled by the bird, the boy stopped. Then out of the clouds, two men flew down, singing,

Behold, a sacred voice is calling you; All over the sky a sacred voice is calling.

As the boy watched, awestruck, the sky-men morphed into geese as they flew back into the clouds. Then a mighty rain roared up. Frightened, the little boy didn't tell anyone about his vision. From time to time, the voices would return over the next few years, but the boy did not pay attention to them. He didn't know what might happen if other people knew he was hearing voices and no other boys seemed to be hearing them.

By the time the boy was nine years old, he had been learning the ways of the warrior on horseback with his bow. One summer evening he was sharing dinner in the teepee of Man Hip when he heard a voice: "It is time; now they are calling you." Hearing the voice, the boy stood up and walked outside to see who was speaking, but there was no one there. He lost his appetite, and his legs began to cramp.

At this time, the boy's people were migrating slowly toward the Rocky Mountains, moving camp each day. Over the course of the next day, riding his horse as his people moved camp, his legs gave out and he became very ill. The next day, he was even more sick and could not ride his horse, so he was put in a pony drag. His whole body became swollen. He was put to rest in his parent's teepee. Here, the boy left his body and had a great vision:

The two cloud men flew down and escorted the boy up into the cloud realm. He met the powers of the West, North, East, and South, in the form of powerful horses. Then he entered a teepee with a flaming rainbow door where the Grandfathers were holding council. The Six Grandfathers introduced themselves to the boy and told him they were here to teach him. They represented the west, north, east, south, the sky, and the earth. From the first four grandfathers, the boy received these gifts:

The cup of water to make live the greening day,
The white wing of cleansing,
The sacred pipe and the power that is peace,
The sacred stick and the nation's hoop.

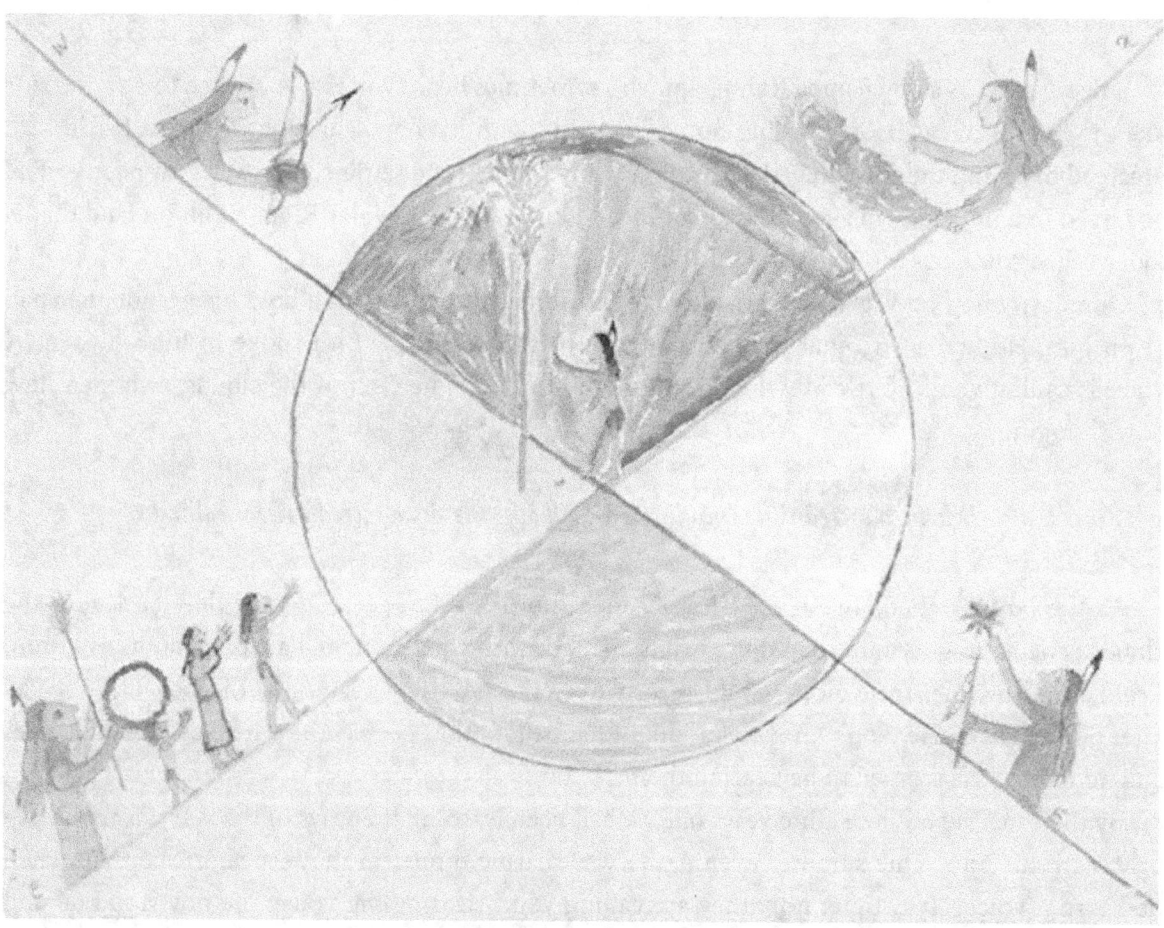

Figure 2.2 "Black Elk under the Tree of Life."[3]

The boy received instructions from each grandfather on how to use these gifts. Here was what the Grandfather of the South had to say:

"Younger brother," he said, "with the powers of the four quarters you shall walk, a relative. Behold, the living center of a nation I shall give you, and with it many you shall save." And I saw that he was holding in his hand a bright red stick that was alive, and as I looked it sprouted at the top and sent forth branches, and on the branches many leaves came out and murmured and in the leaves the birds began to sing. And then for just a little while I thought I saw beneath it in the shade the circled villages of people and every living thing with roots or legs or wings, and all were happy. "It shall stand in the center of the nation's circle," said the Grandfather, "a cane to walk with and a people's heart; and by your powers you shall make it blossom."[4]

The boy received instructions in his vision on the ways of the medicine man, *wičháša wakȟáŋ*. He learned how to heal, and he received great wisdom. He was shown a vision of the next four generations of his people as their way of life was destroyed by the coming white settlers. But most importantly, he was shown how to create the sacred hoop (mandala), how to use the sacred stick (wand), and how to access the life-giving energies of the kosmos in the center of the hoop. At only nine years old, the boy was initiated into the archetype of the Magician. The name he received at birth, Kahnigapi (which means *chosen*) was changed to Black Elk, the name of his father and grandfathers going back four generations who where were all medicine men.[5]

[In my vision], I was still on my bay horse, and once more I felt the riders of the west, the north, the east, the south, behind me in formation, as before, and we were going east. I looked ahead and saw the mountains there with rocks and forests on them, and from the mountains flashed all colors upward to the heavens. Then I was standing on the highest mountain of them all, and round about beneath me was the whole hoop of the world. And while I stood there I saw more than I can tell and I understood more than I saw; for I was seeing in a sacred manner the shapes of all things in the spirit, and the shape of all shapes as they must live together like one being. And I saw that the sacred hoop of my people was one of many hoops that made one circle, wide as daylight and as starlight, and in the center grew one mighty flowering tree to shelter all the children of one mother and one father. And I saw that it was holy.[6]

After receiving the great vision and being initiated as a Magician for his people, the boy returned to his physical body back in his parent's teepee. He has been unconscious for twelve days. The boy recovered full health, but spent the next twelve days apart from his friends and family—he was now no longer a regular boy.

Over the following decades, the Oglala Lakota people suffered death and hardship at the hands of the white settlers. Black Elk's people suffered famine, disease, invasion and war. His people were moved onto reservations where their spirit and culture were stifled.[7]

Black Elk became a healer of the sick, called a *yuwipi man* in Lakota. He worked as an oracle or medium. He also served as *heyókha* or sacred clown.[8] He stepped into his role as spiritual leader for his people, organizing a Horse Dance in the way he had been shown in his vision. This ritual connected the people with the archetypal hoop, the four directions, and the life-giving world tree at the center. As the Magician, Black Elk learned the sacred ways of the kosmos and worked for the benefit of his people.

Later in life, he gave his story in a series of interviews with a white man named John Neihardt.[9] Through this act, Black Elk offered his wisdom as an inspiration for all people and all times.[10] Black Elk's publications not only transmitted a repository of spiritual wisdom to the world, through them, he became "the prophet of the Sioux revitalization movement."[11] In a time when the culture and religion of the Lakota people was in danger of being lost, Black Elk preserved and rallied support for the Lakota traditions.

There is a notion in the Tibetan Buddhist tradition that how a teacher dies is generally their greatest teaching. Shortly before his death at the age of 87, Black Elk told his daughter, "I have a feeling when I die, some sign will be seen. Maybe God will show something. He will be merciful to me and have something shown which will tell of his mercy."[12] On the night of his passing a light show illuminated the sky. It was observed across the United States and Canada. The magazine *Sky and Telescope* reported that "shimmering and darting forms" lit "the landscape as bright as with the moon."[13]

To inspire wonder and awe, this is the magic of the Magician. To reconnect us with *Wakháŋ Tháŋka*, the Great Mystery, and to remember that we are all part of this one sacred life—what greater blessing could we hope to receive?

Prompts for Journaling and Discussion

What is the Magician's relationship with power?

Where does it source and how does he use it?

What mystical experiences have you had?

Tell the story of the most important mystical experience in your life.

The child Black Elk was afraid to share his vision because his people would think he was crazy. What vision or mission have you received that you have not yet shared with the world?

Notes

[1] Photo by John G. Neihardt.

[2] *Black Elk Speaks*, Neihardt.

[3] Drawing by Standing Bear, from *Black Elk Speaks*.

[4] *Black Elk Speaks*, Neihardt.

[5] "He was heir to a family of medicine men, the fourth Black Elk, though the name did not pass to him until sometime after the onset of his visions. His father was the third Black Elk, a medicine man and warrior hailing from a line of healers." *Black Elk: The Life of an American Visionary*, Jackson.

[6] *Black Elk Speaks*, Neihardt.

[7] "The Sioux had been defeated militarily, and now the government waged economic, social, and political war. The old approach of isolating Native Americans on nearly worthless land had not solved the 'Indian problem.' Now the solution was more complex: the government believed that the only way to save the Indian was to turn him into a white man." *Black Elk: The Life of an American Visionary*, Jackson.

[8] "Black Elk performed the ceremony of the *heyókha*—the 'contrary,' or Thunder Clown—sometime after mid-May 1882…. The sacred fool had a long history in most religious cultures: though his role was religious and ceremonial, his 'purpose' was to dissipate excesses of power by mocking them. By behaving in a contrary or backward manner, it was believed, the fools wove a reverse magic that dissipated malevolent forces and countered the dangers of lightning and storm." *Black Elk: The Life of an American Visionary*, Jackson

[9] "Finally, Black Elk turned to Flying Hawk as if he'd made a decision. 'As I sit here, I can feel in this man beside me a strong desire to know the things of the Other World. He has been sent to learn what I know, and I will teach him.'" *Black Elk: The Life of an American Visionary*, Jackson.

[10] "The two commenced a project that started as a personal testament of Plains Indian life from the 1860s to 1890 but ended as one of the twentieth century's most important documents on Native American culture and as a classic of world literature…. Black Elk was doing something unprecedented. According to Charles Eastman, 'Sometimes an old man, standing upon the brink of eternity, might reveal to a chosen few the oracle of his long-past youth.' Yet Black Elk was not merely telling the story of his life. By sharing the details of his untold Vision, he passed along his power. By passing it to Neihardt, he gave it to another culture—the very one that had destroyed the Lakota! Yet a book meant permanence: what could be lost would be preserved. The truth of his Vision would remain long after he and the poet were gone." *Black Elk: The Life of an American Visionary*, Jackson.

[11] *Black Elk: The Life of an American Visionary*, Jackson.

[12] *Black Elk: The Life of an American Visionary*, Jackson.

[13] *Black Elk: The Life of an American Visionary*, Jackson.

| 3 |

Accessing the Magician

Figure 3.1 Alchemist, 16th century, Dresden.

There are many ways to access the Magician and they all begin with intention. Stating the desire to connect, intending to connect, and then following through with our actions is what opens the channel. Here are three examples for how to begin dialogue with the Magician within.

Your Power Spot

Humanity today suffers from a place-corrosive process. Urbanization, centralization, increased mobility (although nomads have proven that not all sorts of moving around destroy the relation of belonging somewhere), the dependence on goods and technologies from where one does not belong, the increase of structural complication of life—all these factors weaken or disrupt the steady belongingness to a place, or even hinder its formation. There seems to be no place for PLACE anymore. But the loss of place is felt, the longing persists, and so we feel the need to articulate what it means to belong to a place. The movement toward the development of a sense of place is strengthened through a tightening of the interrelation between the self and the environment.

—Arne Næss[1]

A power spot is the place where the Magician accesses the *axis mundi*, the center of the world. In this place, the Magician connects with sacred space and life-giving energy. When we find our power spot, we *belong*.

Step 1: Discover your spot.

Go into nature and allow yourself to wander. Meander. Let your intuition guide you to *your special place*. You will know this place because you feel inexplicably drawn to it and, when you're there, you feel centered.

Step 2: Create a relationship with your spot.

Explore the terrain. Put your hands on the earth—get dirty. Take note of all the different plants, insects, and animals who call this place home. Observe them. Listen. Notice the sky and the weather. Say a prayer to connect with the spirits of the land.

Step 3: Make an earth mandala.

Wander around the area and gather objects to make a mandala at the center of your power spot. I like to ask permission of rocks, flowers, sticks, or whatever objects I am gathering—checking in with them to see if they'd like to participate in the earth mandala. Arrange these objects into a symmetrical circular design. Become the Magician creating his altar.

Step 4: Pray.

Pray in whatever way is authentic for you. Recite prayers from spiritual traditions. Sing prayer songs or mantras. Speak from your heart and see what comes through. Pray for yourself. Pray for your loved ones. Pray for the earth and all beings everywhere.

Step 5: Bring offerings.

Return to your power spot regularly. Rhythm is what grows relationship. Bring something from your life to offer to your power spot. Perhaps you can offer loose tobacco, some fresh flowers, or a piece of fruit. It is the act of offering that matters more than the substance.

Over time, with dedication and devotion, your power spot will open and become strong. This place will be a resource for you and a source of connection to nature, the elements, and the Magician within.

Figure 3.2 Dr. Faustus in his power spot

Your Dreams

I have become even more convinced not only that every dream comes in the service of the individual dreamer's health and wholeness while speaking in a universal language of archetypal symbol and metaphor, but also that dreams and dreaming expand the very domain of health and wholeness itself by fostering and reflecting the evolution of human consciousness collectively.

—Jeremy Taylor[2]

Dreaming is a window into the unlimited creativity of the psyche. Jeremy Taylor's first basic assumption about working with dreams is that *all dreams come in the service of health and wholeness.*

Whenever I am able to remember a dream, it means that my unconscious is giving me a message to help me on my path. In this view, nightmares show up because there is a very important message that the unconscious is trying to convey and my psyche is really trying to get the attention of my waking consciousness. Keeping a dream journal anchors more dreams into my awareness, expands the capacity of my recall, and perhaps most interestingly, signals to my unconscious mind that I'm paying attention so that it can deliver messages more clearly.

Step 1: Commit to dream engagement.

Make a strong decision with your whole being that you are interested in the content of your dreams and decide to remember them.

Step 2: Get your journal.

If you use a paper journal, reserve it specifically for content related to your dreams. This is a special item in your life. If you decide to type or voice record your dreams, similarly, make a special demarcation of the device you will use. Place your paper or digital dream journal in a consistent spot next to your bed so you build a routine with it.

Step 3: Journal something every morning.

The best time to journal is immediately upon waking up while the dreams are still fresh. You can also journal in the middle of the night if you wake up after a dream. Record whatever detail you can—even if it is vague or seemingly unimportant. In addition to what happened in the dream, record any emotions, colors, and sensations. Drawing a picture of your dream is a rich experience. If you do not remember anything, make a log for that date with "No dream memories." The consistency of journaling sends a signal to your unconscious mind that you are paying attention and strengthens dream recall.

Step 4: Harvest your dreams.

Occasionally read through your dream journal. Talk about your dreams with your friends and family. Share your dreams with your therapist, coach, or spiritual teacher. Join a dream group. Receiving outside perspectives on your dreams will help you understand their messages. Allow others' interpretations to inform your own synthesis. Most importantly: only you know what your dream means for you.

Your Book

The Tarot deck is the book of archetypes for Western consciousness. Each card is an activating symbol that reaches back into the origins of our culture. When you draw a card, your waking consciousness makes contact with the archetype and the synthesis of the two creates a living message. For this reason, the Tarot is known as the *Book of Life.* It is a dynamically unbound book that connects across layers of consciousness and epochs of humanity.

The first evidence for Tarot decks dates to the 1400s in northern Italy. However, the mythological story of the Tarot goes much farther back. It is said that Thoth, the Egyptian god of knowledge and language, created the Tarot, hence its esoteric name, *the Book of Thoth*. As the messenger god, Thoth evolved into the Greek god Hermes, the Roman god Mercury, and the alchemical figure Hermes Trismegistus. In ancient Egypt, Thoth and the priests who functioned on his behalf would offer initiations into the mysteries of life. The most famous example of these initiations comes from *The Papyrus of Ani*, also known as *The Egyptian Book of the Dead*. This text depicts the journey of Ani in the afterlife. His first test was to have his heart weighed against the Feather of Truth.

> *Thus says Thoth, judge of truth, to the Great Ennead which is in the presence of Osiris: Hear this word of very truth. I have judged the heart of the deceased, and his soul stands as a witness for him. His deeds are righteous in the great balance, and no sin has been found in him.* [3]

When Ani was found to be pure of heart, he passed onward to learn the mysteries of the afterlife. In the "House of Osiris in the Field of Reeds," Ani encountered twenty-one portals. Each portal had a gatekeeper who Ani must name in order to pass. [4]

Figure 3.3 Ani traversing the portals. Papyrus of Ani, plate 11. [5]

The Tarot deck shares this structure. In it are twenty-two major arcana cards. The first card in the sequence is numbered zero and is the archetype of the Fool. Ani is the Fool, who represents you and me as we make the journey. The other major arcana cards are numbered one to twenty-one.

As the Fool, we traverse these twenty-one portals of initiation, following in Ani's footsteps. In the mythos of the Tarot, the major arcana are understood as initiations that were first laid out by the Egyptians.

The next thread of this story traces to the biblical book of Genesis. Before Abraham became the great patriarch of Judaism, Islam, and Christianity, he was known as Abram. In Genesis 15, we hear of Abram's heroic battle and rescue of his brother Lot. On the way back from the battle, he encountered Melchizedek, the king of Salem and a "priest of the most high God." Abram tithes one tenth of his property to Melchizedek, who in turn blessed him. Immediately following this initiation, Abram had a visitation by the Lord, where they made a covenant.

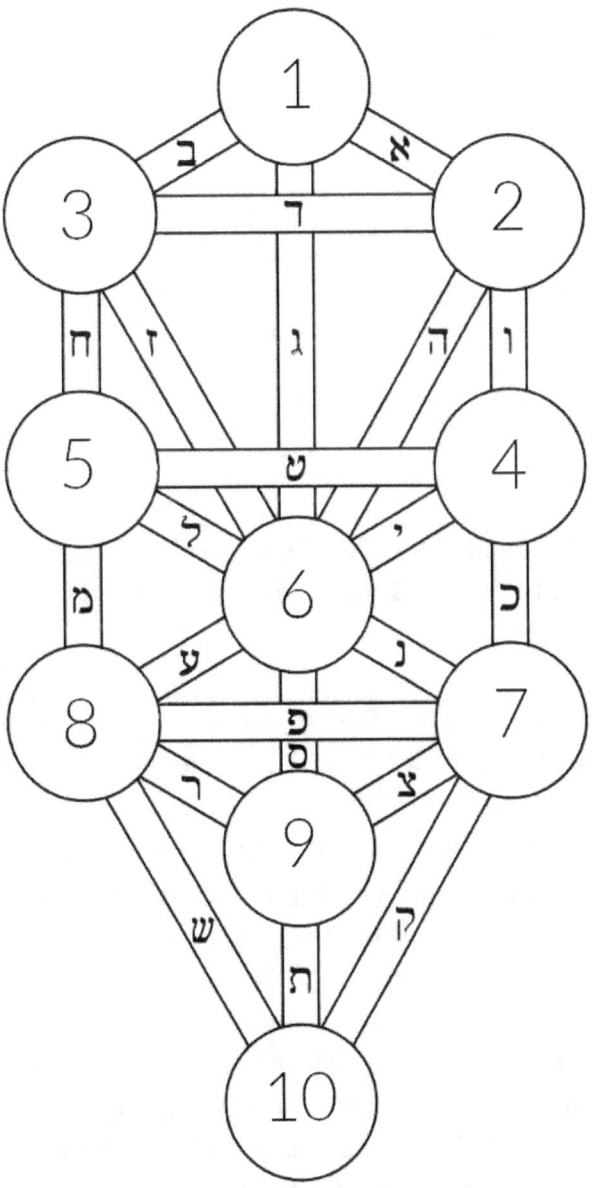

Figure 3.4 The Qabalistic Tree of Life.

[God says to Abram], Look now toward heaven, and tell the stars, if thou be able to number them: and he said unto him, So shall thy seed be.

—Genesis 15:5

It is said that, in this mystical experience, Abram received the transmission of the *Sepher Yetzirah* text. This mystical work lays out the foundational tenets of Jewish mysticism known as Kabbalah. These tenets have been adopted by non-Judaic forms of mysticism including Hermeticism and tarot. These other traditions use the term *Qabalah* as a distinction. The Sepher Yetzirah describes the creation of the world through the numbers one through ten and the twenty-two Hebrew letters of the alphabet.

Ten are the numbers of the ineffable Sephiroth, ten and not nine, ten and not eleven. Learn this wisdom, and be wise in the understanding of it, investigate these numbers, and draw knowledge from them, fix the design in its purity, and pass from it to its Creator seated on his throne.… From the Spirit he made Air and formed for speech twenty-two letters.

—Sepher Yetzirah[6]

The ten spheres plus the twenty-two letters comprise the thirty-two paths of wisdom and are depicted by the mystical symbol of the Qabalistic Tree of Life, illustrated above. One other addition from Qabalah is the belief that the kosmos is comprised of four layers or worlds: Emanation, Creation, Formation, and Action.[7]

Returning to the tarot, the deck has four suits (Swords, Cups, Wands, and Pentacles) that correspond to the four Qabalistic worlds. In each suit, the minor arcana number one to ten and correspond to the ten sacred numbers, or Sephiroth, which are spheres on the Tree of Life. The twenty-two major arcana each correspond with a letter of the Hebrew alphabet and a pathway between spheres on the Tree diagram. Rounding out the full Tarot deck, each suit contains the Kings, Queens, Knights, and Pages, which in the twentieth century have evolved into the arche-types of the Father, Mother, Son, and Daughter.[8] So the Qabalistic Tree of Life can be utilized as a condensed map for the structure of the tarot deck. Thus, the structure of the tarot deck can be mapped both to the mythos of the Egyptian Book of the Dead and to the mystical Qabalah.

To be clear, there is no historical evidence of ancient Egyptians or Hebrews using tarot decks. As I mentioned above, the first decks seemingly appeared in the fifteenth century. However, on a symbolic level today, the tarot is tapping into the structures and archetypes of the mystical roots of Western civilization. In addition to the Egyptian and Qabalistic influences, tarot is connected to Pythagorean number mysticism, Gnosticism, Hermeticism, and Freemasonry. Many of Europe's medieval mystical lineages found a home in the tarot, where they continue to live today.

The tarot deck is a book of symbols that incorporates layer upon layer of meaning in our collective unconscious. As with all of the Magician's power objects, the tarot will become more potent as you spend more time connecting to it. The first initiation into Tarot is to discover your birth cards.

Step 1: Calculate your soul number.

Add the day of your birth, the number of your birth month, and the number of your birth year together. For example: Salvador Dali was born on May 4th, 1904, so: 4 + 5 + 1904 = 1913.

Then add the digits of that number together, so 1 + 9 + 1 + 3 = 14.

If the resulting number has two digits, perform the same operation: 1 + 4 = 5. Salvador Dali's soul number is 5.

Step 2: Find the corresponding major arcana card.

The major arcana listed below are based on the *Tarot of the Spirit* deck. Other tarot decks will use slightly different names. Find the deck that feels most resonant for you. Based on the table below, Salvador Dali's major arcana birth card is *V. The Hierophant*.

I. The Magus	II. The High Priestess	III. The Empress	IV. The Emperor
V. The Hierophant	VI. The Lovers	VII. Chariot	VIII. Strength
IX. The Hermit	X. Wheel of Fortune	XI. Karma	XII. The Hanged Man
XIII. Death	XIV. Temperance	XV. The Devil	XVI. The Tower
XVII. The Star	XVIII. The Moon	XIX. The Sun	XX. Resurrection
XXI. The Universe			

Figure 3.5 The major arcana of tarot.

Step 3: Find your tertiary card(s).

In the example with Salvador Dali, the first reduction of numbers yielded 14. So his secondary birth card is *XIV. Temperance*. Similarly, people with *VI. The Lovers* will have a secondary card of *XV. The Devil* (15 is 1 + 5 = 6), and so on.

You may even have three birth cards. If your birth number reduces to one, then your birth card is the *I. The Magus*. In addition, you will have both *X. The Wheel of Fortune* and *XIX. The Sun* as tertiary birth cards (both reduce to one: 1 + 0 = 1, and 1 + 9 = 10 and 1 + 0 = 1). The same goes for the twos: *II. The High Priestess, XI. Karma,* and *XX. Resurrection,* and the three's: *III. The Empress, XII. The Hanged Man,* and *XXI. The Universe.*

One special rule is if your birth date reduces to 22, then in addition to being 2 + 2 = 4, *IV. The Emperor,* you also qualify as the twenty-second arcana, or *0. The Fool.*

Step 4: Meditate on your birth card(s).

The lowest number is your *soul card*. This is the archetype that is most directly aligned with your soul's work in this lifetime. This card describes your dharma. The tertiary card(s) describe sub-themes in your life and relate to your personality. So, Salvador Dali's dharma was connected to the archetype of *The Hierophant*, the teacher who connects spirit and matter, and his personality sub-theme was that of *Temperance*, walking the path of trials.

Purchase a Tarot deck.[9] Read about your birth cards and make an intentional connection with the archetypes represented there.

Prompts for Journaling and Discussion

How does skepticism work both for and against accessing the magic of the Magician?

Besides those listed here, what other tools help to access your Magician?

What sacred lore or specialized knowledge have you learned to access, and how do you use it?

Notes

[1] *The Ecology of Wisdom: Writings by Arne Naess*, Naess.

[2] *The Wisdom of Your Dreams: Using Dreams to Tap into Your Unconscious and Transform Your Life,* Taylor.

[3] *The Egyptian Book of the Dead*, Goelet et al.

[4] "Ani's version of chapters 146 and 147 are simplified versions of much longer texts which portray as many as 21 entrances, each of which can be passed only after a brief dialogue with each being blocking the way. In the present case, however, this exchange is merely implied. Knowing the names of the gatekeepers appears to be sufficient to give the deceased power of these creatures and thus gain entrance. The complex and threatening names of these beings, as well as Ani's arcane declarations at his arrival before each entrance, connect these two chapters with a genre of texts in which the deceased demonstrate their acquisition of special knowledge and thereby prove the fitness for membership in the community of gods." *The Egyptian Book of the Dead*, Goelet et al.

[5] Zecharia Sitchin Index.

[6] Sepher Yetzirah, or the Book of Creation, Trans. W. W. Westcott and A. Nagy.

[7] "Even every one that is called by my name: for I have created him for my glory, I have formed him; yea, I have made him." Isaiah

43:7 KJV. The four worlds or *Olam* are *Atziluth, Briah, Yetzirah,* and *Assiah.*

[8] Cf. *Tarot of the Spirit*, Eakins.

[9] Tarot decks that explicitly incorporate Qabalistic symbolism include The Rider-Waite Deck, The Golden Dawn Deck, The Builders of Adytum Deck, The Thoth Deck, and Tarot of the Spirit.

| 4 |

The Gift of the Magician: Consciousness

Figure 4.1 Xochipilli, señor de las flores, National Museum of Anthropology

Our normal waking consciousness, rational consciousness as we call it, is but one special type of consciousness, whilst all about it, parted from it by the filmiest of screens, there lie potential forms of consciousness entirely different. We may go through life without suspecting their existence; but apply the requisite stimulus, and at a touch they are there in all their completeness, definite types of mentality which probably somewhere have their field of application and adaptation. No account of the universe in its totality can be final which leaves these other forms of consciousness quite disregarded.

—William James[1]

In Chapter 2, each of the Six Grandfathers imparted a gift to Black Elk in his vision. When I touch the archetypes and develop a relationship with them, they offer gifts. In this series, each of the seven archetypes (Magician, Warrior, Lover, King/Masculine, Queen/Feminine, and Androgyne) has a gift to offer. These gifts come in the form of initiations, and the gift of the Magician is *consciousness.*

As the Magician, I learn to step beyond the known into the mystery. While there are vanishingly few geographical horizons left on earth, the inner landscapes of consciousness offer vast realms for exploration and discovery. The psyche is today's wild frontier. And while mystics throughout the ages have been encouraging us to look within, never before have the spiritual technologies and practices been as accessible as they are today.

Here is an amazing fact: studying consciousness stimulates the development of consciousness. To put it another way, learning about this material is psychoactive. Studying a map for how awareness operates provides a reference for where to look in my experience. When I open my awareness to a new place in my psyche, I am literally expanding my consciousness. Indeed, in the Tibetan Buddhist tradition, the major initiations happen through *pointing-out instructions,* where the teacher shows the student where to look to experience the nature of the mind.[2]

I will begin with an exploration of the psyche, which lays the foundation for our journey. From here, I will take a tour of the states of consciousness, ranging from waking consciousness all the way up to nonduality. Then I will examine how consciousness evolves through a progression of paradigms or worldviews. Finally, I'll delve into archetypes, which will lay out my main thesis of utilizing archetypes for men's work.

At a surface level, the sections that follow offer some maps for understanding consciousness. When they are studied, internalized, and experienced, they constitute the Magician's initiation into the kosmos—his gift of *consciousness.*

Notes

[1] *The Varieties of Religious Experience*, James.

[2] "In a similar way, before pointing-out instructions, the nature of realization—the inherent awakened awareness within—was only a matter of hearsay and speculation. After experiencing the nature of mind, one knows the end point of the path that one is traveling. This gives tremendous inspiration and trust. In addition, by having tasted the immaculate wisdom within, one is less apt to become confused and get lost in sidetracks. And one is less likely to take conditioned experiences and partial realizations for full awakening. As Sogyal Rinpoche says, the experience of pointing out leaves one with a deep inner certainty, relaxation, and joy." *Secret of the Vajra World*, Ray.

| 5 |

The Psyche

Figure 5.1 Feast of the Gods at the Marriage of Cupid and Psyche[1]

We begin with the ego, which is the Latin word for "I." Carl Jung defined the ego as the totality of awareness in waking consciousness. The ego includes my sensory experiences, thoughts, active memories, emotions, and the personality traits that I am aware of. But when I talk about the ego, I mean something more than simply *naked awareness*. The ego is the organizing self (with a small *s*). It is the process capable of self-reflection and, thus, the part of me that knows that I am me. My egoic self is distinct from my environment, from my subconscious instincts and impulses (the *id*), and from my social roles (the *superego*).

Neurobiologically, we understand that the majority of egoic awareness is due to the processing activities of the prefrontal cortex.[2] My brain processes and filters an incredible amount of raw sensory information and sends it to my prefrontal cortex to prioritize, make meaning, and construct plans. This system is tremendously valuable for everyday life: logic, language, complex behavior, modeling scenarios, and executive function all help me survive and thrive as a human.

The ego does not comprise the totality of consciousness, however. With a simple exploration, I can recognize aspects of my psyche of which I am unaware: dream imagery, automatic behaviors and habits, parts of myself that have been exiled or locked away, memories that I've repressed, and so on. From a somatic perspective (meaning, working with the intelligence of the *soma* or body), there are emotions, sensations, tension patterns, bodily functions, unresolved experiences from the past (i.e., trauma), and behavioral patterns (i.e., attachment and character strategies), which are carried out or held by my body without my conscious awareness. Following Jung, I'll define the totality of this unknown material as *the unconscious*.

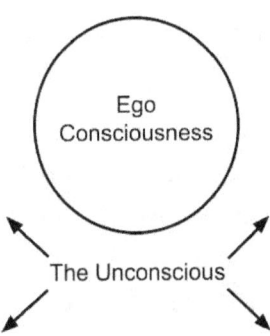

Figure 5.2 Basic map of the psyche

I can draw a definitive circle around my present waking awareness. At any given time, my ego awareness is definable—I am aware of *this*, and I'm not aware of *that*. The unconscious, in contrast, cannot be limited, counted, or bounded, because by definition, it is the psychic material that is unknown. I don't know *how much* I don't know. This is illustrated in the figure above, where the ego is enclosed within a circle and the unconscious is floating in space.

The sum of the ego and the unconscious, which is the totality of one's psychological experience, Jung termed the Self (capital *S*). My ego has its own agendas. Largely, these are comfort, safety, the known, ego glorification, and ego perfection. Similarly, the Self has its own agenda, namely, the integration of all parts of the psyche, including the ego, into *wholeness*. The Self desires to realize the Self. So, my ego's project is ego perfection, and my Self's project is wholeness, both of which are simultaneously being pursued. Sometimes these two projects coexist in harmony, but often they are working against each other.

In addition, Jung mapped out autonomous parts of the unconscious that split off and work for their own agendas—these are called *complexes*. For example, if I strongly repress my sexuality, then my sexual part may form his own subpersonality that emerges when I'm intoxicated and follows his agenda of sexual expression. Put all of these together, and I begin to see myself as a collection of competing aspects of the psyche with different agendas coexisting in a dynamic tension.

Even though the unconscious is unknown, I can still infer several aspects of its structure and content. I have personal psychological material in the unconscious, much of which stems from adverse childhood experiences. I can also identify transpersonal material in the unconscious. The same dream symbols show up for multiple people across cultures and ages. This points to a universal psychic repository that we are all connected to. These symbols are not held by any individual's psyche. Thus, they are transpersonal. Jung called this realm the *collective unconscious*. Importantly, the *unconscious* includes both *subconscious* and *higher-conscious* material that has not been integrated into egoic awareness.

I'll define the *archetypes* as these universal symbols that all humans may access. They constitute forces, instincts, intuitions, *forms and ideals*, mythologies, deities, and primordial principles within the psyche. They exist primarily in the collective unconscious and may constellate into both the personal unconscious and egoic consciousness. Connection between the ego and an archetype is called the *ego-archetype axis*.[3] Throughout this series, we'll be opening our axis for the archetypes of the Magician, Warrior, Lover, King, Queen, and Androgyne. Because archetypes are held in the collective, they are vastly more powerful than any individual psyche. These reservoirs of energy and meaning have the potential to be consciously integrated or unconsciously domineering and destructive.

The *shadow* is a blanket term for the parts of myself that I deny, repress, or exile. Thus, my shadow exists in my unconscious. The shadow represents how and where I suppress my power and my light. Each of the seven archetypes of the psyche listed above holds a shadow. When I am disconnected from an archetype, its shadow becomes an unconscious influencer in my life. As I begin to integrate these powerful energies into the ego, I become an active cocreator and develop the skills to direct the archetypal energies for generative and beneficial purposes.[4]

In figure 5.3, below, these elements are mapped onto the psyche. Only the ego can be defined, so all other aspects are delineated with dotted lines to note their ephemeral and unbounded natures.

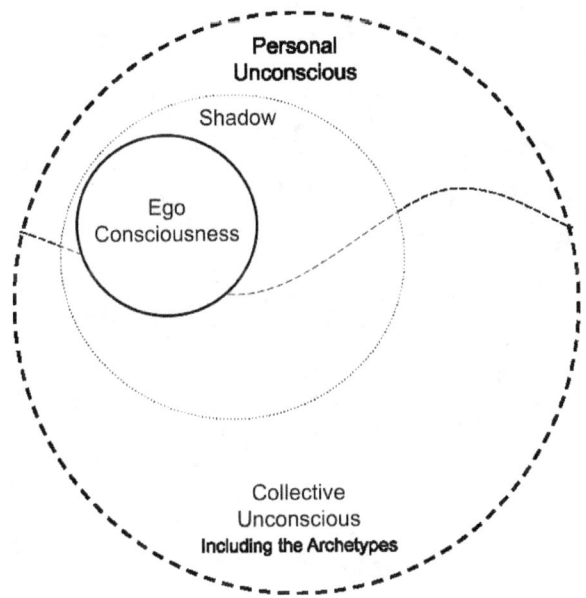

Figure 5.3 Detailed map of the psyche

As I mentioned, the Self has a natural drive toward *wholeness*. It achieves this agenda by integrating the various parts of the psyche into a harmonious and coherent system. "Wholeness" is an archetype itself, which is represented by the symbol of the *mandala*.

From the ego's perspective, this pathway to wholeness of Self entails meeting and loving the aspects of the psyche that are perceived as dangerous, hideous, disgusting, taboo, or shameful. Everything that has been consciously or unconsciously suppressed from the ego will need to be welcomed and accepted. Jung terms this process *individuation*.

One common misconception on the path is that I, as ego, must try to be good by suppressing or transcending my shadow. From the view of the Self, this actually leads to more separation and, thus, greater suffering. Another misconception is that when I become *healed* or *awakened* enough, I will no longer have a shadow. Until the point when my ego completely dissolves into unity consciousness (i.e., conscious and unconscious become one), I will have a shadow. The path is not about getting rid of the shadow, moving beyond it, or purifying it. The task is to love the shadow.[5]

Figure 5.4 Mandala of the Five Dhyani Buddhas. Tibet

This points to an even larger hurdle, which is that my ego would like to be the center. I want to be the owner and controller of the total psyche. It is important to understand that it is not the ego that drives individuation, but the Self. Therefore, from the perspective of my ego, individuation is largely a process of surrender.

> *The ego cannot help discovering that the afflux of unconscious contents has vitalized the personality, enriched it and created a figure that somehow dwarfs the ego in scope and intensity. This experience paralyzes an over-egocentric will and convinces the ego that in spite of all difficulties it is better to be taken down a peg than to get involved in a hopeless struggle in which one is invariably handed the dirty end of the stick. In this way the will, as disposable energy, gradually subordinates itself to the stronger factor, namely to the new totality-figure I call the self.*
>
> —C. G. Jung[6]

My naive picture of the path is of my egoic self-becoming wiser and holier until I become enlightened. Rather, enlightenment becomes me. The unconscious is vastly larger and more powerful than the ego—indeed, it is *all that is.*[7] My ego must be willing to surrender its agenda and control to integrate into the larger whole of the Self. Through the individuation process, the ego learns to braid its will into the larger will and takes its place as a servant of the Self.

Prompts for Journaling and Discussion

What parts of yourself do you deny, repress, or exile?

What parts of yourself do you refuse to give love?

Draw a picture of your shadow.

Which archetypes do you feel most connected to? How do you relate with these archetypes?

Notes

[1] Image: Bartholomeus Spranger, 1587

[2] The prefrontal cortex receives highly processed information from all major forebrain systems, and neurophysiological studies suggest that it synthesizes this into representations of learned task contingencies, concepts and task rules. In short, the prefrontal cortex seems to underlie our internal representations of the 'rules of the game'. This may provide the necessary foundation for the complex behaviour of primates, in whom this structure is most elaborate." "The prefrontal cortex: categories, concepts and cognition," Miller et al.

[3] "We do not want to *be* an archetype. Maturity is getting to a place of strength where none of the archetypes can take us against our wills and possess us. We don't want to let go of any of them either. The archetypal energy we can hold on to will be a *source* for everything we do. And because the source is in the collective psyche, it will never run dry." *The King Within: Accessing the King in the Male Psyche*, Moore and Gillette.

[4] "Archetypal awareness brings greater self-awareness and thus greater personal autonomy. Again, this is the basic rationale for depth psychology, from Freud and Jung onward: to release oneself from the bondage of blind action and unconsciously motivated experience, to recognize and explore the deeper forces in the human psyche and thereby modulate and transform them." *Cosmos and Psyche*, Tarnas.

[5] "The shadow is a living part of the personality and therefore wants to live with it in some form. It cannot be argued out of existence or rationalized into harmlessness." *Collected Works of C. G. Jung, Volume 9 (Part 1)*, Jung.

[6] *On the Nature of the Psyche*, Jung.

[7] "No, the collective unconscious is anything but an incapsulated personal system; it is sheer objectivity, as wide as the world and open to all the world. There I am the object of every subject, in complete reversal of my ordinary consciousness, where I am always the subject that has an object. There I am utterly one with the world, so much a part of it that I forget all too easily who I really am. "Lost in oneself" is a good way of describing this state. But this self is the world, if only a consciousness could see it. That is why we must know who we are." *On the Nature of the Psyche*, Jung.

| 6 |

States of Consciousness

Figure 6.1 Mandala Chandar, woven tapestry, Kashmir 1840

The ordinary waking consciousness is a very useful and, on most occasions, an indispensable state of mind; but it is by no means the only form of consciousness, nor in all circumstances the best. Insofar as he transcends his ordinary self and his ordinary mode of awareness, the mystic is able to enlarge his vision, to look more deeply into the unfathomable miracle of existence.

—Aldous Huxley[1]

In the prior section, I defined *ego* as the contents of waking awareness. In this section, we'll explore the ranges that can be traversed throughout consciousness including and beyond the ego. Each day, I pass seamlessly through different states of consciousness. I dream, I go into deep dreamless sleep, and I wake up to go about my day. A *state of consciousness* is a transitory experience of awareness. My state is defined by the contents of my moment-to-moment reality.

Expanded states of consciousness can be accessed through spiritual practices like meditation and breathwork, they can be induced with psychedelics, and they can happen spontaneously, for example, hiking through the forest or listening to a symphony orchestra. Remarkably, each major mystical tradition describes roughly the same four or five experiential states of consciousness.[2] This gives us reason to believe that states of consciousness are independent of culture, lineage, type of spiritual practice, or historical period in humanity. Inborn in each human is the capacity to access these experiential realms.

The five major states of consciousness are: gross (waking), subtle (dreaming), causal (dreamless sleep), witness (pure awareness, emptiness), and nonduality.

The gross state is my everyday waking consciousness. Here, I identify with my conceptual mind and perceive a world of form and matter. Jung calls it the ego. This is the consciousness that exists in the three-dimensional, physical world with a past, present, and future. The experience of waking consciousness actually has quite a wide range of possibilities. At the contracted end, obsession will completely focus me on a single object, while distraction and overwhelm leave me without any focus. The expansive end of the spectrum includes flow states and creative brainstorming.[3]

The state includes the physical sensations arising in my body, called *enteroception*, and my direct sensory perceptions of my environment (i.e., touch, taste, sound, sight, and smell).

Some folks refer to this as *ordinary consciousness* or *normal consciousness*, which is contrasted to *non-ordinary states of consciousness* or *altered states of consciousness*. I prefer not to use these terms. In my view, dreaming consciousness is just as ordinary and normal as waking consciousness.

The subtle state is my experience of subtle energy, life force, and vitality. In this state, I experience phenomena that are beyond the capacity of science to measure, hence the term *subtle*. As with the gross state, the subtle state contains quite a few layers of experience.

The aliveness of living organisms is variously called *prana, chi, sambhogakaya,* and élan vital. Whereas the gross realm contains the physical breath—the air being breathed—the subtle realm contains the energy of the breath. This life-force energy pervades every living cell. It flows through the body via *meridians* or *nadis.* It collects in centers called *chakras.* This energy is experienced as emotions: grief, fear, anger, joy, and so on. It is also the energy of eroticism, desire, kundalini, and orgasm. The four alchemical elements, fire, water, air, and earth, exist here as qualities of experience, in contrast to the chemical elements of the gross realm. All of these qualities comprise what is sometimes called the *low-subtle realm* or the *pranamaya kosha* in yoga.

At the more refined end of the spectrum, or *high-subtle realm,* are the mental activities and thoughtforms. The content of my thoughts cannot be measured, and yet my thoughts are an experiential reality. Thoughts carry an energy to them that we include in the subtle realm. Vivid memories, dream imagery, imagination, and visualization all fall within this category. In yoga, this is known as the *manomaya kosha.*

What we call *waking consciousness* is actually a nuanced amalgam of the gross state and the subtle state. At any given moment, I am experiencing physical sensations, emotions, and mental energies. Sometimes I may be fully *engrossed* in the physical realm—for example, during strenuous exercise. Other times, I may be totally absorbed in the mental realm—*lost in thought.* In this sense, the subtle state is almost always with me, and there is no need to go somewhere else or transcend somewhere to access it.

As a state of consciousness, the subtle realm is fluid and unbounded. Energy flowing through my body is not constrained by anatomical structures. Subtle energy is fickle, volatile, whimsical, and ephemeral. When I am fully immersed in the subtle realm, for example, during dreaming or orgasm, I experience time and space differently. They lose their *cartesian* orientation—their absolute ordinal nature—and become ever-present now and here.

The causal state is where the archetypes live. This realm holds the most primal and fundamental structures in the kosmos. Following big bang theory, there was a moment when all of the matter in the universe blasted into existence. For this moment of creation to take place, the *causal archetypes* crystalized into the substructure of the universe. These include the dimensionality of space-time, geometric and mathematical principles, the Logos (the creative function of the kosmos), Eros (the drive for parts to develop into wholes), Agape (the drive for wholes to embrace and integrate parts), colors and qualities, forms, and so on. These first principles created the container and set the wheels in motion for the contents to populate the universe.

In addition to the *causal archetypes,* this realm contains the *evolutionary archetypes* that have been developing along the way. For example, the archetype of *The Great Mother* was laid down as a groove in consciousness as soon as life-forms evolved to the point where mothers were gestating and birthing offspring. Prior to that time, there is no reason to believe this archetype existed. As such, we call it an evolutionary archetype—it evolved together with the kosmos and continues to evolve. The seven archetypes in this series, Magician, Warrior, Lover, King, Queen, and

Androgyne, are all evolutionary archetypes. They form a small subset of all the Jungian archetypes. Deities and myths also live in this realm, as they codevelop psychologically and culturally together with humanity.

In the Yogacharya school of Buddhism, there is a layer of consciousness called the *alaya-vijnana*, also known as the collective unconscious or "storehouse" consciousness, that contains a memory of every event in the history of the universe.[4] The storehouse consciousness exists in the causal realm.

Another category of evolutionary structures are the morphic fields. When an electron first met a proton and stabilized into orbit, the morphic field for the hydrogen atom was created. It is a habit or pattern for the behavior of matter that is duplicated and repeated to create a kosmic groove in consciousness. Subatomic structures, atoms, molecules and crystals, physical and astronomical processes, chemical and biological processes, and behavioral instincts are all examples of morphic fields. These may look like the *laws of nature*, but more properly could be understood as *emergent habits of nature*. The layer of consciousness where those habits are inscribed is this causal state.

Again, in my "waking consciousness," I am continually being influenced by one or more archetypes and one or more habits. The causal realm is seamlessly interwoven into reality across all scales. It underlies and pervades my experience even though I'm generally not aware of it.

As a state of consciousness, the causal realm is immense, all-pervading, and transpersonal. When I experience *beauty*, I connect with an experience that is somehow larger or transcending me as witness and the object inspiring the beauty. When the mystic encounters the deity, experience moves beyond description or definition. This vast, transcendent space is the causal state of consciousness.

When I access these higher states, I have what William James termed, a *primary religious experience*. Two of the qualities he gave to it are as follows: (1) *Ineffable*. It is beyond description. I am incapable of relaying the fullness of the experience back in waking consciousness; and (2) *Noetic*. The illumination, revelation, or beatific vision is an order of knowledge beyond factual information. It supersedes and is more authoritative than knowledge gained in the gross realm.[5]

The witness state is what I experience in deep dreamless sleep. It is awareness without any object—simply *pure witnessing*. At this level, all distinction falls away into qualityless awareness. The Buddhist concept of *emptiness* is awareness that is empty of all content.

This is also known as *rigpa*,[6] buddha-mind, and the *dharmakaya* in Buddhist tradition. In yoga, this is variously known as *turiya*,[7] *anandamayakosha*, and is also described by some states of *samadhi*.[8] In Kabbalah, it is *Ayin*.[9] This is a dimension beyond time and space, beyond subject and object, beyond inside and outside. It is pure *I Am*-ness. Total being. The Absolute. Consciousness itself.[10]

I have sometimes said that there is a power in the soul which alone is free.… So now I shall name it in nobler fashion than I ever did before, and yet it disowns the nobler name and mode, for it transcends them. It is free of all names and void of all forms, entirely exempt and free, as God is exempt and free in Himself. It is as completely one and simple as God is one and simple, so that no man can in any way glimpse it.

—Meister Eckhart[11]

This pure witnessing state was famously articulated by the Indian Buddhist sage Nāgārjuna, circa 200 CE. In order to point to the ineffable nature of this state, he offers us four categories that *cannot* be affirmed as true:

1. It exists
2. It is nonexistent
3. It is both existent and
4. It is neither existent nor nonexistent.

None of these four categories apply to the witness state of reality.[12] Nothing whatsoever can be said to define this realm—it transcends any description. Even calling the state *undefinable* is inaccurate because that is itself a definitive label. Understanding this limitation, various mystical traditions have described this state as timeless, infinite, ungraspable, and groundless.

The total consciousness of I Am, pure being, is at the core of all experience. More accurately, it is the pervasive layer underlying all experience.[13] It is the container within which all experience arises. It is the fundamental nature of the mind and *the great space of being.*

Free of karma, I am the fire that burns all karmas. Free of sorrow, I am the fire that removes all sorrow. Free of form, I am the fire that releases all forms. I am the liberating nectar of Self-Knowledge; I am all-pervading like the sky.

Free of sin, I am the fire that burns all sins. Free of prescribed duty, I am the fire that purifies all duties. Unbound, I am the fire that breaks all bondage. I am the liberating nectar of Self-Knowledge; I am all-pervading like the sky.

I am beyond both existence and non-existence; neither pertain to me. I am beyond both union and separation; neither pertain to me. I am beyond both thought and the absence of thought; neither pertain to me. I am the liberating nectar of Self-Knowledge; I am all-pervading like the sky.

—Avadhuta Gita[14]

Nonduality is the union of the witness state with the totality of all phenomena.[15] From the Heart Sutra, *"emptiness is form, form is emptiness. Emptiness is none other than form. Form is none other than emptiness."*[16] Nonduality means "not two." When awareness and the objects of awareness are experienced as a seamless whole, that is nondual consciousness. There is no subject and object, no me and other, no light and dark.

This state is variously referred to as enlightenment, liberation, awakening, and realization. This state can be understood as the true nature of reality. It is called *suchness* or *thusness*—the totality of existence exactly as it is. This state *is*. There was never a time when it was not.

> *In fact, there is no such thing as a path to enlightenment, simply because enlightenment is ever present in all places and at all times. What you can do is to remove any and all illusions, especially the ones you value most and find the most security in, that cloud your perception of Reality. Let go of clinging to your illusions and resisting what is, and Reality will suddenly come into view.*
>
> —Adyashanti[17]

In this state, the interior of awareness becomes continuous with the exteriors of phenomena. More accurately, one perceives the true unified nature of reality without the dualistic filter. Inside perception and cognition are not separate or distinct from outside environment and phenomena. In the Christian tradition, nonduality is referred to as *indistinct union*.[18]

Summary

Each of these states of consciousness is available right here, right now. They are your birthright. They are your nature. Your awareness cannot *not* be somewhere on this ladder of states because it describes the totality of what consciousness can experience.

Informed by this map, I can practice accessing these states of consciousness. This primarily involves clearing away the mental clutter and disidentifying with the discursive voice in my head. Meditation, yoga, chanting, prayer, shamanic trance states, and countless other modalities all work toward the same end: recognition and stability in the I Am of consciousness.

In 2005, Johns Hopkins University released a study where participants were given a high dose of the active ingredient in psychedelic mushrooms to understand the relationship between psychedelics and Primary Religious Experiences described by William James (referenced above). The study found that mystical experiences were not only incredibly meaningful, but that participants showed marked improvements in their daily lives afterward:

More than 60 percent of subjects described the effects of psilocybin in ways that met criteria for a "full mystical experience". One third said the experience was the single most spiritually significant of their lifetimes; and more than two-thirds rated it among their five most meaningful and spiritually significant. Subjects liken it to the importance of the birth of their first child or the death of a parent.

Two months later, 79 percent of subjects reported moderately or greatly increased well-being or life satisfaction compared with those given a placebo at the same test session. A majority said their mood, attitudes and behaviors had changed for the better. Structured interviews with family members, friends and co-workers generally confirmed the subjects' remarks.[19]

Expanded states of consciousness, when we are able to safely access and integrate them, connect us to meaning, purpose, well-being, love, bliss, and grace, just to name a few qualities. The Hopkins study demonstrates that, in the proper circumstances, accessing higher states of consciousness offers significant benefits to quality of life. These experiences provide perspectives beyond our neurotic ego's self-interest—what Chogyam Trungpa calls *basic sanity*.[20]

Practice Accessing States

(Listen to a free guided audio of this section at organicmasculine.com)

The Gross State

Come into a comfortable meditation posture.

> This can be done in two ways. Lie down on your back with your feet on the ground and knees knocked in together. Rest your hands at your sides or on your belly with your elbows on the floor.

> Or sit cross-legged on a meditation cushion. Ensure that your hips are elevated above your knees so your inner thighs can relax. Lengthen your spine up toward the sky. Shoulders are broad. Relax down the back of your body. Slightly tuck in your ribs. Gently lower your chin and bring it back toward your spine so the back of your neck is aligned with your spinal column. Relax your jaw and your eyes. Rest your hands on your thighs or hold one hand in the other at your belly.

Enter into *mindful awareness.*

> Bring your awareness inside yourself. Begin to witness your inner landscape. Mindfulness means simply watching what is happening without needing to do or engage in any way. Take a step back in your awareness to simply observe.

Notice the sensations of your breath.

> Feel the cool air as it enters your nostrils and passes through your sinuses and windpipe and into your lungs. Feel the warm air as it passes back out from lungs to windpipe, to sinuses, through your nostrils. Feel your ribs and chest rising and falling with each breath. Feel your belly expand and contract. Notice the minute shifts your pelvis makes with each breath and the ways your shoulders and upper arms shift with the breath. Feel your whole body participating in each breath.

Feel for tension in your body.

> As you breathe, feel for tension, tightness, or pain arising in your body. Welcome the sensations without needing to do anything about them. Imagine that you are able to breathe directly into this tense part of your body. Gently wrap the in-breath around this place of tension like a soft blanket. On the out-breath, just relax.

Feel for a place of neutrality in your body.

> As you breathe, notice one place that feels neutral—neither good nor bad, neither painful nor pleasurable—just *regular*, just *normal*. Imagine that you are able to breathe directly into

this part of your body. Imagine this place expanding with the in-breath and emptying out on the out-breath. Relax into this neutral place in your body. Notice that this is a safe, sanctuary space for you to inhabit.

Feel for pleasure in your body.
Notice one place in your body that feels good. Breathe into it and wake it up. Exhaling, say "yes" to the pleasure. Take slow, powerful breaths, and give yourself permission to enjoy breathing. Feel the sensations of each in-breath and out-breath and welcome any joy, excitement, or goodness that arises. Smile with your breath.

Breathe with your whole body.
Imagine you are able to inhale air through every pore in your skin directly into all parts of your body. Feel the breath coming into your whole body. Exhale through every pore back out. Feel your whole body breathing. Feel every cell in your body breathing. Breathe as your body.

Notice the feeling of your body on the earth.
Feel the places where your body is touching the cushion or mat. Feel the solidity of the floor and the earth beneath you. Allow yourself to be supported. Feel your body being held. Relax into the earth.

Notice the sounds in your environment.
Welcome in the sounds of your space. Be curious. Really listen. Notice that while the sounds are happening outside of you, the awareness of the sound is happening inside of you. Explore the edge where external sound becomes internal cognition. Breathe with the sounds of your environment.

Open your eyes and notice the colors and shapes of your environment.
Release the interpretations of how objects are defined. Simply observe the colors. Observe the textures. Notice how the brightness or dimness affects your eyes. Notice that while shapes are located outside of you, awareness of shapes is happening inside of you. Explore the edge where external objects become internal cognition. Allow the colors and shapes to wash over you.

Feel your body breathing together with your environment.
Feel your whole body. Breathe as your body. Feel your body in relationship with the earth below. Breathe with the earth. Feel your body in relationship with all the objects, sights, and sounds around you. Breathe with your environment. Become the total awareness of body, earth, and environment.

The Subtle State

Come into a comfortable meditation posture.

Same as above.

Enter into *mindful awareness*.

Same as above.

Notice your mental activity.

From the place of mindful awareness, notice whatever thoughts are happening. Allow them to pass through. Notice how they arise and notice how they pass away. Without engaging the content of your thoughts, observe them as they stream through your consciousness. Notice the qualities of your mental activity: fast or slow, energetic or tired, anxious or relaxed.

Notice your emotions.

From the place of mindful awareness, welcome whatever emotions are present. There is no need to process any of these emotions. Simply acknowledge each emotion as it arises. Notice if there are several emotions and make space for them. Notice if there is not much emotion present. Either way, breathe and be curious.

Feel your emotions.

Let go of observing and come into your body to feel your emotions. Do not overwhelm yourself or pick too much—just feel the amount and intensity that you can handle. Let go into feeling. Open into the fullness and richness of your emotions. Breathe and feel.

Feel the aliveness of your body.

Notice how you experience aliveness. Whatever process is happening is a part of your life force. Everything, including numbness, resistance, depression, and pain are part of aliveness. Say "yes" to your aliveness. Breathe along with your aliveness. Welcome in more and more of your aliveness.

Receive from your aliveness.

Acknowledge the wisdom of your vitality. Allow your life force to do whatever it naturally wants to do. Sing along with it. Support the process of your aliveness. Be nurtured and sustained by your aliveness. Breathe a breath of gratitude for your aliveness.

Become your aliveness.

Immerse into your aliveness. Let go and become to creative, spontaneous unfolding of aliveness itself. Dunk yourself into this aliveness. Each breath is lifeforce. Each thought is lifeforce. Every resistance is lifeforce. Release the illusion of separation and become total aliveness.

The Causal State

Come into a comfortable meditation posture and enter into mindful awareness.

Invoke the archetype of the *Magician*.

Call in the spirit and essence of the Magician to be with you now. Ask the Magician to guide you and show you how to open. Listen for what comes through. Trust your intuition and the quiet guidance that arises. Ask any questions you'd like to ask.

Call in the qualities of the Magician: intellectual genius, exploration, transformation, magic, and mystery. Remember a time when you experienced these qualities in yourself. Find the Magician who lives within you. Welcome the Magician to move through you and to share wisdom with you. Imagine yourself reaching upward with wand in hand to touch the pure bright light of the Magician archetype. Now imagine channeling that essence through your wand into your body. Feel yourself as the Magician in human form.

Repeat this process for any archetypal pattern that you'd like to connect with.

The Witness State

Come into a comfortable meditation posture and enter into mindful awareness.

Breathe into the space of your lower belly.

Slowly and gently breathe into your belly. Find a spot midway between your navel and your pelvic floor, back toward the inside of your spine. Softly breathe and feel. Notice for a dark space about the shape of an egg. Allow your breath to meet the surface of this shape and simply breathe with it. On the out-breath, begin to relax into this space.

Let go into the space of your lower belly.

Imagine that your nostrils are located on the surface of this dark egg in your lower belly. Gently inhale into the egg. On each out-breath, just let go. Without agenda or pressure, feel your way into the center of this space. Keep letting go into it. Deeper and deeper. Softly releasing into this dark, vast space.

If you pop out, come back to feeling your nostrils on the surface of the dark egg near the inside of your spine. Go slow and be gentle. Allow the space to open in its own time.

Once you let go into the space, just keep falling. Notice that there is no up or down, no edge or limit, nothing to hold onto, and no bottom to the space. Space feels different. There is no time. Just an infinite, black, nothing to melt into. Let go completely into the space.

Notice if there was ever a time when this space did not exist. Is it here while you are sleeping? Was it here before you were born? Will there ever be a time when this space does not exist? Will it be here after you die?

Notice if this space is accessible in all places. Is there anywhere in the universe that this space does not pervade and underlie? Is there any edge or limit to this space?

Nonduality

Stabilize in the experience of the *witness state*.

Add back in all other states of consciousness.
  Include your thoughts, personality traits, and neuroses. Include distraction, skepticism, and resistance. Include all emotions.

Allow the perfect unfolding of this moment.
  Add nothing. Subtract nothing. Abide in the suchness of existence. Experience the perfection of each moment unfolding both relatively and in timeless absolute. Surrender to thusness.

Prompts for Journaling and Discussion

Recall a mystical experience you had in as much detail as possible. How has this experience shaped your life?

How does reality function in dream-space: time, location, distance, relationship, and so on?

What clues does this offer about metaphysics and mechanics of the subtle realm?

Describe Enlightenment. Describe *the void*. Describe God. Knowing that these are indescribable, do your best anyway.

Notes

[1] *Moksha*, Huxley.

[2] "Every major meditation tradition recognizes these 4 or 5 major states of consciousness, and likewise has maps of the 4 or 5 major correlative state-stages, or meditative stages, for moving through them, transcending and including them as they go. Significant research has demonstrated that although the surface features of each of these traditions and their state-stages differ considerably from culture to culture, their deep features are in many ways significantly similar. In fact, virtually all of them follow variations on the 4 or 5 major natural states of consciousness given cross-culturally and universally to all human beings." *The Religion of Tomorrow*, Wilber

[3] "The mystique of rock climbing is climbing; you get to the top of a rock glad it's over but really wish it would go on forever. The justification of climbing is climbing, like the justification of poetry is writing; you don't conquer anything except things in yourself.… The act of writing justifies poetry. Climbing is the same: recognizing that you are a flow. The purpose of the flow is to keep on flowing, not looking for a peak or utopia but staying in the flow. It is not a moving up but a continuous flowing; you move up to keep the flow going. There is no possible reason for climbing except the climbing itself; it is a self-communication." *Flow*, Csikszentmihalyi.

[4] "The Buddha distinguishes eight forms of consciousness: the basic five (visual, auditory, olfactory, gustatory, and tactile), along with conceptual consciousness (mano-vijnana), selfconsciousness or will (manas), and repository or storehouse consciousness (alaya-vijnana), which is sometimes referred to in this sutra simply as 'mind.'" *Lankavatara Sutra*, Pine.

[5] C.f. *The Varieties of Religious Experience*.

[6] "The perspective of dzokchen, then, emphasizes primordial enlightenment of the 'mind.' It speaks of ultimate awakening as the recognition of 'mind itself,' by which is meant the untrammeled awareness of the natural state, the 'buddha-mind.' This 'mind,' obviously, is not the ordinary mind of dualistic awareness, the consciousness or 'subject' pole of the subject-object dichotomy. In dzokchen, this ultimate 'mind' translates the Tibetan term rikpa, 'intelligence' or 'naked awareness.' This rikpa is the dharmakaya. It is the flash of awareness that precedes the split into dualistic consciousness of myself, my mind, and the other, the object. It is the first instant of each moment of perception that occurs outside of the I-other framework of the skandhas. If this moment is not 'mind' in the ordinary dualistic sense, then why call it mind at all? This is done in order to make clear that this moment is not nothing, not pure vacuity, but clear, brilliant, and cognizant." *Secret of the Vajra World*, Ray.

[7] "Turiya – literally means 'fourth' state of consciousness, unmanifest state of purusha and prakriti, beyond conscious, subcon-

scious and unconscious mind; supraconsciousness." *Hatha Yoga Pradipika*, Muktibodhananda.

[8] "When time, space and idea (knower, known and knowing) are removed, and the essential nature of thought remains, it is nirvichara or *vichara asamprajnata*. At the culmination of this

samadhi, the chitta is illumined and intellect ceases. Nirvichara develops into ananda or *sanandan* samadhi when chitta has penetrated beyond the subtle existence of the object and there is only awareness of the existence of the vritti 'I am' (aham asmi). It is sattwic ahamkara or ego, a state of pure existence and awareness without word or idea. Ananda becomes asmita when there is no differentiation between the object of consciousness and the consciousness. Awareness and consciousness are absolute but there is still the seed of ego. It is the highest sattwic state of consciousness. *Hatha Yoga Pradipika*, Muktibodhananda.

[9] "The word *nothingness* connotes negativing and non-being, but what the mystic means by divine nothingness is that God is greater than any *thing* one can imagine: it is like *no thing*. Since God's being is incomprehensible and ineffable, the least offensive and most accurate description one can offer is, paradoxically, *nothing*. David ben Abraham ha-Lavan, a fourteenth-century kabbalist, insists that "nothingness [*ayin*] is more existent than all the being [*yesh*] of the world.'" "Ayin: The Concept of Nothingness in Jewish Mysticism," Matt

[10] "Consciousness is a singular of which the plural is unknown; that there is only one thing and that what seems to be a plurality is merely a series of different aspects of this one thing, produced by a deception." Schrödinger.

[11] Sermon 8.

[12] "Previous to its own defining features space does not exist, not even slightly. If it came before its own defining features, it follows that it's featureless. An entity devoid of features can never have existence anywhere. If there is no thing that's without features, to what can features then apply?... If things do not exist, of what can there be nonexistence? And what is there that, being neither an existent nor a nonexistent thing, can have cognizance of existence or nonexistence? Therefore space is neither an existent nor a nonexistent thing; it's not the basis for defining features, nor those very features." *The Root Stanzas of the Middle Way*, Nāgārjuna.

[13] "All of the great meditative traditions maintain that each and every moment your mind actually starts out that way—fully and nakedly present, focused on the timeless Now, being fully present in the Present. And then you start thinking, analyzing, judging, condemning, grasping, feeling, and separating—at once you exist on this side of your face, looking at the world 'out there' as it smashes into you and generally begins to make your life intolerable, full of anxiety, suffering, despair, torment, tears, and terror. Identified with this small, finite, separate self or ego, we have forgotten our true, clear, vast, open, deep, empty, and pure Self, the pure Witness, the pure infinite Observer." *The Religion of Tomorrow*, Wilber.

[14] Translated by Rory Mackay.

[15] "Hence there are really two distinct acts of 'divine union,' two distinct kinds of illumination involved in the Mystic Way: the dual character of the spiritual consciousness brings a dual responsibility in its train. First, there is the union with Life, with the World of Becoming: and parallel with it, the illumination by which the mystic 'gazes upon a more veritable world.' Secondly, there is the union with Being, with the One: and that final, ineffable illumination of pure love which is called the 'knowledge of God.'" *Mysticism: The Preeminent Study in the Nature and Development of Spiritual Consciousness*, Underhill.

[16] "All material forms and all conscious states are to be known as absolutely selfless, without separate identity, luminously pure. The processes of personal awareness do not need to be purified. They are ontologically transparent, or perfectly pure, by their very nature. All the apparently complex forms of functional interdependence remain utterly simple, indivisible, pristine, open and free. Universal transparency is what manifests as both form and consciousness. Material forms are empty of the slightest substantial self-existence, and luminous emptiness of self-existence is precisely what is manifest as material forms. In the same way, conscious states are empty of the slightest independent self-existence, and luminous emptiness of self-existence is precisely what is manifest as conscious states." *Mother of the Buddhas*, Hixon.

[17] *The Way of Liberation.*

[18] "Indistinct union refers to the way in which during the experience one is still completely united to God while at the same time not recognizing oneself is a position separate from God. There is only God all around, within and without, in a kind of 'indistinct' nature, without at the same time this oneness being an undifferentiated mush. Rather it is a dynamic vision and opening to the Kingdom of Heaven on Earth, where God is 'all in all.'" "Indistinct Union: An Integral Introduction to Nonduality in Christianity," Dierkes.

[19] "Psilocybin can occasion mystical-type experiences having substantial and sustained personal meaning and spiritual significance," Griffiths et al.

[20] "Fundamental security comes from realizing that you have broken through something. You reflect back and realize that you used to be extraordinarily paranoid and neurotic, watching each step you made, thinking you might lose your sanity, that situations were always threatening in some way. Now you are free of all those fears and preconceptions. You discover that you have something to give rather than having to demand from others, having to grasp all the time. For the first time, you are a rich person, you contain basic sanity. You have something to offer, you are able to work with your fellow sentient beings, you do not have to reassure yourself anymore." *The Myth of Freedom and the Way of Meditation*, Trungpa.

| 7 |

The Evolving Kosmos

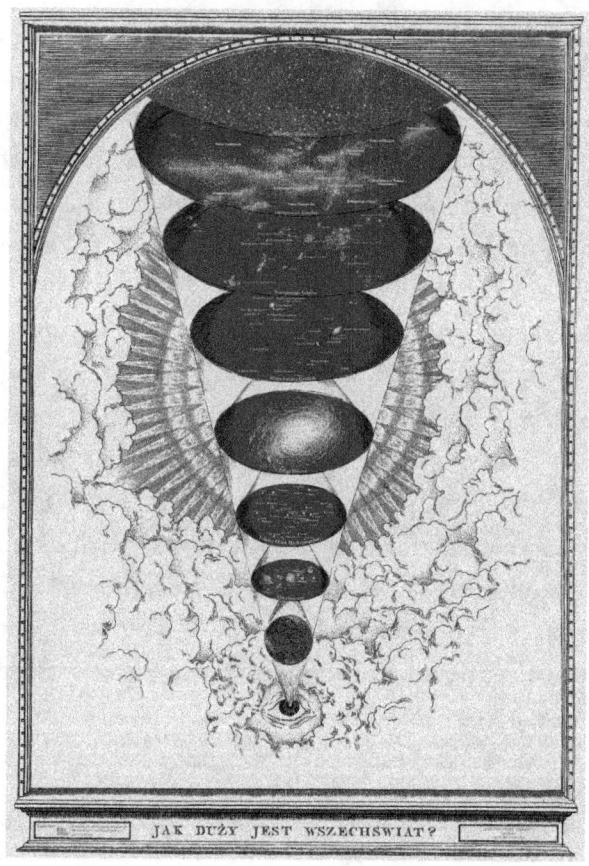

Figure 7.1 "How Big is the Universe?"[1]

The kosmos is the totality of the interior realms of consciousness together with the exterior phenomenal universe. From moment to moment, the kosmos is changing. When I look closely, I discover the change has a directionality: kosmos is in a process of evolution. As we shall explore in this chapter, the evolutionary drive is toward greater degrees of wholeness and complexity. This drive of becoming is called *Eros*.

Western culture tends to view the universe as a collection of things in motion. This is the foundation of *scientific materialism* that emerged in the eighteenth century. The *process* view of the kosmos, on the other hand, holds that reality *is* the evolutionary process itself. This view was articulated by Alfred North Whitehead at the beginning of the twentieth century. And now, at the cutting edge of our understanding is the *holonic* view of the kosmos that sees every *thing* and every *process* as a holon. A holon is an entity that is whole in itself, that contains parts, and that is itself part of a larger whole: a whole-part. The kosmos can be viewed as a collection of nested whole-parts in an ongoing process of evolution.

Because the kosmos includes all consciousness, from nondual enlightenment to my most trivial thoughts, I can say that the kosmos is conscious(!) and the consciousness of the kosmos is not separate from me. I am one individuated locus of consciousness and form within this vast tapestry of consciousness and form. All of me, all of us, and all of the kosmos are in a process of self-becoming. In the broadest sense, this is what I mean by the *evolution of consciousness.* Throughout this chapter, we'll examine concrete examples for how this process works.

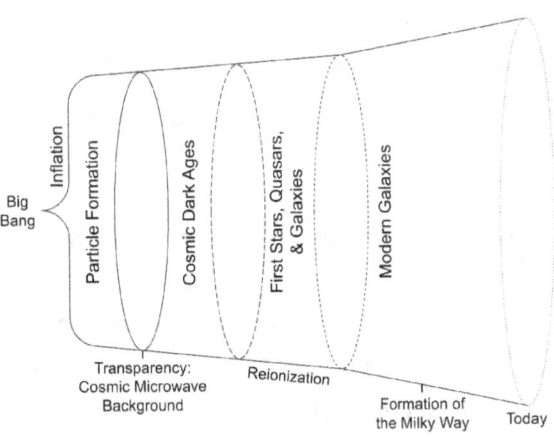

Figure 7.2 History of the physical universe

When I learned how to look through an evolutionary lens, I began to see this process happening at every layer and level of existence. Evolution occurs along four concurrent trajectories: the physical universe, biological life, cultural evolution, and psychological evolution. The *evolution of consciousness* encompasses all four of these developmental lines of the kosmos, though I tend to focus on the psychological and cultural aspects of consciousness most.

These four evolutionary processes sequentially build upon each other. The physical universe needed to mature to a certain point for biological life to emerge. The biosphere rests on the foundation of the physiosphere. Similarly, cultural and psychological evolutions required a certain maturation of biological life in order to emerge (i.e., to develop into humans). So, the advancement of human consciousness, both individually and collectively, rests on the more fundamental process of biological evolution, which rests on the even more fundamental process of physical evolution.

I. Evolution of the Physical Universe

Let's briefly consider the evolution of the physical universe. Our best guess is that the universe originated billions of years ago from an infinitely dense point, called the big bang (fig 7.2). Moments after the big bang, the universe expanded rapidly and uniformly in a theorized period called *inflation*.[2] From there, the energy permeating space condensed into particles as the universe expanded and cooled. Within the first three minutes, the whole stage was set. All matter and energy, their distribution throughout space, the four primary forces: strong, weak, electromagnetic, and gravitational, and the key constants like the speed of light were all in place.[3] Over the next 13.7 billion years, these basic particles will do some pretty magnificent things.

As space expanded and cooled, electrons slowed enough to be captured by protons into orbit, forming atoms. At this transition, the universe became transparent to light. We measure this today as the cosmic microwave background radiation. This moment of phase change from roaming protons and electrons into atoms marked the universe's shift from a light-filled soup into darkness. Atoms then coalesced into massive clouds of gas that eventually ignited into the first stars and quasars. These stars collected into galaxies and superclusters of galaxies. Until this point, the universe had only two elements: hydrogen and helium. Massive stars fused all the heavier elements in their cores and spewed them back out through supernova explosions.

As more and more stars lit up the universe, the free-floating gas charged back up, and electrons disconnected from protons in a process called *reionization*. However, by this time, space had expanded and cooled enough that it remained transparent to light, as it is today. Eventually, our Milky Way galaxy formed, our sun accreted enough matter to ignite, and in its accretion disc, the earth and other planets in our solar system formed.

In the superstructure of the universe, we see an evolutionary movement from undifferentiated cosmic soup, to particles, to galaxies with stars and planets. In the microstructure, we see a similar complexification from undifferentiated light, to subatomic particles, to hydrogen and helium, to the heavier elements (fig. 7.3). On both macro and micro scales, the physical universe has been in a 13.7-billion-year process of evolution.[4]

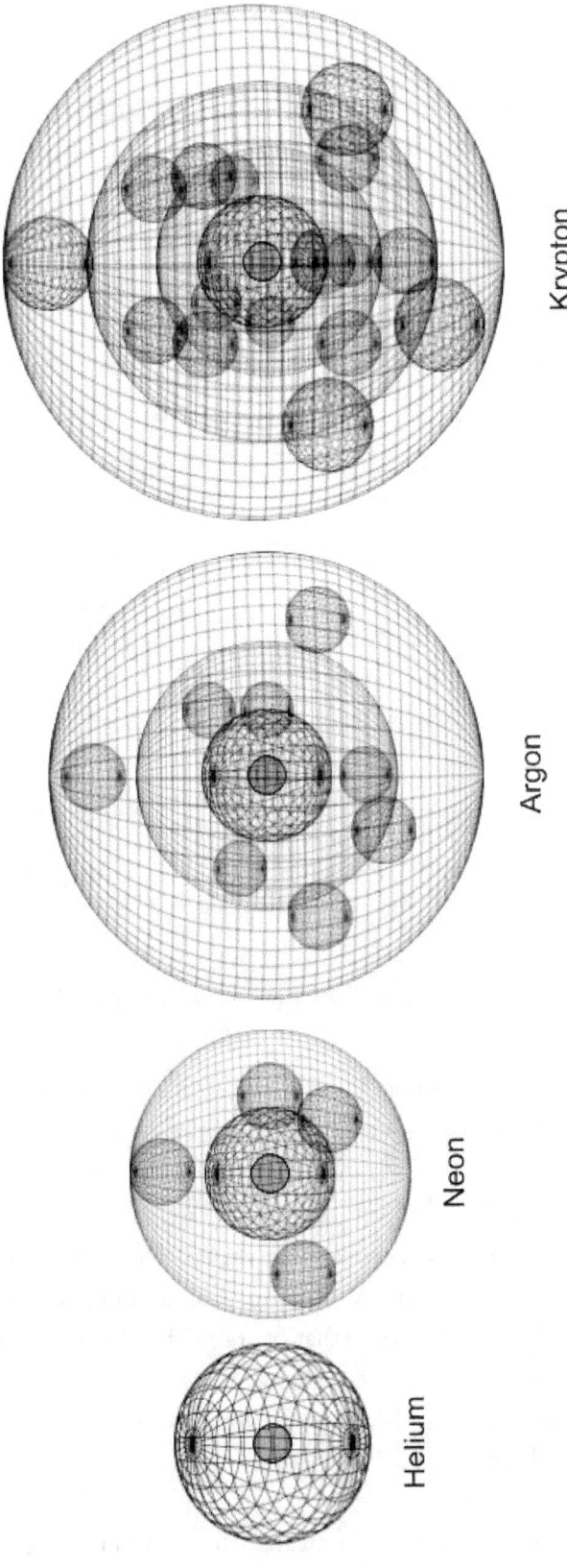

Figure 7.3 Electron geometries of noble gases

II. Evolution of Biological Life

The emergence of biological life marked a categorical shift in the progression of the universe. Our best scientific guesses propose that a soup of organic material self-organized into a system capable of self-reproduction around 3.7 billion years ago (fig. 7.4).

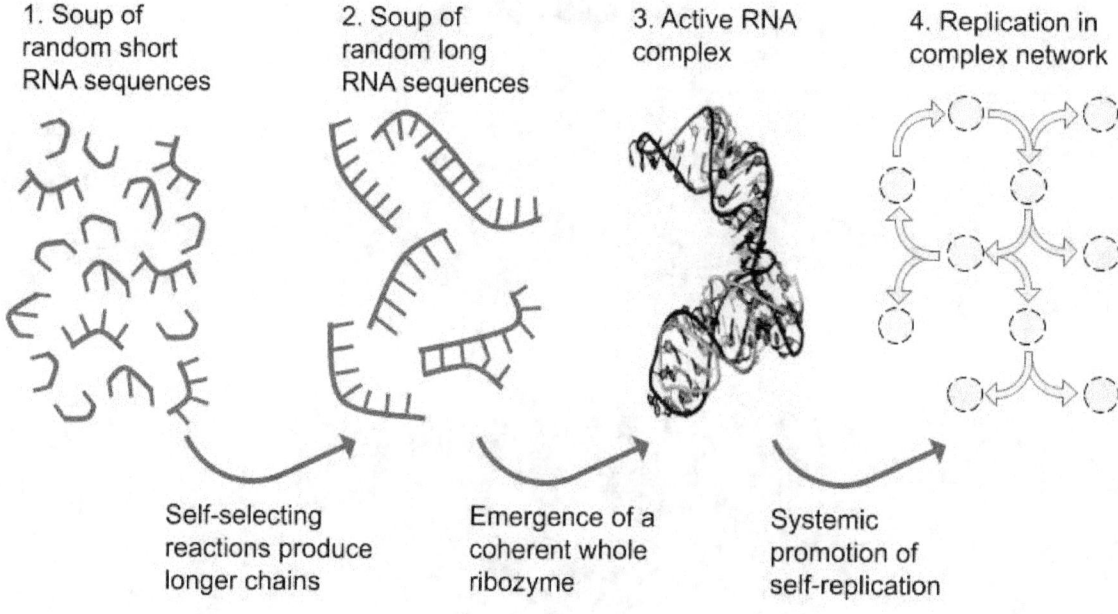

1. Soup of random short RNA sequences

2. Soup of random long RNA sequences

3. Active RNA complex

4. Replication in complex network

Self-selecting reactions produce longer chains

Emergence of a coherent whole ribozyme

Systemic promotion of self-replication

Figure 7.4 Theoretical model for the formation of RNA molecules[5]

The processes of life are fundamentally different from nonbiological systems. The reason for this is that life inherently incorporates self-referential complexities that are beyond physical systems. Imagine that each strand of DNA is a cookbook. In the cookbook are recipes for how to make a cell wall, how to make a ribosome, an endoplasmic reticulum, and a golgi body. In addition, the recipe book has a recipe for how to make this very DNA book, including this very recipe, including this very step here, now. There is an astounding amount of symbolic meaning packed into each strand of DNA. It is a chemical code that contains the blueprint for all of itself.

Over the course of the twentieth century, systems theorists, cyberneticists, chaos theorists, and biologists teamed up to make remarkable strides in understanding how biological life operates. Here is how we characterize living organisms:

• Each organism is an open system. This means it is a bounded entity that is continually in exchange with its environment. Organisms eat food and dispel waste.

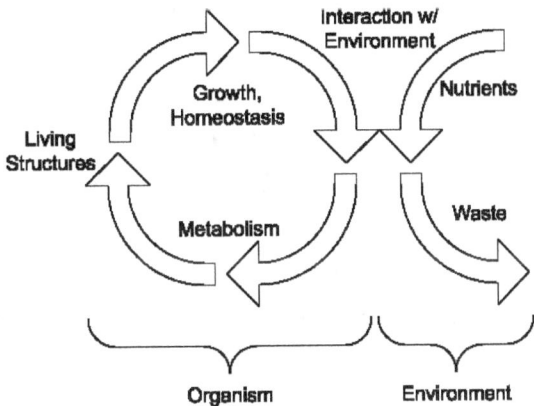

Figure 7.5 Organism as an open system

- These bounded, open systems balance in states that are far from equilibrium. This adaptive capacity has been described scientifically as a *dissipative structure*. The open systems of organisms operate differently from closed systems. According to the second law of thermodynamics, entropy is always increasing for closed systems. This means most systems in the universe are always moving toward thermal equilibrium and maximum randomness. Living systems, on the other hand, create islands of order that exist far from equilibrium.[6]

- Organisms are self-organizing. Each organism assembles itself. It displays systemic properties where the pattern that governs the organism contains a level of complexity beyond the sum of the parts. Organisms display emergent behaviors and operate according to network effects and interactions.

- Organisms are self-regulating. This is known as *homeostasis*. Organisms maintain themselves through internally adaptive processes and in ongoing relationship with their environment. This requires a degree of *prehension* or sensing of the total system, together with a degree of agency to respond to changing conditions. Organisms are adaptive.

- Aliveness is nonlocalized. Individual atoms and molecules do not hold the property of aliveness. Rather, the *livingness* of an organism must be understood holistically at the level of the organism itself. No subpart or local region of an organism determines its aliveness.[7]

- Organisms are population forming. These groups of organisms interact in complex ways. Flocks of geese, hives of bees, and societies of humans all display emergent group-level phenomena that cannot be understood solely at the level of interacting individuals. Groups of organisms hold collective awareness and intelligence. Members within populations compete, cooperate, and diversify roles within the groups.

- Organisms are generational. While individual organisms have a finite life span, the pattern of the organism is passed down from parent to offspring. Biological life passes down information through generations via the genome. Life remembers. In addition, generational reproduction carries forward the adaptations from individual organisms, mixes genes, and creates opportunities for genetic mutation. And because organisms compete and selectively reproduce, the most successful features of life are dynamically carried forward. Reproduction enables biological evolution.

- Organisms incorporate biofield energy. This final point is not listed in biology textbooks because *scientific materialism* does not incorporate or account for the realms of consciousness discussed in the previous chapter. Science only measures the gross realm. However, the *aliveness* of biological life is subtle energy. It is prana, chi, *elan vital,* or *entelechy.* The complexification of living systems have interwoven the more expansive subtle realm of consciousness into its processes. Systems with more depth embody more complex consciousness. Life's marriage of the subtle and gross realms represents a profound advancement in the consciousness of the kosmos.

To be clear, the subtle realm is coextensive with the entire physical universe. There is not a single speck of space dust that does not participate in the subtle realm, however faintly. But the incorporation of subtle energy into a meaningful pattern is fundamentally beyond the capacity of purely physical systems to hold. The organizing pattern within a living system operates throughout both the gross physical domain and the subtle energetic domain. Subtle energy is intrinsically woven into the pattern of life.

> *Living systems are characterized by a remarkably complex organization which endows them with the capacity to respond to external stimuli, to bind or release energy (metabolism), to grow, to differentiate, and to replicate. Biological systems have the further remarkable property that they are open systems, which maintain a steady-state balance in spite of much input and output. This homeostasis is made possible by elaborate feedback mechanisms, unknown in their precision in any inanimate system.*
>
> —Ernst Mayr[8]

Life-forms organize and reproduce in a continual process of creation that advances their own self-systems, a property termed *autopoiesis.*[9] *Auto* means "self" and *poiesis* means "creation," stemming from the same root as the word *poetry.* Biological life creates itself. So I'll define a living system as *an autonomous process of self-organization.*[10]

Biological life further interconnects across species to form ecosystems and ultimately a planetary system. These macro-systems exhibit recursive complexities toward homeostasis, just like the organisms that comprise them. One striking example on the planetary scale is the observation that over the past four billion years, the sun has become about 25 percent hotter, and yet life on Earth has adapted to keep itself within the narrow band of livable conditions with liquid water. This observation led James Lovelock to propose that the biosphere of earth is one living system, known as the Gaia hypothesis.[11]

Over the past 3.7 billion years, biological life has undergone a process of complexification into greater expressions of wholeness. Simple prokaryotic cells eventually incorporated the nucleus and mitochondria to give rise to eukaryotic cells. Single-celled organisms gave rise to multicellular organisms. Life diversified into fungi, plants, and animals; and life-systems evolved greater relational complexity (for example, the co-arisal of flowers and pollinators) and ecosystems.

III. The Evolution of Psychological and Social Consciousness

As far as we know, humans hold a unique trait among biological life: the capacity for self-reflection. In the same way that recursive complexity of organic matter is a distinguishing feature of biological life, recursive complexity of awareness (i.e., self-consciousness) is the feature that distinguishes human consciousness. The realm of purely physical processes is known as the *physiosphere*, biological life occupies the *biosphere*, and the *noosphere* describes the realm of human consciousness. The emergence of this type of awareness in the evolution of life is called the *point of reflection*:

> *Reflection is, as the word indicates, the power acquired by a consciousness to turn in upon itself, to take possession of itself as of an object endowed with its own particular consistence and value: no longer merely to know, but to know oneself; no longer merely to know, but to know that one knows.… The being who is the object of his own reflection, in consequence of that very doubling back upon himself, becomes in a flash able to raise himself into a new sphere. In reality, another world is born. Abstraction, logic, reasoned choice and inventions, mathematics, art, calculation of space and time, anxieties and dreams of love—all these activities of inner life are nothing else than the effervescence of the newly-formed centre as it explodes onto itself.*
>
> —Teilhard de Chardin[12]

With the emergence of humans, the inner psychological landscapes of consciousness blossomed into the kosmos. This point of reflection ushered in the self-aware ego for life on earth. Just as life systems are autonomous self-organizing processes of organic matter, the ego is an autonomous self-organizing process of thoughtforms. The ego is essentially a repeated and habitual focusing of attention inward, or "self-ward," so that consciousness becomes individuated. This self-organizing process is an interweaving of thoughts, identities, beliefs, personality traits, and memories. The self-reflective center organizes and interprets sensory perception, manages priorities, makes plans, and directs behavior.

Egoic consciousness can be understood as an even richer interweaving of the gross physical realm with the subtle energetic realm. Biological life is made *alive* by the incorporation of biofield energy, which occupies the lower spectrum of the subtle realm (termed in yoga, the *pranamaya kosha*). At the high end of the subtle realm are the thoughtforms (i.e., the *manomaya kosha*). As sensory and cognitive feedback mechanisms evolved more complexity, organisms began to access the *high subtle realm*. A mind is made *sentient* by the incorporation of thoughtforms from the high subtle realm into the awareness of the living system.

Each individual human undergoes a developmental process of psychological maturation. As the infant grows into child and then adult, the ego emerges, gains agency, and matures. What is developing is the awareness of *who I am*—which is to say, an evolution of consciousness. This psychic space is experienced within each individual. It is our inner landscape, the psyche. Psychological consciousness is subjective rather than objective and qualitative rather than quantitative. Over the past century, developmental psychology has been studying how consciousness matures in individuals. I'll examine a few of these models in the following section on *paradigms*.

Codeveloping together with the individual egoic consciousness is collective consciousness. This is formed by the language, customs, culture, symbols, and meanings that are held between members of a culture. While psychology is subjective, culture is *intersubjective*. Culture can be understood as an autonomous self-organizing process that is constituted by relationships. Western civilization has progressed from premodern, modern, and now into postmodern phases in its evolution.

Cultural consciousness influences and is influenced by psychological consciousness. They have co-evolved throughout human history and they codevelop within each individual. In fact, these two realms are constantly interacting. So even though these two evolutionary categories are distinct, they are best understood when studied as a whole.

Summary

In summary, the distinct evolutionary pathways in the kosmos are physical, biological, and social/ psychological. These three processes exist in a hierarchy where matter forms the foundation for life, and life forms the foundation for subjective and intersubjective consciousness. Each progressive layer carries an increasing degree of complexity, and the system as a whole displays an *organized complexity*. The *kosmos*, as the totality of each layer of reality woven together, is in a process of evolution through these concurrent processes.[13] From Whitehead's perspective, the evolutionary process *is* the kosmos.[14] In this view, I am not separate from the kosmos. There is no *inside me* that is apart from the *outside world*. My individuated consciousness is one aspect of the total consciousness of the kosmos. Just as I am on a journey of evolution to know myself, the kosmos is on an evolutionary journey of awakening.

The evolutionary process itself is the development of a Truth of existence concealed here in an original Inconscience and brought out from it by an emerging Consciousness which rises from gradation to gradation of its self-unfolding until it can manifest in itself the integral reality of things and a total self-knowledge.

—Sri Aurobindo[15]

IV.   The Cosmogenetic Principle

Over the last two hundred years, Western philosophy, biology, psychology, and cosmology have been honing in on exactly how the process of evolution works. In 1850, Darwin published his *Origin of the Species* for biological evolution. Around the same time, anthropology and social-evolutionary theories began to emerge. Freud published his psychosexual development theory in 1909—the first developmental model for psychology. And the idea of an evolving universe entered the scientific arena in 1931 with the big bang theory, proposed by Georges Lemaître. The underlying process appears to be a universal pattern woven across physical systems, biological systems, and social/psychological systems.

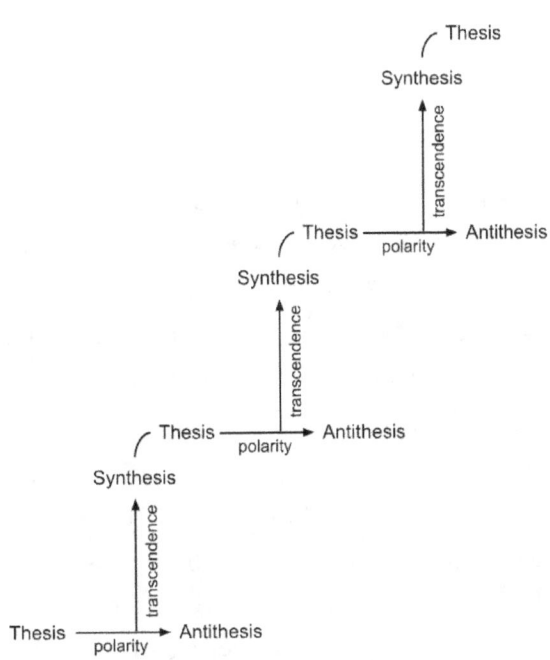

Figure 7.6 The dialectic of progress: thesis, antithesis, and synthesis

The mechanism of evolution was first termed the *dialectic of progress*. Although the dialectic is often attributed to the German philosopher Hegel, who undoubtedly employed its methodology in his philosophy, the terms *thesis, antithesis,* and *synthesis* are properly attributed to his contemporary Johann Fichte. This dialectic describes a three-part process. The first step is any proposition or manifest object: *thesis.* This is followed by the second proposition, which negates or opposes the first: *antithesis.* Polarity arises through contrast. Finally, the third proposition resolves the conflict by transcending to a new level: *synthesis.* Each synthesis then becomes the initial thesis for the next layer of development (fig. 7.6).

In more contemporary usage, the dialectic has been superseded by the *cosmogenetic principle,* introduced by Brian Swimme and Thomas Berry. They substitute the terms *differentiation, autopoiesis* (meaning self-creation), and *communion* as the activities of the dialectic. These three terms have many interpretations and are offered as broad themes for the underlying tripart process. This is the evolutionary engine of our continuously growing kosmos.

We now know that we live in a cosmogenesis, an ongoing, developing reality. Our extension of the Cosmological Principle, which we will call for clarity the Cosmogenetic Principle, assumes that every point in the universe is the same as every other point, and additionally, that the dynamics of evolution are the same at every point in the universe.... The Cosmogenetic Principle states that the evolution of the universe will be characterized by differentiation, autopoiesis, and communion throughout time and space and at every level of reality.

—Swimme and Berry[16]

Every entity, whether a proton, a cell, a human, or a galaxy is subject to these three drives. First, each unit becomes its own coherent self. Every whole entity in the cosmos is completely unique and original. This is the first step of *differentiation.* Second, each entity engages with both internal and external forces that cause change. Nothing is static, and there are no isolated islands in our universe. This is *autopoiesis.* Finally, each entity becomes a part of a larger whole that transcends to a new level of complexity. This is *communion.*

For yet another lens on the kosmic process of advancement, we can turn to systems theory. In this perspective, the most fundamental way to understand the kosmos is through *holons.* Every process and thing in existence is simultaneously both a whole in itself and part of something larger. Every entity is a whole/part. The property of being both a whole and a part, depending on one's perspective, is called a *holon.*[17] Whether we are considering a materialistic view of a kosmos made of *things,* or a process-oriented view of the kosmos, every thing and every process is both a part and a whole—a holon. Each holon contains subholons cascading downward without end (*transfinitely*). And each holon is a part of larger and larger wholes ranging upward without end. The entire kosmos, inclusive of all phenomena and all consciousness, is continually being superseded moment by moment by a more complex, more developed kosmos that contains and transcends each moment that came before. There is no lower limit and no upper limit. We are all holons, living in a holonic kosmos.

At the beginning of this chapter, I introduced the term *Eros*, which is the universal drive toward greater wholeness and complexity. Each holon is subject to this fundamental drive of becoming. Each holon reaches upward. In equal measure, the kosmos exhibits a universal capacity for wholes to reach down and embrace parts, which we call *Agape*. Every holon, across every scale, naturally reaches downward. These two drives, Eros and Agape, exist in a dynamic tension. They are another way to understand the polarity of thesis-antithesis and differentiation-autopoiesis in the process of evolution. The third phase in this framework is known as either *transcend and include* or *negate and preserve*. The third step of *synthesis* or *communion* is achieved by advancing to a new level, *transcending*, while *including* the parts from the previous level. In moving to a higher level, the prior state is *negated*, while the component parts are *preserved*. Ken Wilber likens this process to the successive viewpoints that become available as we climb a ladder:

In short, each structure-rung in the ladder generates a different View of the world around it (just as if you were climbing a real ladder). With each next-higher stage of development, the self steps off the previous structure-rung, loses the View of the world from that previous rung, steps up to the next higher structure-rung, and begins to see the world from that new and higher View. Again, just as when climbing a real ladder, the climber (or self-sense) loses the View from the previous rung—but the previous rung itself remains in existence (all the way back to the first rung). Thus, development is "transcend and include," or "negate and preserve"—the successive Views (or structure-stages) are negated and transcended (as the self steps up to the new and higher rung and its View), but the structure-rungs themselves are included and preserved (all rungs remain in existence).

—Ken Wilber[18]

The cosmogenetic principle describes how the universe developed from subatomic particles and light into galaxies, stars, planets, biological life, and humans. This process is completely *original*. Each one of us is a uniquely *original* process of becoming interwoven into the grand becoming of the kosmos. That which constitutes us sources from the *origin*. As holonic beings, it is our nature to *originate* new creations. This is the *original* nature of our evolving reality, which Whitehead described as "the creative advance into novelty." Every holon is original, sources from the origin, and originates new holons. We participate in an original kosmos. Across every scale, this kosmos is evolving through a three-part process: *cosmogenesis*.

V. Panexperientialism

Each and every phenomenon in the kosmos is known to exist because it has some interaction with other holons. In any interaction, there is an external, relational, ontological component. The *otherness* of the phenomena is registered "out there." Simultaneously, there is an internal *feeling* or *prehension* that constitutes an *interior* of experience. This inner aspect is subjective, experiential, and epistemological. Each holon contains both an exterior and an interior.

For humans, this is easy to recognize. We have both physical bodies and a psychological self that is conscious. Similarly for animals, we can recognize an interior awareness. Even for plants that grow toward the sun, there is some degree of awareness (known as *phototropism*). When we look down the chain of complexity of life-forms, there is no place where we can draw the line and say, "Consciousness is no longer present below here." Continuing downward from the biosphere into the physiosphere, every planet, rock, and subatomic particle in some way *prehends* its physical interactions.[19] The proposition of panexperientialism is that the interiority of experience is universal. This duality of interior and exterior is a fundamental aspect of holons.

> The central tenet of panexperientialism is that experience goes "all the way down." "Pan" means "all of," "the whole," or "universal"—therefore "panexperience" means experience as an ingredient all through the universe, permeating all levels of being. Not just human brains, but individual cells, individual molecules, individual atoms, and even individual subatomic particles incorporate a capacity for "feeling," a degree of subjective interiority. According to panexperientialism, all individuals possess this capacity.
> —Christian de Quincey[20]

Thus, the entire holonic kosmos is dynamically inter-experiencing itself across all scales and levels of complexity in each moment.

The final aspect to incorporate into our picture of the evolving kosmos is the formation of communities. I mentioned above that organisms are population forming. We gather into colonies, schools, herds, and tribes, which have emergent properties. Analogously at the physical level, beaches, atmospheres, planetary systems, and superclusters of galaxies display emergent properties. And in the noosphere, human consciousness forms into paradigms and cultures (these will be the primary topic of the next chapter). At each level of evolutionary process, holons gather into communities whose patterns supersede the interactions of the individuals. Each community has both a phenomenal exterior and an intersubjective interior. Thus, our kosmos consists of holons with interiors and exteriors, forming *communities of holons* with collective interiors and collective exteriors.

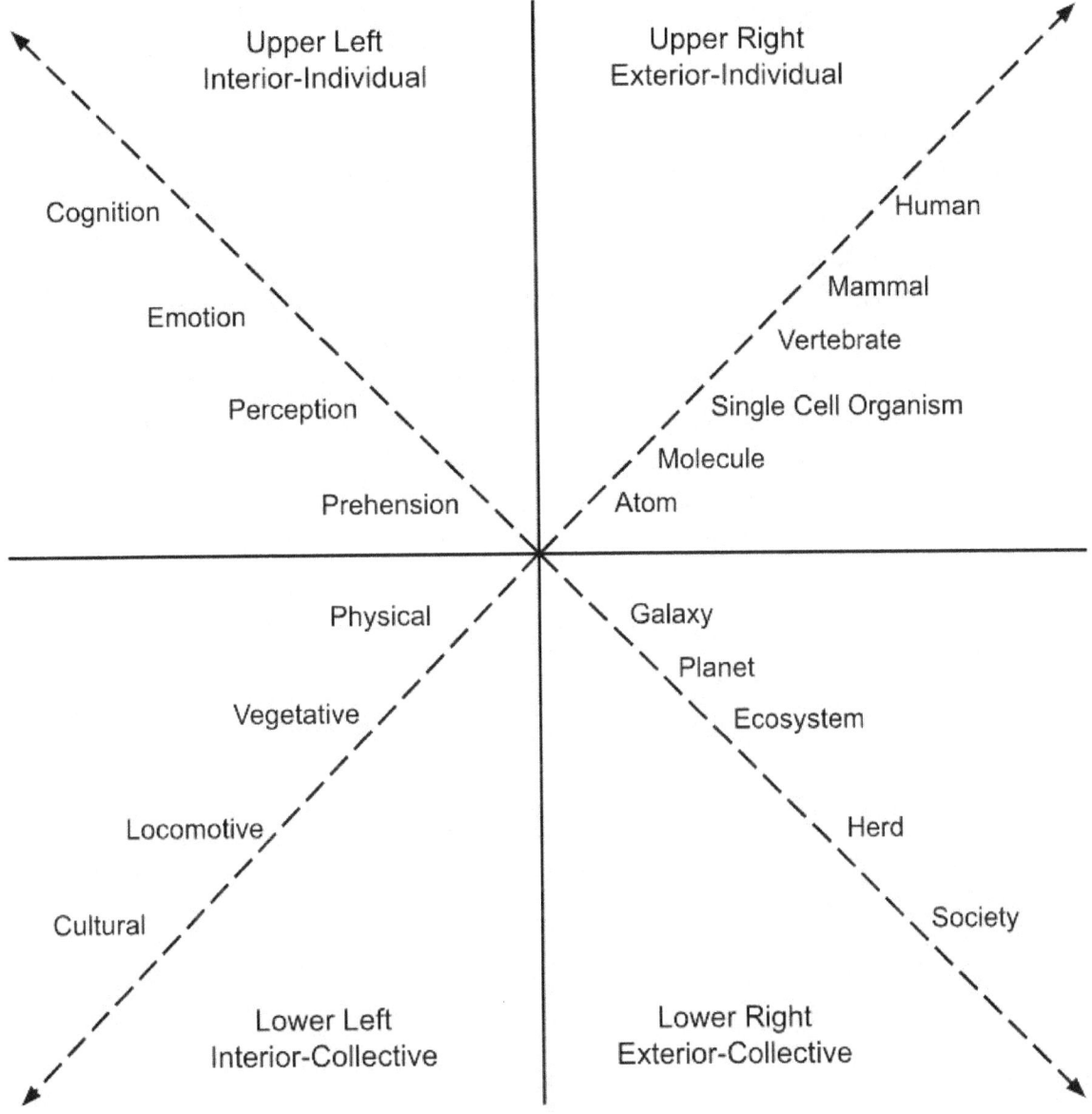

Figure 7.7 The four-quadrant model[21]

We can plot this as a graph with four quadrants (above). Each quadrant represents one aspect of a holon: interior-individual, exterior-individual, interior-collective, and exterior-collective. Every holon occupies a position somewhere in each of these four quadrants.

This four-quadrant model forms the foundation of Ken Wilber's integral theory. Here it is explained in his words:

To very briefly review, the 4 quadrants are (i) the interior of the individual (the "I" space, which is accessed by introspection and meditation, and contains thoughts, images, ideas, feelings, insights, emotions, satori, and the repressed submergent and emergent unconscious; this Upper Left quadrant includes structures and states of consciousness, as well as shadow material); (ii) the exterior of the individual (the "it" space, which is seen objectively by observation—a typical "scientific" view of the organism, which, in humans, contains atoms, molecules, cells, organ systems, lungs, kidneys, a triune brain with neurotransmitters, and so forth, plus the individual as seen from an "objective" or "exterior" view; for example, a fern, tree, frog, ape, and so forth, along with the individual's objective behavior, all in their singular, individual, objective forms); (iii) the interior of the collective (the "we" space, which contains shared values, ethics, worldviews, meanings, semantics, mutual resonance, and so forth); and (iv) the exterior of the collective (the "its" space— systems and collective structures, social institutions, family structures, organizations, environmental surroundings and ecological systems, techno-economic modes of production—foraging, farming, industrial, informational, and so on; the elements in the Lower Right quadrant are often referred to by sociologists as PESTLE—political, economic, social, technological, legal, environmental).

—Ken Wilber[22]

This four-quadrant graph contains every holon in the kosmos, ranging from the most rudimentary at the center to the most complex at the periphery. This is our evolving kosmos as we know it.

Prompts for Journaling and Discussion

Give examples of how you observe evolution unfolding for the physical universe (physiosphere), organic life (biosphere), and human consciousness (noosphere).

What parts or sub-holons had to come together to form the wholeness of you as a human?

What larger wholes do you participate in as a part?

In what ways are you original?

Notes

[1] Igor Kubik, 2020 CC BY-SA 4.0

[2] "The inflationary scenario supposes that at some time during the early history of the Universe, a very large dark energy density existed, which led to a rapidly accelerating expansion of the Universe.... During the inflationary epoch, the Universe expands by a factor of 1043 or more. At about 200ts, the inflationary epoch ends, and Act II begins. Act II is a standard Big Bang model, but with initial conditions set during the inflationary epoch. For example, a very small patch can become isothermal, and inflation makes the small isothermal patch into a huge isothermal patch, which expands to become much bigger than the observable Universe." *Origin and Evolution of the Universe*, Zuckerman and Malkan.

[3] "At the end of the first three minutes the contents of the universe were mostly in the form of light, neutrinos, and antineutrinos. There was still a small amount of nuclear material, now consisting of about 73 percent hydrogen and 27 percent helium, and an equally small number of electrons left over from the era of electron-positron annihilation. This matter continued to rush apart, becoming steadily cooler and less dense. Much later, after a few hundred thousand years, it would become cool enough for electrons to join with nuclei to form atoms of hydrogen and helium. The resulting gas would begin under the influence of gravitation to form clumps, which would ultimately condense to form the galaxies and stars of the present universe." *The First Three Minutes*, Weinberg.

[4] "It is the progression of the Universe from the great symmetry and simplicity we imagine for the Big Bang, through the building of the particles we see today, with their complicated relationships, through the synthesis of the chemical elements, first in a pervasive hot plasma and then in the cores of stars, and most recently to the invention of biology and life. That is what the phrase 'evolution of the universe' means to me." *Origin and Evolution of the Universe*, Zuckerman and Malkan.

[5] Adapted from "Structured sequences emerge from random pool when replicated by templated ligation," Kudella et al.

[6] "The crucial breakthrough occurred for Prigogine during the early 1960s, when he realized that systems far from equilibrium must be described by nonlinear equations. The clear recognition of this link between 'far from equilibrium' and 'nonlinearity' opened an avenue of research for Prigogine that would culminate a decade later in his theory of "dissipative structures."... Prigogine's concept of a dissipative structure introduced a radical change in this view by showing that in open systems dissipation becomes a source of order." *The Systems View of Life*, Capra and Pier.

[7] "The unifying principle of an organism as a mode of being of the organism is integral with but distinct from the entire range of physical components of the organism. It is the source of spontaneity, its self-manifesting power." *The Universe Story*, Swimme and Berry.

[8] *Toward a New Philosophy of Biology: Observations of an Evolutionist*, Mayr.

[9] "An autopoietic machine is a machine organized (defined as a unity) as a network of processes of production (transformation and destruction) of components which: (i) through their interactions and transformations continuously regenerate and realize the network of processes (relations) that produced them; and (ii) constitute it (the machine) as a concrete unity in space in which they (the components) exist by specifying the topological domain of its realization as such a It follows that an autopoietic machine continuously generates and specifies its own organization through its own operation as a system of production of its own components." *Autopoiesis and Cognition the Realization of the Living*, Maturana.

[10] "Since all components of an autopoietic network are produced by other components in the network, the entire system is *organizationally closed*, even though it is open with regard to the flow of energy and matter. This organization closure implies that a living system is self-organizing in the sense that its order and behavior are not imposed by the environment but are established by the system itself. In other words, living systems are autonomous." *The Web of Life: A New Synthesis of Mind and Matter*, Capra.

[11] "The process of self-regulation is the key to Lovelock's idea. He knew from astrophysics that the heat of the Sun has increased by 25% since life began on Earth and that, in spite of this increase, the Earth's surface temperature has remained constant, at a level comfortable for life, during those 4 billion years. What if the Earth were able to regulate its temperature, he asked, as well as other planetary conditions – the composition of its atmosphere, the salinity of its oceans, and so on – just as living organisms are able to self-regulate and keep their body temperature and other variables constant? Lovelock realized that this hypothesis amounted to a radical break with conventional science. Rather than seeing the Earth as a dead planet, composed of inanimate rocks, oceans, and atmosphere, he proposed to consider it as a complex system, 'comprising all of life and all of its environment tightly coupled so as to form a self-regulating entity' (Lovelock 1991)." *The Systems View of Life*, Capra and Luisi.

[12] *The Phenomenon of Man*, Teilhard de Chardin.

[13] "One kind of evolution prepares the ground for the next. Out of the conditions created by evolution in the physical realm emerge

the conditions that permit biological evolution to take off. And out of the conditions created by biological evolution come the conditions that allow human beings - and many other species - to evolve certain social forms of organization." *Evolution: The Grand Synthesis*, Laszlo.

[14] "The process itself is the constitution of the actual entity." *Process and Reality*, Whitehead.

[15] *The Life Divine*.

[16] *The Universe Story*.

[17] "In a systems view of the universe, we recognize and describe whole systems (sometimes called *holons*) arranged in an ordered series, in such a way that the parts of a whole at one level are wholes at the level 'below,' and are themselves part of wholes at the level 'above.'" *Ecology of Consciousness*, Metzner.

[18] *The Religion of Tomorrow*.

[19] "The 'prehension' of one actual entity by another actual entity is the complete transaction, analysable into the objectification of the former entity as one of the data for the latter, and into the fully clothed feeling whereby the datum is absorbed into the subjective satisfaction- 'clothed' with the various elements of its 'subjective form.'" *Process and Reality*, Whitehead.

[20] "Consciousness All the Way Down? A Critique of Panexperientialism."

[21] Adapted from Ken Wilber

[22] *The Religion of Tomorrow.*

| 8 |

Paradigms of Consciousness: First Tier

Figure 8.1 Evolution in the Past, 1912, Knipe.

Briefly, what I am proposing is that the psychology of the mature human being is an unfolding, emergent, oscillating, spiraling process marked by progressive subordination of older, lower-order behavior systems to newer, higher-order systems as [humanity]'s existential problems change.

—Clare Graves[1]

In this chapter, we'll explore the universal stages that human consciousness evolves through, both in individuals and collectives. Before we dive into those details, I want to take a moment to distinguish what is evolving from what's not evolving. The *states of consciousness*, described in chapter 6, are not undergoing evolution. Indeed, the pure witness realm of absolute *I Am*-ness that the Buddha experienced 2,500 years ago is the exact same consciousness that you or I could experience today. The prana of the subtle realm that Patanjali described is the same prana that we feel today. States of consciousness are the containers for experience, and they do not evolve. These states were required *a priori* in order for the kosmos to come into existence through the big bang.

Distinct from the *state*, there is a second aspect of consciousness undergoing evolutionary development: our faculty for making meaning of reality. Humans weave together coherent *worldviews* or *paradigms of consciousness* (I will use these two terms interchangeably).[2] A paradigm is an organizing story about the nature of self and reality. Paradigms contain the values, assumptions, beliefs, myths, identities, and purpose for an individual or a culture.[3] The paradigm is the interpretive lens through which we translate reality, and becomes the mechanism by which we define reality.[4] Paradigms are emergent morphic fields that have developed together with humans and the advancement of the kosmos. This means there are two axes of consciousness: expansion into greater *states* of awareness (being) and evolution through *paradigms* (becoming).

States are something we can look at; structures [or paradigms] are things we look through.

—Ken Wilber[5]

Paradigms of consciousness are discrete and sticky. By this I mean, individuals and cultures tend to cohere into the bucket of a single paradigm. Just like living systems, each paradigm is an autonomous process of self-organization. A worldview is a coherent, homeostatic framework that lives in the subjective and intersubjective fields of consciousness. Paradigms are also called *stages* and *structures* of consciousness because they arrange themselves in a progression, like rungs on a ladder.[6] Paradigms have also been termed *memes* because they pass themselves down through culture in the same way the genes pass down inherited traits through generations of organisms.[7]

Paradigms undergo a process of evolution as they assimilate new symbols, language, and myths by humanity over time. This evolution tends to be slow and self-reinforcing. The core values of the paradigm remain constant while the ways that the paradigm interprets the present reality shifts to align to the core values.

What is more striking is that individuals and collectives will change lenses in a jump called the *paradigm shift*. This has variously been described as *the lightning flash*, the *scales falling from the eyes*, the *eureka* moment, *the quantum leap*, rebirth (i.e., *Renaissance*), and revolution. Humans and cultures make the evolutionary journey by jumping from one paradigm to the next.

Each paradigm is itself a coherent whole. It is a valid, internally consistent story about the world and the individual's place in it. Additionally, each paradigm forms a *part* of the next more complex paradigm. This means that paradigms are holons of the noosphere.

Paradigms exist in a progression like rungs on a ladder. Each paradigm becomes the foundation for the next more advanced paradigm to build upon and each layer forms a *part* of the layer above. The needs of each paradigm must be met before one moves higher. We call this progressive pathway a *growth hierarchy*, where actors move through sequential stages of development in a system.[8]

Growth hierarchies, by the way, are distinct from *dominator hierarchies*, which describe a social structure where certain members exert power over others within the group. Dominator hierarchies describe a form of collective suffering, for example, within hegemonic masculinity. In contrast, growth hierarchies describe how the kosmos advances through progressively more complex stages toward wholeness and actualization.[9]

A system of holons, arranged in a growth hierarchy, is known as a holarchy. As we shall presently explore, paradigms exist in a holarchy. Individuals and collectives grow from paradigmatic holon to holon along this developmental ladder. *Integral philosophy* postulates that human consciousness is in a process of evolution through successive paradigms.[10] In addition, the term *integral* refers to a specific stage that humans may reach on the developmental staircase, which we'll explore in-depth, below.[11]

One hallmark of integral philosophy is the capacity to make connections and create new unities. So instead of arguing for a single correct developmental model, the integral approach is to compare *all* developmental models and look for commonalities. The integral meta-theory (i.e., theory of theories) claims that all humans across all cultures develop through a similar series of milestones. There is one common pathway that consciousness evolves through in humans, which becomes apparent when we compare developmental models.

Because my paradigm is the lens through which I view the world, it is challenging to see the paradigm itself. My assumptions, values, and beliefs determine *how* I see. Like the fish without a concept of water, I am so immersed within my worldview that I experience it as a given. Once I am able to observe my paradigm, I can take a step back and use a wider lens. My subjective lens filters the objective world. When I shift from using my paradigm as the subjective viewing instrument to an objective focus of study, I am able to "see" the filters for the first time. Looking *at* my paradigmatic lens is one of the primary mechanisms for growth. The current subjective paradigm becomes an object in the next paradigm.

The root or 'deep structure' of any principle of mental organization is the subject-object relationship. 'Object' refers to those elements of our knowing or organizing that we can reflect on, handle, look at, be responsible for, relate to each other, take control of, internalize, assimilate, or otherwise operate upon.... 'Subject' refers to those elements of our knowing or organizing that we are identified with, tied to, fused with or embedded in. We have object, we are subject.... The relation of [organizing principles (i.e., paradigms)] is transformative, qualitative, and incorporative. Each successive principle subsumes or encompasses the prior principle. That which was subject becomes object to the next principle. The new principle is a higher order principle (more complex, more inclusive) that makes the prior principle into an element or tool of its system.

—Robert Kegan[12]

Each paradigm is *transcended and included* as I grow. I move to a higher level (transcend) while incorporating the cognitive capacities of the lower level (include). As I step to a higher paradigm the old organizing story is *negated* by the next story while the developmental gifts are *preserved* as a part of the larger whole. In this way, studying consciousness stimulates the evolution of consciousness. That is to say, learning about paradigms is "psychoactive." With this in mind, let's take a look at the paradigms mapped out by integral philosophy.

The paradigms that have developed within Western culture are: archaic, magic/tribal, mythic/traditional, mental/modern, and plural/postmodern. These are known as *first-tier paradigms*, and they form a developmental ladder (fig. 8.2, below). Each of these paradigms exists within both intersubjective culture and subjective individual psyches. Because integral theory looks at paradigms across many traditions and schools of thought, the rainbow-color scheme was introduced to reference developmental levels in a system-neutral language. The upward arrow indicates the hierarchical progression of these paradigms and also suggests that more paradigms exist above plural/postmodern. Indeed, there are more structures of consciousness higher up, and we'll be exploring them later. In this chapter, we'll begin at the bottom of this ladder and work our way up.

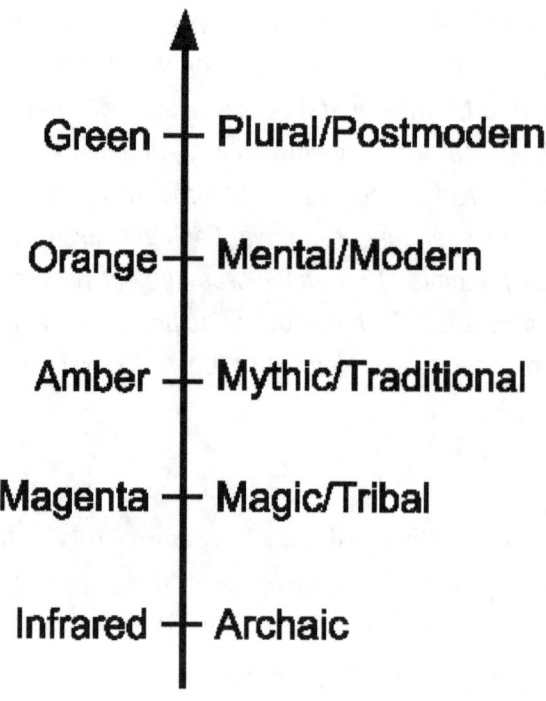

Figure 8.2 First-tier paradigms of consciousness

When I say that each paradigm is a *whole*, I mean that each of these developmental stages is valid, valuable, and worthy of dignity. By examining the staircase, we can see the essential beauty of each step. In addition, each paradigm is *necessary* because it forms the foundation for higher paradigms to be built upon.

It is important to remember that we are not using these paradigms to pigeonhole people. Paradigms don't define individual people or cultures; they define *types of consciousness* held by people. Higher levels represent greater complexity, but not greater value. Each paradigm has its necessary place in the staircase, and so is an equally valuable member of the larger whole. Similarly, people are each intrinsically valuable and lovable, regardless of the complexity of consciousness they hold. Steve McIntosh offers a moving illustration on this point:

> *In our estimates of children, we don't value second-graders less than sixth-graders. We recognize that sixth-graders are more educated and more independent, but certainly not more valuable in an absolute sense. And when it comes to the stages of consciousness, we likewise recognize that every human has a core value as an individual that must be respected, regardless of their level of development.*
>
> —Steve McIntosh[13]

The Archaic Paradigm

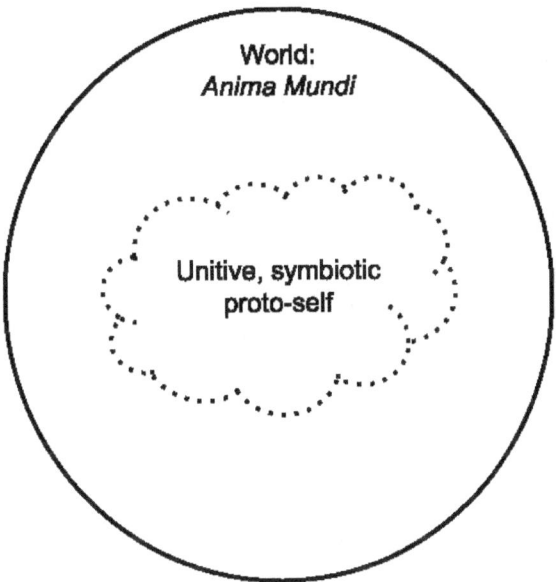

Figure 8.3 Archaic psyche in relation with the world

The archaic paradigm is defined by total immersion into the environment. This is the paradigm each of us was born into. At archaic, I have little or no notion of a separate egoic self. The infant is embedded within the archetype of the Great Mother. Here, my consciousness is undifferentiated from the *anima mundi*—the living world soul. Consciousness is fully immersed in the environment with only a rudimentary distinction between inside feelings and outside stimuli. My focus here is on basic needs and survival. This is the earliest, most primal stage of human consciousness. It is what the first humans experienced and developed through prior to the creation of culture. For this reason, the color is infrared—it's the foundation that lies beneath the visible spectrum.

Each paradigm has its own understanding of the self and the world, sometimes called a life-world:

> *The concept of "life-world" (Lebenswelt) was formulated by philosophers of the European phenomenological school. It includes both the Mitwelt ("with-world") of relations and the Umwelt ("Around-world") or environment. This life-world is what we are presently aware of and identified with.... The philosophical and psychological conundrums associated with the concept of "self" can best be avoided, I have come to think, if we combine the indigenous and phenomenological notion of "life-world" with a systems view: the self is a system of relations that we can also call the life-world.*
>
> —Ralph Metzner[14]

The self and the world codevelop and must be understood together. At archaic, I illustrate the life-world as a solid circle (fig. 8.3). The circle is the archetypal symbol for wholeness, and the *anima mundi* of the archaic world is a unified whole. As we shall see, not every paradigm experiences the wholeness of the world. While the world is whole, the self at this level is not well-defined, and so I've illustrated it as a dotted-line cloud at the center. Again, as we progress through the paradigms, we'll observe an evolution of the self-system at the center of the life-world.

The Magic/Tribal Paradigm

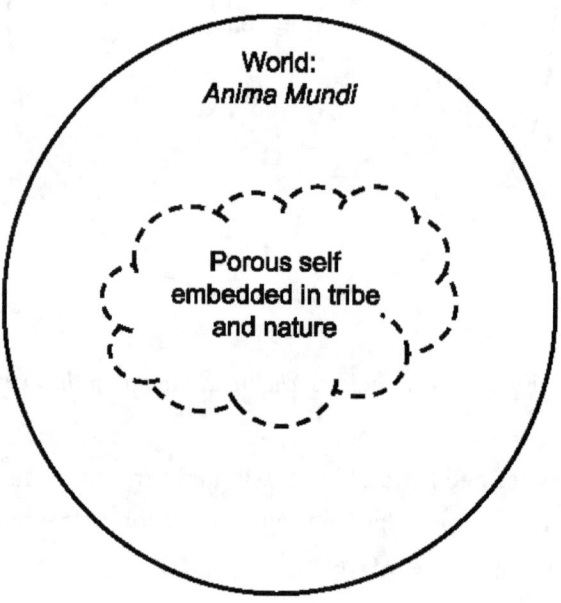

Figure 8.4 Magic/tribal psyche in relation with the world

Self	Dreamlike self with subject/object fluidity
Nature	Living spirit world, *anima mundi*
Values	Safety
Motivation	Fear and emotions
Truth	Will of the gods, shamans, & chiefs
Spirituality	Animism, shamanism

Figure 8.5 Defining aspects of the magic/tribal paradigm

In the magic paradigm, my psyche emerges and separates from the environment in a dreamlike way. While there is a distinct "me," it is porous and fluid. My psyche experiences aspects of nature as magical subjective beings and there is a continuity between the outer and inner landscapes— known as *participation mystique*.[15] In the magic/tribal paradigm, the *anima mundi* of the archaic paradigm develops more personality: the world becomes a rich tapestry of signs, symbols, spirits, and omens. The natural world is *animistic*, meaning objects take on subjective qualities, for example "the rocks are alive." Individual agency holds *magical realism*, meaning the subjective mind has special power over objects, for example, "the word *curse* has the power to cause harm." Objects in the environment actively *participate* with me, for example, "the moon follows me as I walk."

The collective-level organization of the magic paradigm is into tribal units. As has been studied extensively by anthropologists, tribal cultures across the world and throughout history utilize a remarkably uniform structure. Every single one of us has ancestors who lived in some sort of a clan or tribe. Usually, the tribe is two hundred people or fewer, and the bonds are very strong family and kinship relationships. This paradigm is focused on safety needs—protection from the elements, security, law, and basic well-being. Fear is a strong motivating factor for actions taken by the group.

In this paradigm, the needs of the group overshadow the needs of the individuals. There may even be conflation or merging of individual and collective will. Typically, the dictates of the spirit gods, shamans, and leaders of the tribe determine truth and morality. The culture may contain powerful rituals to connect with the larger forces of nature, spirits, and gods. The religious expressions at Magical tend to be forms of animism or shamanism.

The Mythic/Traditional Paradigm

Self	The hero, the chosen one
Nature	To be conquered and ruled, or evil
Values	Belonging, conforming, tradition
Motivation	Loyalty, salvation
Truth	Monotheistic God, religion, myths
Spirituality	Organized religion

Figure 8.6 Defining aspects of the mythic/traditional paradigm

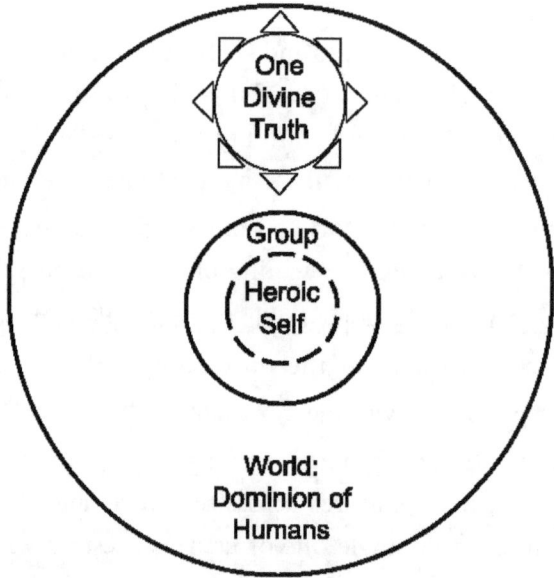

Figure 8.7 Mythic/traditional psyche in relation with the world

In the mythic/traditional paradigm, my ego emerges as an individual self. Here, I inhabit the hero or heroine who navigates a world defined by myths. The hero's journey is one of personal empowerment that moves toward glory. Along the way, I must subdue or conquer the monsters that inhabit a hostile outside world.

In the myths or religious doctrines that define this paradigm, there is a singular transcendent truth that is revealed through providence to the hero or the chosen people. This transcendent truth is the source of moral guidelines that must be followed to reach salvation. Religious examples of the transcendent truth include God, Yahweh, Allah, the Buddha, and so on, together with the religious leaders and institutions that work on behalf of that truth. In addition to organized religion, salvation may be found through loyalty to a team, company, political party, or nation. Adherence to the transcendent truth within the group guarantees salvation in this life or more commonly, in the next. Failure to comply leads to damnation, excommunication, or destruction. Outsiders are not privy to the one transcendent truth. Thus, they are either evil or are here to be saved by conversion into the in-group. The mythic/traditional paradigm tends to hold strongly black-and-white dichotomies: forces are either good or evil, and you are either with us or against us. The view of the natural world is either that it is here as the divine being's gift to the chosen people or that nature is the *Devil's playground*—a realm of evil and temptation that must be transcended.

The strongest drive in this paradigm is loyalty to the group. I define myself in relation to the group. In Ego Development Theory, this paradigm is called *conformist consciousness*.[16] Belonging to the group and conforming to group norms are my strongest values. My individual identity can be merged or *con-fused* with the group identity. In the diagram above, the self is more defined than in the previous two paradigms but is still enclosed by a dashed line that exists within the closed circle of the social group. I source self-worth by my status within the group. In addition, I assume the status of the group as my status. For example, when my favorite sports team wins, I become a winner. Faith in the transcendent truth, duty to the family or group, and respect for authority are also core values. Dependence on group decision-making, obedience to group norms, caretaking, pleasing, and keeping up social appearances are all typical behaviors in mythic/traditional paradigm. These are based on the core need to belong.

At the collective level, mythic/traditional groups take the form of organized religions, political parties, unions, sports teams, military organizations, or any type of group that shares a mythology. Whereas tribal groups are familial or small enough that each member would personally know everyone, mythic/traditional groups can be millions or even billions of people, where membership is conferred through sharing a transcendent truth. Because these groups value the one transcendent truth above all, the stories and myths about this truth become sacred themselves. In order to preserve these myths, the groups place a strong emphasis on tradition and family values. At the extremes of this paradigm are all forms of fascism, fundamentalism, solipsism, ethnocentrism, and, of course, hegemonic masculinity. However, it's important to recognize that there are also many healthy, tolerant groups at the mythic/traditional paradigm of consciousness, and this paradigm is an essential step on the developmental pathway. By population, this is the largest paradigm in humanity today.

In human evolution, this paradigm emerged together with domestication, civilization, and monotheistic religions. In order to preserve the myths that maintain belief in the transcendent truth, these cultures value oral tradition, the written word, codes, and laws. Other historical developments from this paradigm include morality, commerce, and social and political institutions. All of these social structures are necessary as a foundation for the next paradigm to build upon.

The Mental/Modern Paradigm

Self	The rational mind
Nature	Governed by science, resource extraction
Values	Logic, achievement
Motivation	Competition, prestige
Truth	Science and philosophy
Spirituality	Agnosticism, atheism

Figure 8.8 Defining aspects of the mental/modern paradigm

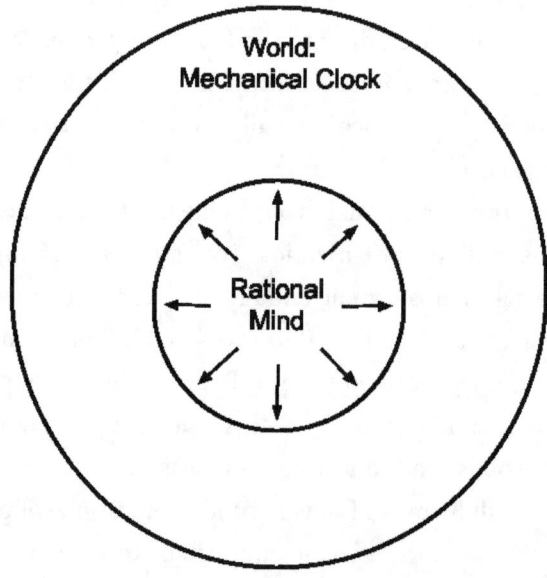

Figure 8.9 Mental/modern psyche in relation with the world

Cogito ergo sum! "I think therefore I am." This is the proud proclamation of the mental/ modern paradigm. The centerpiece of this paradigm is the rational mind with its capacity to comprehend the universe through logic, reasoning, and the scientific method. Psychologically, this stage represents the fruition and fullness of the egoic self. At this stage, my ego has emerged as a truly independent, individualistic, self-aware entity. My focus is on competition, achievement, and status. I am satisfying *esteem needs* from within *achievement consciousness.*

Historically, this stage developed in Western culture during the 1700s in what is known as the Enlightenment:

> *The whole development of thought occupied exactly two generations. It commenced with Galileo and ended with Newton's Principia; and Newton was born in the year that Galileo died. Also the lives of Descartes and Huyghens fall within the period occupied by these great terminal figures. The issue of the combined labors of these four men has some right to be considered as the greatest single intellectual success which mankind has achieved.*
>
> —Alfred North Whitehead[17]

The paradigm that was founded during the Enlightenment is known as *scientific materialism.* In this worldview, the universe is composed of physical stuff acting according to natural laws. The universe is reducible to a complex mechanical clock. These laws are described by mathematics and are discernable through the scientific method.

Historically, this new paradigm dethroned the dogmatism of the Christian Church and the oppressive feudalism of European monarchies. With it came liberal values, *The Social Contract, The Rights of Man*, and the American and French revolutions. The mental/modern paradigm ushered in democracy and a new age for humanity. Modern medicine, modern science, the industrial revolution, and modern capitalism all ensued from this level of consciousness—what we now call *modernity*. With these institutional changes came a rise of the middle class and massive advances in human rights, education, material wealth, and quality of life.

Reason emerged as the supreme arbiter of truth, and so the mental/modern paradigm rejected the dictates of organized religion and with it, much of spirituality. Rationalism, skepticism, and objectivity are gifts of this paradigm. Atheism and agnosticism are natural and healthy belief systems at mental/modern.[18] It is an advancement from religious ideology and superstition into an evidence-based world that I can test and determine for myself.

Today, scientific materialism reigns supreme as the most powerful and influential Western (and, arguably, global) paradigm. The majority of our institutions including science, schools, government, and business ascribe to this worldview. To the extent that politics and media are not engrossed in the mythic/traditional structure one step below, these institutions also function within scientific materialism. Corporate culture and a large swath of the tech industry occupy this paradigm.

At this stage I gain the capacity to think for myself, a drive to advance and succeed, and an intellectual curiosity to know and understand the world. The collective benefits have included liberal values, representative government, and unprecedented progress through technology, science, and commerce.

The pathologies of this paradigm have been commensurate with the benefits. Individuals at this level suffer through greed, moral bankruptcy, perfectionism, workaholism, and disconnection from the wisdom sources of nature, spirituality, and cultural heritage. Egoic superiority, one-upmanship (i.e., always getting the final word), and ultra-rationalism are also traits in this paradigm. Collective pathologies include the large-scale destruction wrought by WWI and WWII, the existential threat of nuclear war, the continued colonization and exploitation of marginalized humans, and consumerism. Perhaps humanity's most pressing crisis today is the accelerating mass extinction event caused by ecosystem collapse, biodiversity loss, and climate change, which have emerged in the wake of industrialization and globalization.[19]

Just as the pathologies of feudalism and the Church provided the impetus for the rise of modernity, the ills of capitalism and scientific materialism have spurred the rise of the next paradigm in an attempt to deal with these issues. However, it is equally important to recognize that the gifts of the prior paradigm are necessary in order for the new paradigm to emerge. The agricultural systems and moral fabric laid down by the mythic/traditional paradigm had to be there—and today still need to be here—in order for the mental/modern paradigm to function. The education, quality of life, and material wealth of the mental/modern paradigm are necessary for the emergence of postmodernity. Each subsequent paradigm transcends the prior one while including it as a part of the more complex, more holistic new paradigm.

The Plural/Postmodern Paradigm

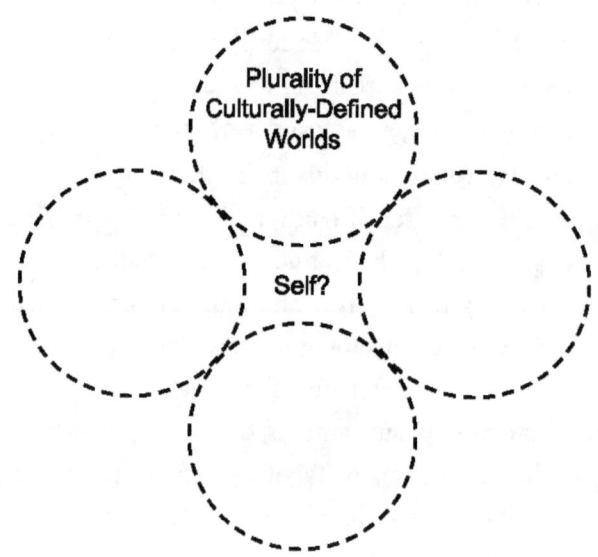

Figure 8.10 Plural/postmodern psyche in relation with the world

Self	Socially constructed and deconstructed
Nature	Victim of humanity's greed
Values	Sensitivity
Motivation	Inclusion, sustainability
Truth	No "Truth," relativism
Spirituality	Humanitarianism, New Age

Figure 8.11 Defining aspects of the plural/postmodern paradigm

At the plural/postmodern paradigm, greater degrees of self-awareness allow me to recognize that my identity is largely constructed by personal, familial, and cultural conditioning. Biases and privileges that were previously invisible to me now come into view. I become aware of my natural tendencies for *defensive self-deception* and *culturally biased distortion*. Socialized identity-layers like race, gender, and class begin to peel back from the self. These identities are *deconstructed*. In this paradigm, I feel a pull inward to find the authentic me, and a strong skepticism of the existing social order.[20] I begin the process of *self-authoring*, where I behave and identify according to my internally referenced values.

I now reframe the singular transcendent truth of the mythic/traditional paradigm and the scientific objective truth of the mental/modern paradigm as *relative truths* that largely depend on the context of the observer. My world now holds a plurality of truths instead of any single "Truth." I begin to recognize different parts within my psyche that hold different truths. "Whatever is true for you" supplants objective truth. In plural/postmodernism, I hold a moral relativism that is sensitive to each individual's experience and the experiences of marginalized groups. This can extend into "truth can never be found" and even "there is no truth."

> *In the worst case, postmodern individualists claim with absolute certainty that there is no position from which to judge anything. They do not recognize the inherent self-contradiction in this stance which values or privileges this idea over all others, which of course is a form of judgment and hierarchical ordering of value.*
>
> —Susanne Cook-Greuter[21]

In this paradigm, I move beyond purely rational ways of knowing to include emotional, psychological, and subjective ways of knowing. In addition, the plural/postmodern psyche begins to think in terms of systems, emergent solutions, and holistic frameworks.

The core value of this paradigm is sensitivity.[22] I become increasingly aware of my internal landscape and begin to welcome the emotions that I had marginalized or suppressed in the previous paradigms. I also become more sensitive to the emotional states and experiences of others. At this paradigm, I'm careful not to push my interpretation onto anyone else. Instead, I am intensely interested in listening, feeling, and *centering* the experiences of others. The importance of feeling brings an increased interest in present experience and ongoing process rather than the future-oriented achievement focus of the mental/modern paradigm.

At the collective level, postmodernism arose in the 1960s and has been gathering momentum ever since. The "counterculture" of the sixties was largely a reaction *against* the wars, industrial-degradation, consumerism, social oppression, and morality of the prior two paradigms: traditional and modern. Postmodernism has birthed the environmentalist, feminist, and civil rights movements. More recently, these trends have continued with indigenous rights, gay and trans rights, the *#metoo* movement, and *black lives matter*. Social activism and nonviolent political change are hallmarks of this paradigm.

With my new focus on sensitivity, I make space for marginalized voices. Plural/postmodernism welcomes and celebrates alternative and traditional medicines, Eastern religions, and New Age spirituality. I have a new interest in indigenous, neo-shamanic, and native cultures and practices. In this paradigm, I'm fostering reparation, social and restorative justice, environmental sustainability, and social inclusivity.

Within critical academia, Jacques Derrida's idea of *deconstruction* and Michel Foucault's theories on power structures form the core of postmodernism. The soft sciences in academia, including literature, the arts, humanities, cultural studies, gender studies, and media studies largely occupy the plural/postmodern paradigm.

Many of the scientific advancements of the twentieth century have corroborated the plural/postmodern paradigm. Einstein's special theory of relativity states that all inertial frames of reference are equivalent. There is no such thing as an objective *Cartesian frame* that we can lay down on reality. All phenomena depend on the observer. Similarly, the Heisenberg uncertainty principle in quantum mechanics shows how, at small scales, there is an indeterminacy of position and direction that is fundamentally influenced by the act of observation. Chaos theory describes systems of such high complexity that no ordering principle or causal determinacy is possible. Fractal geometry (pictured below) generates infinitely complex shapes out of very simple equations, changing the mathematical understanding of complexity itself. The neatly ordered mechanical clock of scientific materialism has been superseded by postmodernism's chaotic, emergent, fuzzy, statistical, systems worldview.

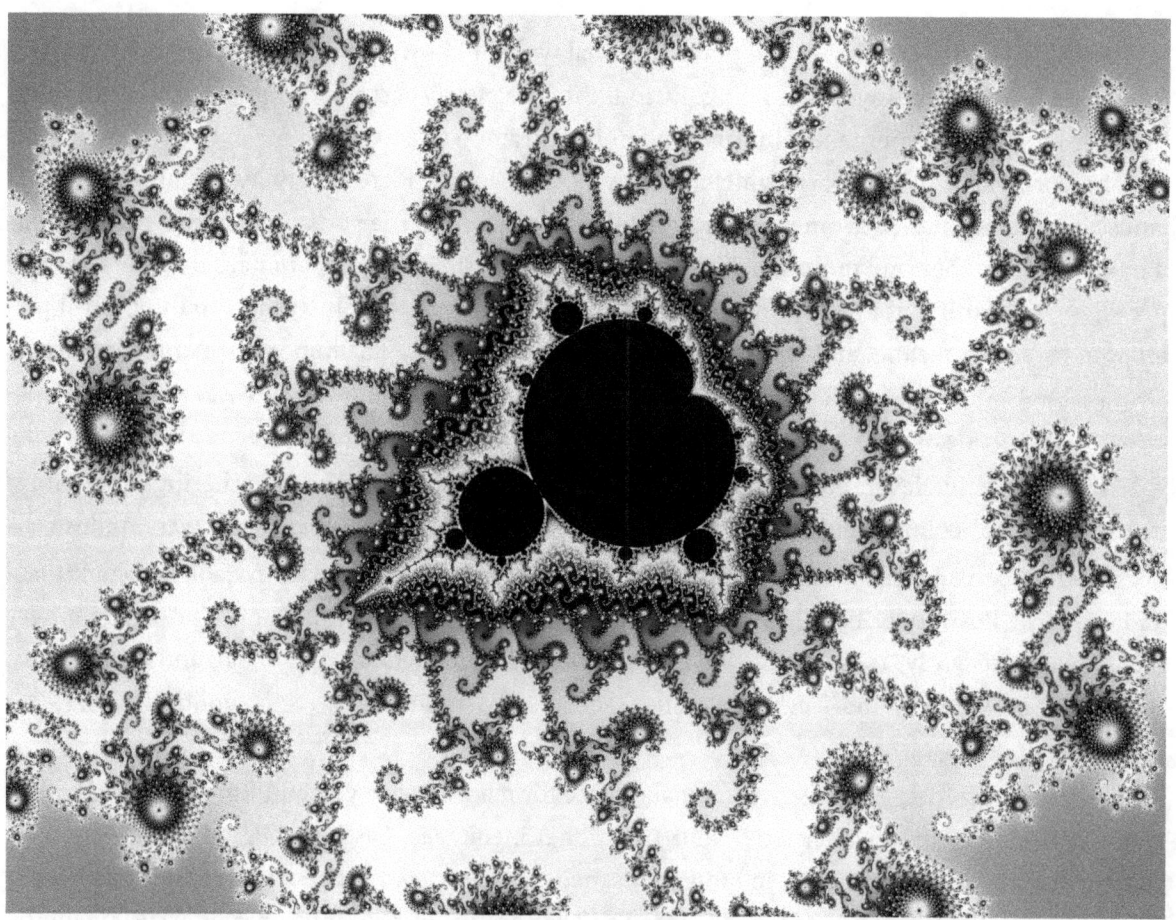

Figure 8.12 The Mandelbrot set[23]

The belief that in every complex system the behavior of the whole can be understood in its entirety by the properties of its parts is central to the Cartesian paradigm. This was Descartes' celebrated method of analytic thinking, which has been an essential characteristic of modern scientific thought.... The great shock of twentieth-century science has been that systems cannot be understood by analysis.

—Fritjof Capra[24]

In contrast to the starkly anti-spiritual objectivism of the mental/modern paradigm, the plural/postmodern paradigm holds a variety of stances on spirituality. Atheism and nihilism are both at home here. Plural/postmodernism is strongly antihierarchical, so religious institutions (and by extension their spiritual practices) are generally the target of this paradigm's dismantling program. However, the spiritualities that have been marginalized or pushed to the fringes are now welcomed in and *centered*. New Age spirituality, psychedelic-informed spirituality, paganism, neo-shamanic practices, and indigenous wisdom traditions are all embraced by postmodernism. The humanitarian, cultural, or restorative justice aspects of marginalized cultures are often more of a focus than the spiritual practices themselves. It is also worth noting that Buddhism's *emptiness* and *no-self* metaphysics aligns with the deconstructive paradigm of postmodernism. In figure 8.10, above, the single circle of the world has transformed into a multiplicity of worlds and there is no shape to define the self.

The gifts of plural/postmodernism include a world-centric moral compass, increased valuation of diversity, and a drive toward activism. The culturally given identity layers are deconstructed to make space for individual authenticity. The core value of sensitivity leads to greater emotional intelligence and psychological healing. There is a renewed interest in the earth and spirituality.

The pathologies of this paradigm include an *anything-goes* moral relativism and deconstruction into chaos, oblivion, and nihilism. This paradigm can be very focused against modernism and traditionalism, without recognizing that the existence of postmodernism rests upon the continued support of the paradigms that precede it. The sensitivity of postmodernism makes it good at identifying harm, but weak to effect real change among entrenched interests. In addition, this paradigm can get caught within the *drama triangle*, viewing self, marginalized groups, and the earth through the lens of victimhood.[25] While it is a crucial step to recognize that harm has been done, this paradigm has a challenge moving from victimhood back into empowerment.

The Drama Triangle

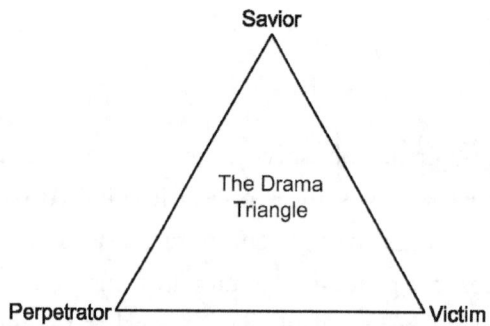

Figure 8.13 The drama triangle

The drama triangle is a framework for understanding the roles we can inhabit in relationships from a place of disempowerment. The three roles are the *victim,* who is the recipient of wrong-doing or abuse, the *perpetrator,* who is the agent causing harm to the victim, and the *savior,* the one who rescues the victim and punishes the perpetrator. As long as I am inhabiting one of these roles, I will view others primarily as one of these roles. The dynamics between each role includes an assumption of blame for power imbalances. The victim is innocent and powerless, the perpetrator wields power for personal gain, and the savior must use their power to save the victim.

Most fairy tales, action stories, and dramas utilize this framework for good storytelling. There is a hero, a villain, and the innocent bystanders. In the story, when a character shifts roles, for example, when the supposed savior actually turns out to be the villain, this creates dramatic tension. In human relationships, these roles are all about emotional drama, blame, and perpetuating the story of unfairness. This system describes how suffering perpetuates itself through relational disempowerment.

As long as I'm in one of these roles, I'm not in my sovereignty, and I'm not able to view others in their sovereignty. As a victim, I'm invested in blaming others, and I'm looking for someone to save me instead of centering in my power and taking responsibility for my situation. As a perpetrator, I am acting out my wounds and pathologies upon others without recognizing the essential human dignity that they possess. In the perpetrator role, I am unable or unwilling to acknowledge the sovereignty of others. As the savior, I view myself as the benevolent police and judge. I use my goodness in order to condemn the perpetrator, and my righteous power is required to save the powerless victim.

The sensitivity of the plural/postmodern paradigm cares about those who have been victimized. *Save the Earth, save the whales,* and *save the rainforests* are prime examples. I am able to identify and commiserate with the victims of hegemonic masculinity and capitalism. This is a necessary and powerful step toward addressing systemic abuses. We need to bring injustice into the light of our collective awareness in order for change to happen.

The next step is to move beyond blaming and role-based identifications. As long as I view someone as a perpetrator foremost, actual forgiveness is impossible. As long as I see myself as a victim, I will be stuck with my story of disempowerment. This is where the plural/postmodern paradigm is prone to becoming stuck, and as we shall see, it is the integral paradigm that provides the crucial step into wholeness that restores sovereignty and releases the grip of the drama triangle.

Summary of Tier I Paradigms

In Western culture today, there are three main cultural factions: mythic/traditional, mental/modern, and plural/postmodern. Each faction operates within its own paradigm with distinct needs, motivations, self-systems, and worldviews. These three paradigms are systemically interdependent and interwoven into society to a degree that they cannot be separated from each other. In addition, each faction receives tremendous benefit from the other two factions. Despite all of this, there is a power struggle between cultural factions for the direction and values of our society. Each faction argues for its core values within its worldview. The worldviews and values of the other two factions seem ignorant, insane, or evil. Integral philosophy gives us a framework to understand these social forces. As we shall see in the next section, the integral paradigm offers solutions that transcend and include all the paradigms that have come before.

In addition to the cultural lenses, the first-tier paradigms give us a tool to explore and understand our inner landscapes and to find commonality with all people. I can recognize that we are all on the same developmental ladder. In addition, I hold all of these paradigms within myself. My center of gravity tends to reside within one paradigm most of the time. However, in different contexts, I may shift paradigms. Humans contain multiple lines of intelligence, including rational, emotional, relational, and sexual intelligences. Each developmental line will progress along the ladder and different lines may exist within different paradigms. Understanding these paradigms and self-locating on the axis is a powerful method for advancing along the pathway.

It is important to note the limits that apply to this meta-theory of the evolution of paradigms. For starters, this system carries the cultural biases of the individuals who created it: largely educated, white, academic, Westerners (myself included). Our claim is that while the cultural specifics vary, the deep features of each paradigm are universal. We have good reason to believe that this developmental ladder applies to all humans and societies (see, for example, *Rising Tide: Gender Equality and Cultural Change around the World*, by Inglehard and Norris, who identify cultural and gender evolutionary progressions across countries using United Nations survey data). However, the interpretations and categorizations are subject to the worldviews of those who are creating the theories. In addition, there are varying degrees of evidence backing for the individual theories that comprise the meta-model. Notably, Ego-Development theory is data-driven. Many of the other theories are not. Finally, this system is prone to be overly prescriptive of a singular developmental pathway, and runs the risk of further marginalizing folks, for example with neurodivergence, who do not fit the ideal human implicit in the meta-theory.

Prompts for Journaling and Discussion

Find the place where each paradigm lives within yourself by filling out the table below:

	Mythic/Traditional	Mental/Modern	Plural/Postmodern
Favorite Books			
Favorite Movies			
Favorite Celebrities			
Favorite Leaders			

Create a Personal Self-World Map[26]

1. On a large piece of paper, draw a shape to represent the structure of the kosmos that you live in.
2. Within the kosmos, draw another shape to represent List your full name given at birth and any other names you have used.
3. Draw your relationship with your body image, sex, heritage, and any other features of your physical body.
4. Add a name, symbol, color, or shape to represent each of your core family relations—parents, siblings, partners, children, grandparents, grandchildren, and so on.
5. Draw or list all other humans whose names you know and are connected to by friendship, work, or shared interest.
6. Draw or list the souls of deceased ancestors, friends, and Add in any spirit guides, angels, or spiritual beings who do not occupy physical form.
7. Draw or list your important relationships with nonhuman This includes animals, pets, plants, and neo-shamanic spirits of animal and plant allies.
8. Draw or list your relationships with collective groups including family, communities, subcultures, nationality, religion, and so on.
9. Draw or list the significant places in your life, including current residence, childhood home, workplaces, schools, ancestry, and so on.

10. Once you have drawn your self-world Compare it to the diagrams above for each paradigm. Which paradigm does your self-world most resemble?

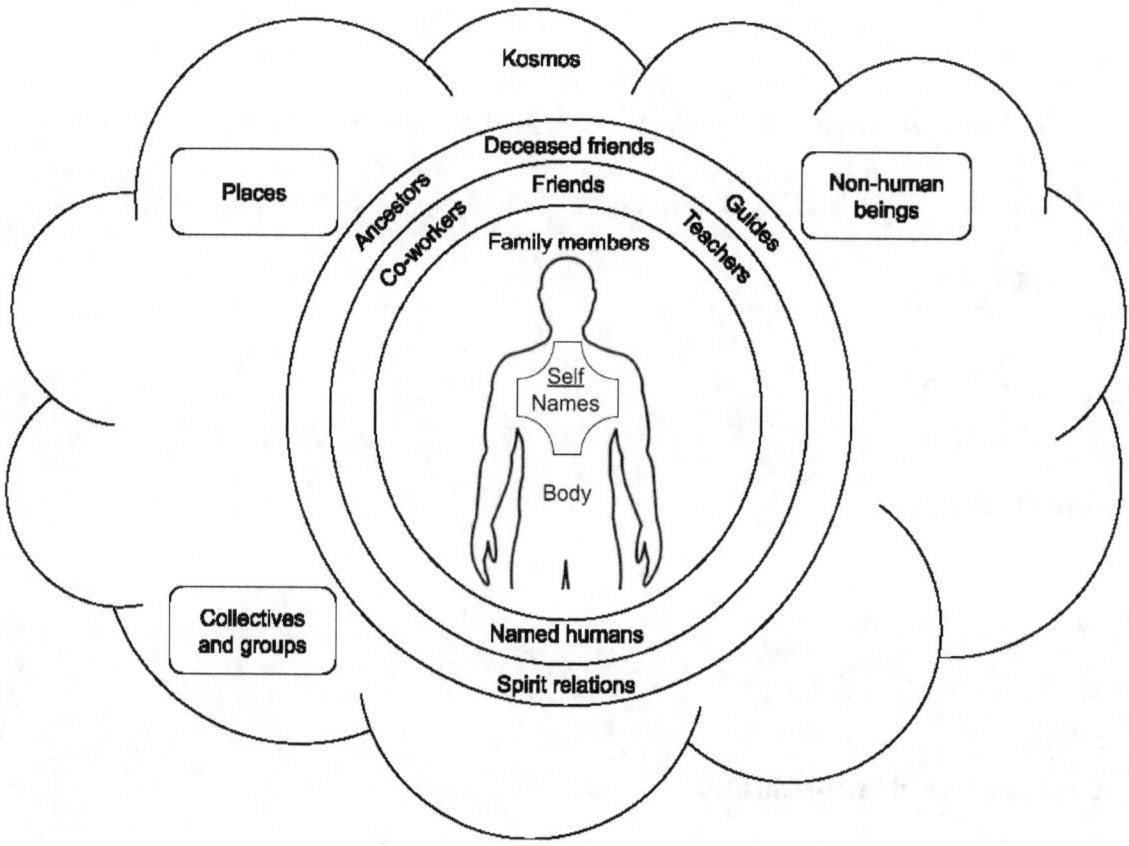

Figure 8.14 Sample skeleton of a self-world map

Notes

[1] Quoted in *Spiral Dynamics: Mastering Values, Leadership, and Change*, Beck and Cowen.

[2] Scientific paradigms were first described by Thomas Kuhn, who defined them as "a constellation of achievements - concepts, values, techniques, etc. - shared by a scientific community and used by that community to define legitimate problems and solutions." *The Structure of Scientific Revolutions*, Kuhn. Technically, a paradigm is a set of practices, or *praxis*, for engaging with the world, occupying the inter-objective realm, while a worldview holds the theories and meanings, or *theoria*, occupying the inter-sujective realm.

[3] "A worldview, as I define it, is a coherent set of values and ideals that persists across multiple generations. Worldviews are large-scale cultural agreements about what is good, true, and beautiful. They give meaning to reality and help us understand the world. In fact, worldviews are arguably the basic units of cultural analysis and interpretation—the most fundamental structures of cultural evolution." *Developmental Politics: How America Can Grow Into a Better Version of Itself*, McIntosh.

[4] "Our world view is not simply the way we look at the world. It reaches inward to constitute our innermost being, and outward to constitute the world. It mirrors but also reinforces and even forges the structures, armorings, and possibilities of our interior life. It deeply configures our psychic and somatic experience, the patterns of our sensing, knowing, and interacting with the world. No less potently, our world view—our beliefs and theories, our maps, our metaphors, our myths, our interpretive assumptions—constellates our outer reality, shaping and working the world's malleable potentials in a thousand ways of subtly reciprocal interaction. World views create worlds." *Cosmos and Psyche*, Tarnas.

[5] *The Religion of Tomorrow*, Wilber.

[6] "According to integral philosophy, each stage of consciousness is a natural epistemology, an organic way of making meaning with its own distinct view of the world that arises from a specific set of problematic life conditions and their corresponding solutions. These stages function as living dynamic systems that organize both entire human societies as well as the minds of the individuals who participate in those societies." *Integral Consciousness and the Future of Evolution*, McIntosh.

[7] "A meme contains behavioral instructions that are passed from one generation to the next, social artifacts, and value-laden symbols that glue together social systems. Like an intellectual virus, a meme reproduces itself through concepts like dress styles, language trends, popular cultural norms, architectural designs, art forms, religious expressions, social movements, economic models, and moral statements of how living should be done." *Spiral Dynamics: Mastering Values, Leadership, and Change*, Beck and Cowen.

[8] "Since each new ego stage or frame of reference builds on the previous one and integrates it, no one can skip a stage." "Ego Development: Inferring the Client's Frame of Reference," Young-Eisendrath.

[9] "In dominator hierarchies, with each higher level, the few dominate and oppress the many. In actualization or growth hierarchies, each higher level is more and more inclusive." *The Religion of Tomorrow*, Wilber.

[10] The term *integral* was first used by the Indian sage Sri Aurobindo in 1914 (quoted above). It was subsequently employed by the Swiss philosopher Jean Gebser in 1939 to describe a new integral structure of consciousness in humanity. Today, integral theory has been popularized by polymath Ken Wilber.

[11] "Integral theory posits that evolution is not limited to the exterior forms of reality (matter and organisms), but is also evident in the interior spaces of reality, namely in the development of culture and consciousness. An integral view of history maintains that the collective consciousness of the human race has evolved through pre-modern, modern and post-modern structures, and is emerging into a new structure of consciousness, the integral stage, which is characterized by an ability to think and act from multiple worldviews." "A Quick Intro to Integral Theory," dailyevolver.com

[12] *In over Our Heads: The Mental Demands of Modern Life.*

[13] *Integral Consciousness and the Future of Evolution.*

[14] *The Ecology of Consciousness.*

[15] "Lévy Bruhl's participation mystique is more descriptive of this condition, since it aptly formulates the primordial relation of the primitive to the object. His objects have a dynamic animation, they are charged with soul-stuff or soul-force (and not always possessed of souls, as the animist theory supposes), so that they have a direct psychic effect upon him, producing what is practically a dynamic identification with the object. In certain primitive languages articles of personal use have a gender denoting 'alive' (the suffix of animation)." *Psychological Types*, Jung.

[16] "The Conformist stage 3 describes persons with an early adolescent frame of mind. Their self-identity is defined by their relationship to a group. This leads to confused boundaries between oneself and the group (whether family, team or nation). Being part of this larger entity allows one to be protected and share in its power. The price for inclusion is loyalty and obedience." *Ego Development: Nine Levels of Increasing Embrace*, Cook-Greuter.

[17] *Science and the Modern World.*

[18] "Agnosticism and atheism, when they are achieved as a result of selfauthorship (i.e., after growing out of a traditional environment), are most often expressions of this level of development." *Streams of Wisdom: An Advanced Guide to Integral Spiritual Development*, DiPerna.

[19] "Nature across most of the globe has now been significantly altered by multiple human drivers, with the great majority of indicators of ecosystems and biodiversity showing rapid decline. Seventy-five per cent of the land surface is significantly altered, 66 per cent of the ocean area is experiencing increasing cumulative impacts, and over 85 per cent of wetlands (area) has been lost.… Approximately half the live coral cover on coral reefs has been lost since the 1870s, with accelerating losses in recent decades due to climate change exacerbating other drivers.… The global rate of species extinction is already at least tens to hundreds of times higher than the average rate over the past 10 million years and is accelerating." The Global Assessment Report on

Biodiversity and Ecosystem Services. Intergovernmental Science-Policy Platform on Biodiversity and Ecosystem Services.

[20] "Individualists distrust conventional wisdom and the hyper-rational tenets of the Conscientious stage. They need to distance themselves from all that went before. In this case, one must reevaluate the self-adopted, yet sanctioned role identities of society and redefine oneself uniquely and independently of them based on one's own experience and conclusions. When one fully realizes that most prior meaning making was socially and culturally conditioned, scientific certainty and the judgmental frame of mind break down. Moreover, Individualists learn to consciously scrutinize their beliefs in order to test their assumptions or to relish the novel mental freedom such a maneuver allows." *Ego Development: Nine Levels of Increasing Embrace*, Cook-Greuter.

[21] *Ego Development: Nine Levels of Increasing Embrace.*

[22] "This quasi-transcendent binding element was eventually discovered through postmodernism's uniquely emergent strength: an enhanced sensitivity to the feelings of others. As a result of this enhanced sensitivity, postmodernists are afforded increased access to the subjective interiority of other people. And this enlarged sense of empathy for the feelings of others has now become the cornerstone of postmodernity's moral system. The rise of postmodernity thus marks the beginning of a new era of sensitivity—a new ethic of care that now defines the moral community of progressive culture. Postmodernism's moral sensitivity finds its focus in a deep concern for the perceived victims of Western civilization. Postmodern morality is accordingly focused on righting the wrongs that the globally ascendant culture of modernism has inflicted on the world." *Integral Consciousness and the Future of Evolution*, McIntosh.

[23] Source: Wolfgang Beyer, Creative Commons

[24] *The Web of Life: A New Synthesis of Mind and Matter.*

[25] "Due to this opening to a deeper interior, the postmodern self easily experiences a sense of victimization by virtue of its increased sensitivity and capacity for self-reflection on its own inner fragmentation and limited patterns." "A Deep Integral View on the Future of Gender," Debold, from *Integral Voices on Sex, Gender, and Sexuality*, Nicholson.

[26] Adapted from Metzner, *Ecology of Consciousness.*

| 9 |

Paradigms of Consciousness: Second Tier

Figure 9.1 Black Marble: Earth at night[1]

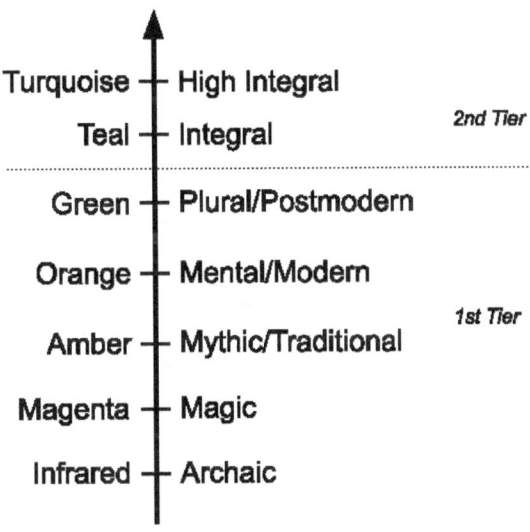

Figure 9.2 First- and second-tier paradigms

The first tier, spanning infrared to green, is where about 90 percent of American adults reside today. Each paradigm in tier one can only recognize the validity of its own perspective—and this is the defining quality of tier one. From any of these vantage points, I recognize only one valid worldview, and it's the one I inhabit. The way I see the world is the one correct way, and everyone else is either crazy or stupid. This doesn't mean that I can't be tolerant of people different from me in tier one. What it means is that I do not recognize the validity of other paradigms or how they complement each other.

Crossing the dotted line into tier two, integral, means for the first time I can *see* the lens of my paradigm. I gain conscious awareness of this previously invisible viewing instrument that colors my entire reality. Further, I can now recognize the lenses of all the other paradigms. With this new awareness, I recognize that each step is simultaneously a valid whole and a valuable part (i.e., a *holon*), and that these paradigms form stairs on a developmental staircase that must be sequentially climbed (a *growth holarchy*). Here, I recognize that each human exists on a given step on their path of growth. I may not abide by the actions of individuals in tier one, but I am now able to hold them with compassion and dignity. Recall that paradigms don't define humans, they define the consciousness humans inhabit. Integral consciousness appreciates the unique contributions of each step on the staircase. This represents a monumental expansion in perspective (i.e., a new tier in consciousness).

At present, our culture's collective consciousness has only developed up to plural/postmodernism. So, as we examine the integral and high integral paradigms, keep in mind that they are still forming.[2] Paradigms above tier one have only been accessed by a small but growing number of individuals. Excitingly, as more folks move into higher tiers, we are literally creating morphic fields for these evolutionary structures of consciousness. Ken Wilber has posited that once integral consciousness reaches about ten percent of the population, our culture will undergo a tipping point where these new values will permeate the collective.[3] By reading and contemplating this chapter, you are taking bold steps into integral consciousness. Learning about this material, digesting it, and forming your own perspective on it is the process through which your consciousness is evolving.

The Integral Paradigm

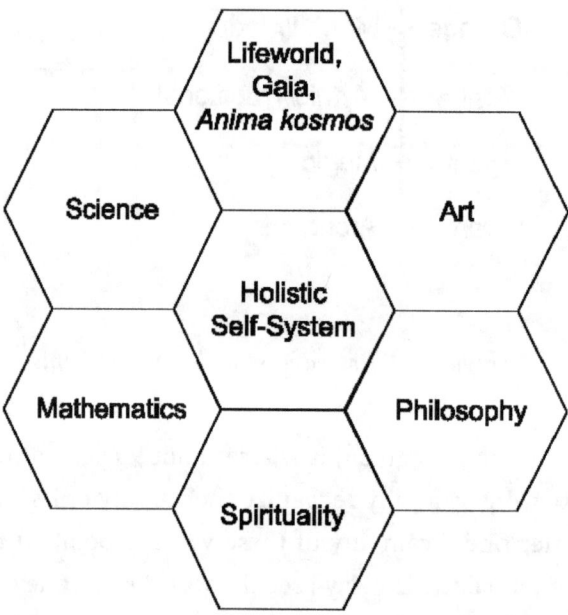

Figure 9.3 Integral psyche in relation with the world

Self	Holistic self-system
Nature	Web of life, Gaia
Values	Self-actualization, evolution
Motivation	Wholeness, interconnection
Truth	Integration of science and spirituality
Spirituality	Panexperientialism

Figure 9.4 Defining aspects of the integral paradigm

Once again, we are not strangers in an alien, mechanistic universe. The grand synthesis of evolution reintegrates us with nature. Our distant ancestors considered themselves an organic part of all that exists, expressing their belief through myth and confirming it through magic. Our not-so-distant forebears thought they knew better and put man above nature, and indeed beyond it. Now we are back in the embrace, indeed in the womb, of a creative universe, capable of bringing forth life and even consciousness.

—Ervin László[4]

At the integral paradigm, I am able to find my core self and make a coherent whole of all my different internal parts. I view the self as the regulator of my self-system that is embedded within relational, cultural, and natural systems. The self holds a high degree of both autonomy and interdependence. Whereas at plural/postmodern, the parts of my psyche may be chaotic, contradictory, or without a center, at integral, my self has found center and is able to "integrate" and own all the disparate psychological parts. At integral, I am more capable of holding internal contradiction or paradox. With a stronger sense of the *authentic self* comes greater resilience to be with strong emotions and integrate shadow aspects of my psyche.

I am able to see that the lens of my worldview gives meaning to reality. With an increased level of sovereignty, I am able to intentionally generate meaning in my life. I begin to choose the story I tell about self and world. Integral is also known as *autonomous* for this capacity to generate meaning.[5] This leads to *self-actualization*, which is the core value of integral. Instead of being motivated by a core *need*, as in the first-tier paradigms, enough of my needs are now met that my core motivation becomes the opportunity to actualize. I direct my energies both inwardly and outwardly on the process of evolution itself. At integral, I am driven by a self-determination to blossom into my fullest expression. With this comes a greater degree of self-responsibility. I now hold greater integrity and inner conviction for how I show up in the world. At integral, I actively seek out feedback and mirroring from others. In addition, I require solitary time to tend to my rapidly unfolding inner landscape.

At plural/postmodern, I am able to recognize the cultural conditioning that obstructs access to my authentic self and I'm focused on deconstructing those outer, false layers. Having done this work of peeling back the false identities, at integral I am now in connection with my *organic self* or *authentic self.* From this center, I am able to invite deeply intimate relationships with others and the world. At integral, I recognize my self-system within an ever-expanding context of cultural, historical, and natural systems.[6] The integral focus is on creating larger unities and understanding the interrelation and evolution of holons (i.e., parts and wholes). My integral self marvels at its part and participation within culture and within natural systems.[7] I undergo an embedding back into the continuous wholeness of reality.

> *The Integral View sees itself as intrinsically interwoven with the entire universe, an interconnected, seamless, vital, living, creative, and conscious Kosmos.… Integral levels themselves are creative and highly conscious; each moment is new, fresh, spontaneous, and alive. It is the first stage that integrates, or better, recognizes, the already existing prior union of knowing and feeling, consciousness and being, epistemology and ontology.*
>
> —Ken Wilber[8]

In addition to my personal growth and self-actualization, I begin to show a deep interest in the development of others. Therapists, coaches, and consultants are common occupations for folks at integral. I view life as an open-ended journey where I recognize that each individual is on a path of self-discovery. I am intensely interested in supporting both individuals and culture on their evolutionary journeys.

The integral paradigm is able to recognize that the polarization between factions in our culture are conflicts between worldviews. Instead of fighting harder, the integral approach is to recognize the validity of each paradigm, to support it to become a healthy, generative part of society, and to enable upward mobility for members within each paradigm. At integral, I recognize that fighting against paradigms pushes its members into extremism and absolutism. Supporting the needs of each first-tier paradigm, therefore, is the key to a healthy society and offers a new hope for the large-scale issues facing humanity today.

> *Of all the values of the integral worldview, that which it most esteems is the value of evolution itself. And with this exaltation of the value of evolution comes the ideal of "the prime directive." The prime directive is to work to maintain the health and sustainability of the entire channel of cultural evolution, the spiral of development as a whole. Because every infant begins life at the level of archaic consciousness, the flow of evolution through the levels is unceasing. So the prime directive instructs us that for cultural evolution to be sustainable, the enduring contributions of each stage of the system must be healthy and functioning within the greater society. Caring for the spiral as a whole means preserving the evolutionary opportunities for every person, regardless of that person's place in the sequence of evolution.*
>
> —Steve McIntosh[9]

At integral consciousness, I am fascinated by how each paradigm constructs identity, culture, and reality. I want to understand how individuals shift paradigms. Figure 9.5, below, charts the paradigms of consciousness across different categories and components of society. While the chart is obviously not exhaustive and presents my own interpretations, it offers a heuristic to understand how each paradigm creates a coherent worldview and how various social categories develop along the ladder.

How Paradigms Construct Culture

	Magic	Mythic/ Traditional	Mental/ Modern	Plural/ Postmodern	Integral
Race	Tribal group	Ethnocentrism	Meritocracy, Basic rights	Decolonization, Inclusion	Liberation-transformation[10]
Gender	Archetypal roles	Traditional roles	Meritocracy, Basic rights	Gender deconstruction	"Conscious" masc/fem[11]
Politics	Tribal units, Warriors	Patriotism, Conservatism	Democracy, Liberalism	Progressive	Global governance[12]
Economy	Barter and raid	Monarchy, Imperialism	Capitalism	Welfare State	Learning organizations
Resource Use	Nomadic, Reciprocity	Conquering, Agriculture	Industrialism, Consumerism	Conservation, Save the earth	Integral ecologies[13]
Religion	Animism, Shamanism	Monotheism	Atheism, Utilitarianism	New-age, Humanitarian	Panexperiential
Morality	Self-interest	Conventional, Conformity	Ethical Principles	Relativism	Developm't'l, Interbeing[14]
Social Order	Survival of fittest, Tribal	Dominator hierarchy	Meritocracy, Technocracy	Deconstruction, Anarchy	Growth hierarchy
Social Geometry	Pea pod	Pyramid	Cartesian Grid	Antistructure, No center	Honeycomb lattice
Body	Power object	Dangerous, Sinful	Machine	Emotional teacher	Pleasure-flow

Figure 9.5 Social constructs across paradigms

The giant leap into tier two and the integral paradigm brings with it a radical revitalization of spirituality (fig. 9.6). I am reborn into a sacred world. The *anima mundi* of the archaic and magical levels re-emerges as the *anima kosmos*, the *living kosmos*, at integral. At first this realization is intellectual: I am recognizing spiritual truths everywhere. As I progress toward high integral, the sacred becomes increasingly experiential and immersive. This can come as a profound revelation after the agnosticism and atheism of mental/modernism, and the anti-religious-establishment zeal of plural/postmodernism. Integral affirms the existence of the sacred, whether it be mystical, spiritual, Divine, Tao, or Buddha nature. In fact, at integral I am discovering truths across spiritual traditions. Unlike the Magic and Traditional paradigms, integral spirituality is not dependent on any external authority. Rather, at this level, I am accessing spirituality through an ever-expanding self and then corroborating my internal experiences through the cannons of spiritual traditions.

A core tenet of this workbook is that the organic androgyne, feminine, and masculine are accessed through their respective archetypes. As we saw in chapter 5, these evolutionary archetypes exist in the causal realm of consciousness. Therefore, I must expand my state of consciousness in order to access them. As I've already noted, these archetypes are unbounded sources of life-giving, creative, ordering energies—they offer tangible benefits. I gain access to these archetypes through sacred practices, which become an increasingly core focus in the integral paradigm.

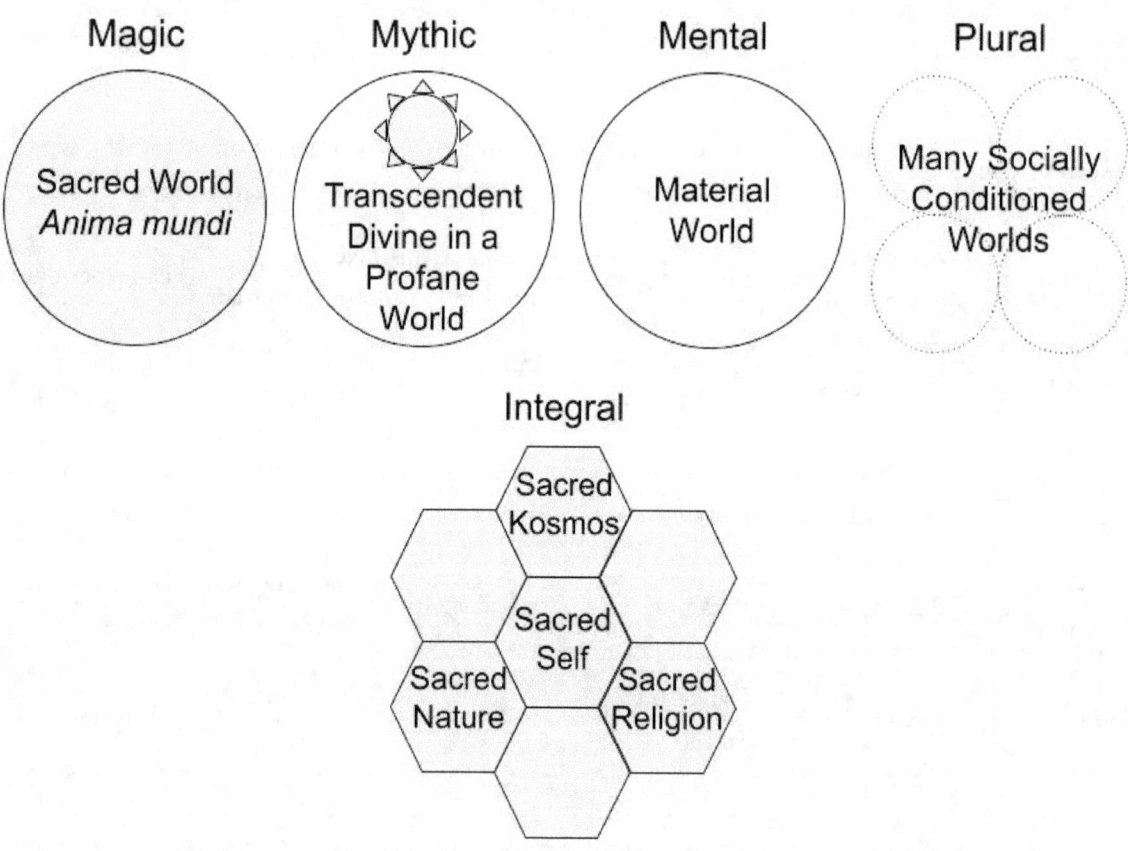

Figure 9.6 Access to the sacred across paradigms

Let's take a closer look at how each paradigm relates to the sacred.

The archaic and magic paradigms incorporate spirituality through a magical experience of the environment. Everything is alive, and everything has a spirit or soul. The imaginal and fantastical qualities of the world impart a spirituality that is immediate, personal, and interactive.

The mythic/traditional paradigm utilizes organized religion. A core message at this structure is that there is one spiritual truth. A chosen group of people have access to this one truth and all other people are excluded or condemned. Here, spirituality is woven into organized religion that creates an identity and a sense of belonging within the community of practitioners. The mythic/traditional paradigm understands the power of archetypal energies. However, organized religions have generally blocked direct access to the *transcendent truth* for lay practitioners—instead the transcendent is communicated to the congregation by the priestly class.

The mental/modern paradigm categorically denies the sacred. Here, *scientific materialism* reigns supreme. In this worldview, what is real is that which is measurable and replicable. The workings of the universe operate according to logic, mathematics, and reason. There is no space for the *divine hand*, for *Buddha nature*, or for angels, miracles, psychic phenomena, and the like. Per Nietzsche, "God is dead. God remains dead. And we have killed him."[15]

The plural/postmodern paradigm is nuanced. When the sacred is described in terms like truth, absolute, noetic, Divine, and God (which it often is by spiritual practitioners), this absolutism is rejected by the pluralist paradigm. Any sweeping definitive claims about reality, metaphysics, or spirituality are intensely scrutinized. These claims, and the authority of anyone preaching them are antithetical to the deconstructionism and relativism of postmodernism. However, postmodernism does welcome the culturally non-centered spiritual traditions. My focus at this paradigm is on the cultural and interpersonal aspects of spiritual traditions rather than the primary spiritual experience itself. In addition, the *everything goes* relativism can open the door for superstition and *woo-woo* without spiritual rigor. At core, people come first in postmodernity, and the sacred is generally either secondary or nonexistent.

Integral brings a powerful revitalization of spirituality. In sharp contrast to the three prior paradigms that populate most of Western culture today, integral posits that spiritual truth is real, it is directly accessible by each individual, and it is fundamentally interwoven into every aspect of existence. This is a massive leap and promises a much-needed *Great Turning* for Western civilization.[16]

Integral spirituality reaches down to include and synthesize spirituality from all prior paradigms. Because the integral paradigm is interested in supporting each paradigm that came before it, instead of fighting or destroying them, integral is uniquely available to receive each one's gifts. Truths are discovered and celebrated within indigenous spiritualities, organized religions, science and philosophy, and New Age mysticism—literally every paradigm represented in our culture. Instead of asserting a single spiritual truth, at integral, I find common truths across traditions. A hallmark of the integral paradigm is the reconciliation of science and spirituality into a larger whole. The science-versus-religion debate is re-understood as a paradigm clash between the traditional and modern paradigms. From the broader integral perspective, I am able to understand how scientists and mystics are describing the same underlying patterns with different languages and lenses. I harvest the objective truths from science and the subjective truths of religion and *integrate* them together. Integral consciousness doesn't care about the singular correct system, it's about finding truth through synergistic connections between *all* systems and traditions—this is why the honeycomb lattice represents the visual symbol for integral.

Personally, when I first shifted into integral, I began to experience spirituality viscerally in myself after spending most of my adult life as an agnostic-atheist. I began to find spiritual truth across religious traditions, including the Catholic faith that I had been raised in and rebelled against. I began to experience the earth as a spiritual being. I could see how science sheds light on spiritual truth. All of which is to say, at integral, spirituality has become a core aspect of *the lens* through which I interpret my reality, choose my values, and identify myself.

One key insight is that it is possible to be scientific about subjective experiences. The mystical, spiritual, and psychological aspects of consciousness are qualitative, not quantitative, and thus, not scientifically measurable. However, I do experience these phenomena as real, and I can be scientific about how I study subjective phenomena. This approach is known as *radical empiricism*:[17]

> *It is not where or how observations are made that makes a field of study 'scientific'; it is what is done with the observations afterward. Repeated systematic observations from the same observer and replicated observations from others, is what distinguishes the scientific method from casual or haphazard observations.… It is possible to be objective about subjective experience using the accepted cannons of the scientific method.*
>
> —Metzner[18]

Today, most major world religions have sub-groups represented by integral teachers and communities.[19] Integral spirituality is inclusive across traditions, yet rigorous about authentic practices. The cultural inclusivity of plural/postmodernism gives way to integral's prioritization on the experiential realms that a tradition accesses.

The hallmark of integral spirituality is known as *panexperientialism*, which is defined in the previous chapter. From this core tenet, arises a variety of integral spiritualities including panpsychism,[20] nature mysticism and the Great Web of Life, Indra's Net,[21] and cosmic consciousness.

The collective benefits of the integral paradigm are still largely in potential. At present, only a small integral subculture has developed, so the social and environmental advancements are not yet measurable. Just as modernity arose to address the issues that traditionalism could not solve, and postmodernity arose to address the issues of the previous two paradigms, the promise of integral is that it will offer meaningful solutions to today's pressing issues. The Enlightenment of the 1700s was a massive revolution across all layers and levels of Western civilization. The arrival of integral is predicted to be an even larger change because it represents humanity's first ever step into a new tier of consciousness.

At the individual level however, we can measure the benefits of integral. Individuals here source worth from within, self-direct life circumstances toward growth and fulfillment, feel a sense of belonging to humanity and the earth, and have a strong center of gravity to ride the inevitable waves of life.

The primary pathology of integral is a fanatical devotion to "integral" and "evolution." Personally, my shadows at integral include spiritual materialism,[22] believing I'm *chosen* or *special*, becoming addicted to the god realms and bliss realms, believing that I'm so *woke, healed, ascended,* or *conscious* that I hide my shadows and stop growing (i.e., spiritual bypassing),[23] and using my voice arrogantly to tell people how to heal and how to grow.

Prompts for Journaling and Discussion

Integral comes online through the process of embracing all prior paradigms. To the extent that I hold judgments of others or myself at these paradigms, I am holding myself back from integral. To work these edges, fill out the table below:

	Mythic/ Traditional	Mental/ Rational	Plural/ Postmodern
What I judge in others			
What I judge in myself			
What I am ready to forgive			
What I can celebrate			

The High Integral Paradigm

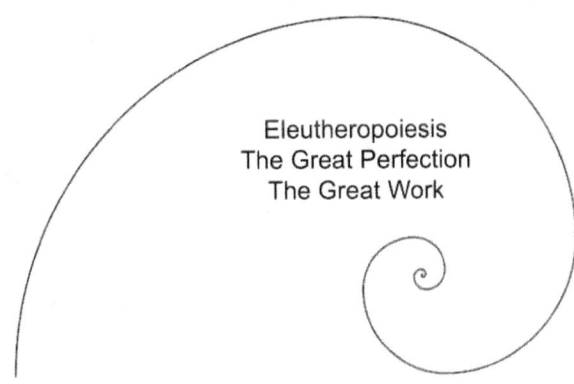

Eleutheropoiesis
The Great Perfection
The Great Work

Figure 9.7 The high integral psyche in relation with the world

Self	Kosmo-centric process	**Motivation**	Construct and ego transparency
Nature	Web of life	**Truth**	Present experience
Values	Compassion	**Spirituality**	Eleutheropoiesis

Figure 9.8 Defining aspects of the high integral paradigm

In the high integral paradigm of consciousness, I become more and more aware of the processes of my ego: how I select for comfort and safety, how I work toward self-aggrandizement and perfection, and my attempts to own, control, track, and understand reality. The ego becomes increasingly transparent to itself. Thus, this paradigm is referred to as *ego aware*. High integral is also known as *construct aware* because individuals at this level understand the ways that language and concepts construct a seemingly permanent and objective world out of the dynamic ungraspable flow of reality. Whereas at integral, I am aware of the embedded interconnectedness of reality, at high integral, I experience this interconnectedness directly. I am actively dismantling the last vestiges of a "separate" ego.

Ego-aware folks may come to feel that the automatic judgment habit that constitutes much of ordinary functioning as a major barrier to deeper self-acceptance and embrace of others. They observe the habits of mind such as the tendency to endlessly analyze and reflect in order to create ever more accurate theories of life and nature. All of these endeavors can now be understood as partial defenses against knowing the impermanence of the embodied self. Thus, at the Ego-aware stage not just cultural conditioning is seen through, but the predicament of living in language.

—Susan Cook-Greuter[24]

The core value of high integral is compassion. At integral, I carry an enthusiasm, and often an agenda, for the evolution of society and its members. By contrast, at high integral, I appreciate the perfection of each person exactly as they are with acceptance and compassion. I hold reverence toward the perfection of the whole evolutionary staircase. I am able to allow the processes to move through myself and others rather than inserting my agendas for growth and actualization.

At high integral, I am able to accept even more of my humanity and messiness. The integral drive toward wholeness means I am invested in holding myself together and presenting myself as *whole* or *evolved*. By high integral, my ego's attempts at self-perfection, positive presentation, and managing my own process are seen with more humor. My practice becomes staying present for whatever the unfolding of life may bring.

The gift that the Master is to her people goes beyond her leadership, mentoring, and tending to the community soul. Her very being is a gift of wholeness. The core value in her life, which arises from her psychospiritual center of gravity, is the desire that every thing and every creature be allowed its true place, so that the world functions in its fullness, in accordance with its comprehensive destiny. She appreciates that each species, each habitat, and each social issue is related to all others. She understands that everything is alive, that it all fits together, and that we are all participants and reflections of the whole.

—Bill Plotkin[25]

With this paradigm comes increasing humility, humor, serendipity, awe, and wonder at the marvels of the kosmos. The self is experienced as a spiral that goes infinitely deep and infinitely wide. The center is the self, but paradoxically, the center is also the entire kosmos. This process is undefinable and ungraspable and yet viscerally unfolding with each successive moment. Because relatively few humans reside in this paradigm, individuals may feel isolated or alone in their experience here.[26]

Eleutheropoiesis

In 1972, Humberto Maturana invented the word *autopoiesis* to describe the autonomous self-organization of living systems. "This was a word without a history. A word that could directly mean what takes place in the dynamics of the autonomy proper to living systems."[27] We use language to create reality. What has not yet been named, cannot be said to exist. In the high integral paradigm, I recognize the importance of *semiotics*—or the study of symbols. Neologizing (i.e., the creation of new words) goes hand in hand with experiencing new realms.

Maturana's insight was that living systems needed a new word. *Auto* means "self." *Poiesis* means "creation." Living systems self-create, and we now call this *autopoiesis.*

Just as the kosmos took a giant leap from physical evolution to biological life, the next step through the *point of reflection* was equally profound. Human consciousness represents another new category of evolution (actually two categories: the subjective psychospiritual, and the intersubjective cultural). The core nature of the consciousness that humans hold is that they *create freedom.* Following Maturana's precedent, the new word being introduced here to describe human systems is *eleutheropoiesis.* It is our nature to move to ever more creative expressions of freedom. *Eleutheria* is the Greek term for "liberty" and, again, *poiesis* means "creation."

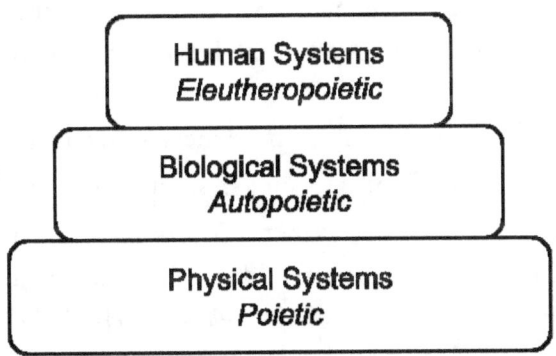

Figure 9.9 Three typologies of evolution

Dynamic systems operate on three levels: structure, pattern, and process. The structure is the individual components. The pattern is the organization of the system. The process describes how the holon is changing over time. Process is whatever is happening now. The way that structures influence the pattern, and the way the pattern changes the structural components is described by the process. In the modern paradigm, I'm seeing the structures of the physical universe via scientific materialism. At postmodern, I'm able to see systems with invisible, yet discernable patterns that hold emergent properties. In integral, I'm focused on the process or the evolution that is unfolding. But at integral, I believe I need to "do" the process. Here at high integral, I understand the inherent perfection of the process itself. It is the nature of human consciousness to self-liberate, and my role is to work in service to this eleutheropoietic process.

With this more expansive view, comes a greater understanding of the nature of freedom. Eleutheropoiesis exhibits three types of freedom: *freedom from, freedom to,* and *freedom as.* The first-tier paradigms are focused on freedom from types of suffering and bondage. Integral is focused on the freedom to self-actualize. In high integral, my focus is on freedom as myself, exactly as I am, and to support others to be exactly as they are.

High Integral	Freedom as the kosmos
Integral	Freedom to actualize
First Tier	Freedom from bondage & meeting core needs

Figure 9.10 Developmental foci of eleutheropoiesis

At the earlier stages of human evolution, eleutheropoiesis focuses on liberation from suffering and oppression. Individuals and cultures move from the safety needs of tribalism, to the belonging needs of traditional, to the achievement needs of modernity, to the sensitivity needs of post-modernism. These first-tier needs correspond to the first five stages Maslow's hierarchy of needs, outlined below.

Crossing into the second tier, my focus shifts from meeting my *needs* to expanding my *capacities.* In Maslow's model, the integral paradigm is focused first on *aesthetics* and then on *self-actualization,* both of which are functions of agency rather than need. In high integral (and presumably higher paradigms), the egoic self becomes less central and the freedom expands into the being and be-coming of life and kosmos. Maslow calls this *transcendence.* Each higher step brings both a greater degree of freedom and a broader understanding of what freedom means.

The high integral paradigm generates a new perspective on *free will.* Earlier egoic paradigms understand free will variously—the freedom to be represented in politics (modern), the freedom from cultural conditioning (postmodern), and the freedom to self-determine (integral). In each case though, free will applies to the egoic self's capacity to choose. High integral individuals are disenchanted from the egoic self, and so the freedom of will is re-comprehended as the freedom of the kosmos itself. The will of the self and the kosmos braid together in increasing harmony. One might ask, "In what sense is the kosmos free?" At high integral, the evolutionary kosmos holds the freedom to be and to become. This represents the leading edge of eleutheropoiesis: the creative self-liberation of reality.

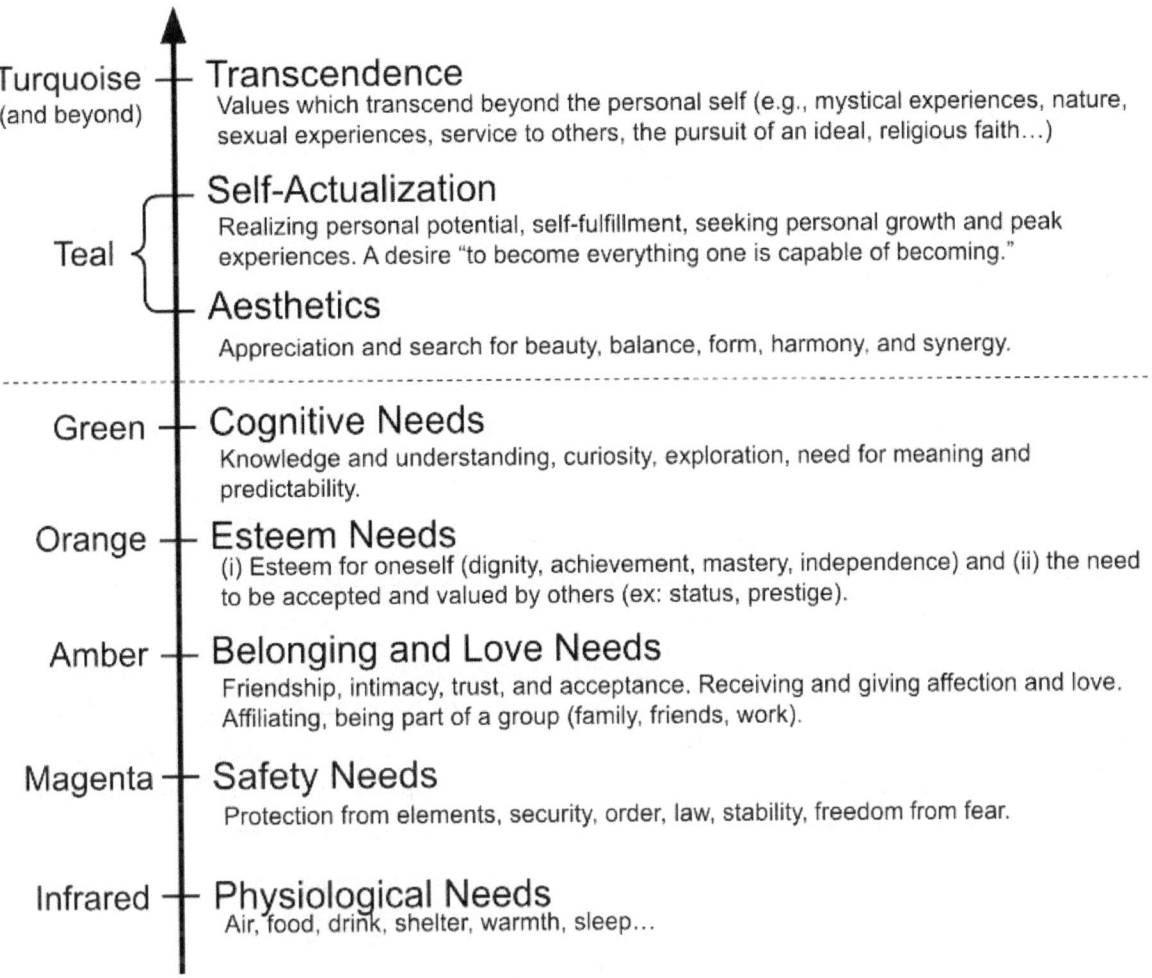

Turquoise (and beyond)

Transcendence
Values which transcend beyond the personal self (e.g., mystical experiences, nature, sexual experiences, service to others, the pursuit of an ideal, religious faith…)

Teal {

Self-Actualization
Realizing personal potential, self-fulfillment, seeking personal growth and peak experiences. A desire "to become everything one is capable of becoming."

Aesthetics
Appreciation and search for beauty, balance, form, harmony, and synergy.

Green

Cognitive Needs
Knowledge and understanding, curiosity, exploration, need for meaning and predictability.

Orange

Esteem Needs
(i) Esteem for oneself (dignity, achievement, mastery, independence) and (ii) the need to be accepted and valued by others (ex: status, prestige).

Amber

Belonging and Love Needs
Friendship, intimacy, trust, and acceptance. Receiving and giving affection and love. Affiliating, being part of a group (family, friends, work).

Magenta

Safety Needs
Protection from elements, security, order, law, stability, freedom from fear.

Infrared

Physiological Needs
Air, food, drink, shelter, warmth, sleep…

Figure 9.11 Maslow's hierarchy of needs[28]

This One Being and Consciousness is involved here in Matter. Evolution is the process by which it liberates itself: consciousness appears in what seems to be inconscient and once having appeared is self-impelled to grow higher and at the same time to enlarge and develop towards a greater and greater perfection. Life is the first step of this release of consciousness; mind [i.e., ego] is the second; but the evolution does not finish with mind, it awaits a release into something greater, a consciousness which is spiritual and supramental.

—Sri Aurobindo[29]

Eleutheropoiesis is represented in a number of spiritual traditions. Kabbalah of Jewish mysticism uses the concept of the Great Work of creation whereby the Divine essence densifies into form, which then evolves back toward unity so that "God may behold the face of God." Dzogchen of Tibetan Buddhism is known as *the great perfection,* where the *suchness* of reality is experienced in utter perfection.[30] In the mythology of the Kalachakra Tantra, when Shakyamuni Buddha attained enlightenment, he looked out through the eyes of all beings at all times. In this moment of total awareness and infinite compassion, he reimagined the universe in such a way that all beings move as efficiently and directly toward realization while still preserving their individual freedom. In the Kalachakra cosmology, we now inhabit this reimagined, maximally compassionate world. In each case, the nature of reality is understood as self-liberative. This is the essential view of the high integral paradigm: liberation through compassionate abiding.

Agape

In this exploration of paradigms, I have been exclusively focused on the action of Eros. This has been variously described as the drive to become, the creative advance into novelty, and the evolutionary process toward greater complexity and wholeness. Eros is our inborn longing to return to Spirit and to transcend. However, Eros represents only half of the developmental journey of realization. The other half of this process is known as Agape, which is the downward efflux or involution from Spirit into matter. Agape is the immanent, inclusive, downward drive. It is the embrace of smaller parts by larger wholes. This downward flow of creation balances Eros' upward drive from parts toward larger wholes. Together, they form a unified circle with unmanifest Spirit (aka God or Buddha nature) at the apex and the most basic forms of matter at the bottom.

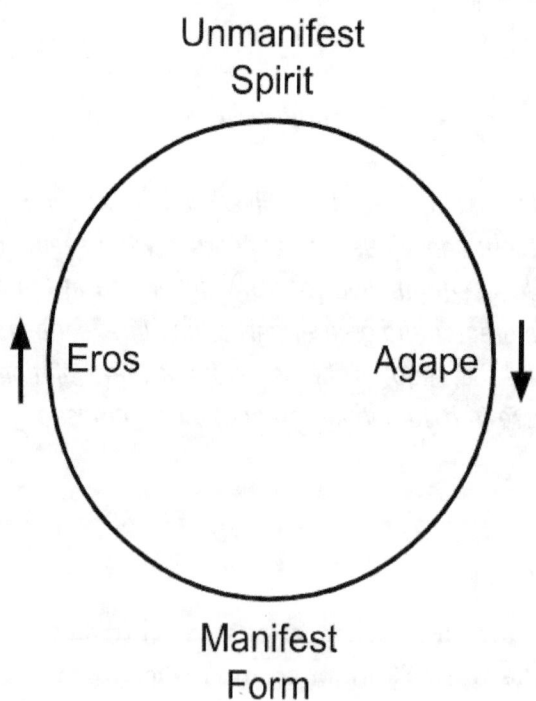

Figure 9.12 Eros and Agape

Eros is the love of the lower reaching up to the higher (Ascent); Agape is the love of the higher reaching down to the lower (Descent). In individual development, one ascends via Eros (or expanding to a higher and wider identity), and then integrates via Agape (or reaching down to embrace with care all lower holons), so that balanced development transcends but includes—it is negation and preservation, ascent and descent, Eros and Agape.

—Ken Wilber[31]

The graph illustrates wholeness which transcends duality. Unmanifest Spirit is absolute and pervades all things. And yet, that remains only half of existence. Spirit alone is still not the totality. The relative, imperfect world of traffic jams and taxes is the sacred manifestation that compliments and completes the unmanifest perfection of Spirit.

It is as true to say that God is permanent and the World fluent, as that the World is permanent and God is fluent. It is as true to say that God is one and the World many, as the World is one and God many. It is as true to say that, in comparison with the World, God is actual eminently, as that, in comparison with God, the World is actual eminently. It is as true to say that the World is immanent in God, as that God is immanent in the World. It is as true to say that God transcends the World, as that the World transcends God. It is as true to say that God creates the World, as that the World creates God.

—Alfred North Whitehead[32]

Another way to understand Agape is *compassion.* Having experienced the singular consciousness that unites us all into a One, compassion is the recognition of that One light in the Many. And compassion, Agape, the love of the many, *is* high integral's revelation and core value. This new, more holistic worldview balances integral's core values of evolution, Eros, and self-actualization.

As conscious cocreators of the grand tapestry of the kosmos, our task is to reach toward greater measures of realization to the same degree that we offer the best parts of our lives to all beings everywhere. In Buddhism, this is known as the path of the Bodhisattva.

Transpersonal Contemplations

(Listen to a free guided audio of this section at organicmasculine.com)

I Am Human

I am my body
I am the totality of my organs I am my tissue
I am my cells I am my DNA
I am the combined DNA of my parents

I am (_Full given name_)
I am the beloved child of (_Mother's full given name_),
and I am the beloved child of (_Father's full given name_)
I am the beloved grandchild of...etc....

I am the present expression of my ancestors I am my genes
I am my ethnicity I am my heritage
I am countless generations of humans

I am (_Full given name_)
I am the beloved parent of (_child's full given name_)
I am the present expression of my descendants

I am my culture
I am the present expression of all culture that came before me
I am the present expression of all future culture
I am the past and future of humanity, expressing now

I am primate I am mammal I am animal
I am an unbroken chain of life-form giving birth to life-form
all the way back to the first organism
I am nature
I am the present evolution of life
I am life in my process of becoming I am life

I Am Elemental

I am breathing
I am feeling my breath I am my breath
I am living breath
I am assimilating oxygen
I am releasing carbon dioxide
I am the molecules of air in my lungs
I am the molecules of air I've just breathed out
I am the air in the room
I am the atmosphere
I am atmosphere breathing
I am living, breathing atmosphere I am breathing

I am water
I am salivating
I am circulating my blood
I am 70 percent water
I am the water that I drink
I am the water that I urinate
I am living water
I am alive water
I am rain
I am river
I am ocean
I am the living water of this planet
I am water

I am digesting my food
I am my food
I am the aliveness of food
I am the plants that grew my food
I am the soil that grew the plants
I am the waste that fertilizes the soil
I am the aliveness of plants, humans, soil
I am ecosystem
I am living earth

I am the energy of my body
I am sugar, fat, and protein

I am the energy of plants
I am photosynthesis
I am the light of the sun
I am light

I am the space that my body occupies
The atoms of my body are 99 percent empty space
I am a speck of matter in empty space
I am energy bound in space
I am light extended through space
I am the awareness of space
I am space

I Am Relationship

I am an individual
I am an individuated consciousness
I perceive, I feel, I cognize, I emote, and I act

I am in relationship with my environment
I am in relationship with my home
I am in relationship with my belongings
I am relationship with place

Everything I am taking in is through relationship
Everything I am offering out is through relationship
I am a locus of experience in relationship

I am in relationship with family
I am in relationship with friends
I am in relationship with colleagues
I am social relationship

Every social identity I hold is known through relationship
Every social behavior I make is through relationship
I am a locus of experience in relationship

Every memory from my past is an imprint from relationship
Every future plan is a possibility for relationship

I am a web of relational fields
I am the experience within which relationship unfolds
I am the experience of relationship
I am a process of relational evolution

I Am Consciousness

I am my body
I am 30 trillion cells
I am one million cells dying and being born each second
I am a trillion, trillion, trillion atoms
I am two-thirds hydrogen, one-quarter oxygen, and one-tenth carbon
I have been blown out from the belly of a star
Someday I will return to the belly of a star
I am the aliveness of the sun
I am the solar system
I am the Milky Way
I am living kosmos
I am this living, breathing, body

I am intelligent
I am intelligence
I am wise
I am wisdom
I am loving
I am love
I am living
I am life
I am conscious
I am consciousness

I witness the universe
I witness myself
I witness time
I witness now
I am the witness and that which is witnessed
I am ever-present
I am eternal
I am change
I am ever-new

I am here, and I am now
I am (_Full given name_)

Prompts for Journaling and Discussion

Where do you hold agendas for your own growth and evolution?

Where do you hold agendas for the growth and evolution of other people and groups?

What does compassion mean to you?

Notes

[1] NASA Earth Observatory image by Joshua Stevens, 2023

[2] "The kind of historically significant worldviews that we've been discussing do not fully come into their own until they exist both in the consciousness of individuals as well as in the cultural structures of societies." *Integral Consciousness and the Future of Evolution*, McIntosh.

[3] "And now, today (2015), we are on the verge of a tipping-point of 10 percent of the population reaching this 'monumental leap of meaning,' the emergence of this entirely new tier, the emergence of the Integral levels." *The Religion of Tomorrow*, Wilber.

[4] *Evolution: The Grand Synthesis.*

[5] "The crucial new capacity is to realize one's power to generate meaning and to tell a new story. This is possible now precisely because one understands that meaning is an interpretation we bring to experience. We all tell stories about what is happening all the time. Autonomous persons consciously commit to actively create a meaningful life for themselves and for others through *self-determination* and *self-actualization* within constantly shifting contexts." *Ego Development: Nine Levels of Increasing Embrace*, Cook-Greuter.

[6] "Those at an Integral stage have found a center within themselves with regard to their own personal beliefs, yet find that they can move seamlessly into a trans-lineage space that transcends and includes their own native system of thought." *Streams of Wisdom: An Advanced Guide to Integral Spiritual Development*, DiPerna.

[7] "Not to be mistaken with a New Age lexicon of pseudoscience and pseudomysticism, or a GREEN [postmodern] bond with only those people who share the same values, TURQUOISE [integral] defines a world community more broadly. In part, a Gaia view emerges, one that centers on life itself - all forms of life (not just humans). Every person, every creature, every species belongs. The planet itself is seen as a single ecosystem. Individuals are not separated; neither are national boundaries, ethnic peculiarities, nor elitist privileges allowed to divide people destructively." *Spiral Dynamics: Mastering Values, Leadership, and Change*, Beck and Cowen.

[8] *The Religion of Tomorrow.*

[9] *Integral Consciousness and the Future of Evolution.*

[10] "Integral approaches to change are those founded on the integration of liberation and transformation methodologies an on the on-going use of practices that develop skills which, together, support the process of consciousness-in-action toward well-being. Integral change approaches are intended to liberate and transform the practitioner who, in turn, becomes a force and a resource for liberatory-transformative change of others." *Consciousness-in-Action*, Rosado.

[11] I put conscious in quotations here. As we will explore in chapter 11, all expressions of gender are conscious. However, at Integral, individuals begin to intentionally engage with gender

and tend to apply the descriptor, conscious. The same applies to the term sacred masculine and feminine.

[12] "The basic outlines and goals of an integral world federation would be to provide democratic oversight of the global economy, protect the world's environment, establish a universal bill of human rights, preserve cultural diversity, and bring an eventual end to war, disease, and poverty." *Integral Consciousness and the Future of Evolution,* McIntosh.

[13] "Those first three approaches (environmental, social, and mental) represent the multiple ecologies that have emerged since the field began, drawing from the biophysical sciences, social sciences, and humanities. The integral approach brings together those multiple ecologies to present a new vision of the Earth, a vision in which humans and Earth are situated in the processes of the evolutionary becoming of the universe, which is to say, processes of cosmogenesis." "The History and Future of Integral Ecologies," Mickey et al. from *The Variety of Integral Ecologies: Nature, Culture, and Knowledge in the Planetary Era.*

[14] "Interbeing is the understanding that nothing exists separately from anything else. We are all interconnected. By taking care of another person, you take care of yourself. By taking care of yourself, you take care of the other person. Happiness and safety are not individual matters. If you suffer, I suffer. If you are not safe, I am not safe. There is no way for me to be truly happy if you are suffering. If you can smile, I can smile too. The understanding of interbeing is very important. It helps us to remove the illusion of loneliness, and transform the anger that comes from the feeling of separation." *How to Fight,* Hanh

[15] Nietzsche, *The Gay Science.*

[16] "[The Great Turning] involves the emergence of new and creative human responses that enable the transition from the Industrial Growth Society to a Life-Sustaining Society. The central plot is about joining together to act for the sake of life and the Earth." *Coming Back to Life,* Macy and Brown.

[17] "To be radical, an empiricism must neither admit into its constructions any element that is not directly experienced, nor exclude from them any element that is directly experienced. For such a philosophy, *the relations that connect experience must themselves be experienced relations, and any kind of relation experienced must be accounted as 'real' as anything else in the system.*" *Essays in Radical Empiricism,* William James.

[18] *Ecology of Consciousness.*

[19] "Other examples of Integral levels of spiritual intelligence can be found in the work of Sally Kempton (Hindu Tantra), Father Thomas Keating (contemplative Christianity), and Daniel P. Brown (Mahamudra and Dzogchen teachings of Buddhism)." *Streams of Wisdom: An Advanced Guide to Integral Spiritual Development,* DiPerna

[20] "All that exists, throughout all time and beyond, is one infinite divine Consciousness, free and blissful, which projects within the field of its awareness a vast multiplicity of apparently differentiated subjects and objects: each object an actualization of a timeless potentiality inherent in the Light of Consciousness, and each subject, you and I, the same plus a contracted locus

of self-awareness. The creation, a divine play, is the result of the natural impulse within Consciousness to express the totality of its self-knowledge in action, an impulse arising from love. The unbounded Light of Consciousness contracts into finite embodied loci of awareness out of its own free will. When those finite subjects then identify with the limited and circumscribed cognitions and circumstances that make up this phase of their existence, instead of identifying with the transindividual overarching pulsation of pure Awareness that is their true nature, they experience what they call 'suffering.' To rectify this, some feel an inner urge to take up the path of spiritual wisdom and yogic practice, the purpose of which is to undermine their misidentification and directly reveal within the immediacy of awareness the fact that the divine powers of Consciousness, Bliss, Willing, Knowing, and Acting comprise the totality of individual experience as well - thereby triggering a recognition that one's real identity is that of the highest Divinity, the Whole in every part. This experiential insight is repeated and reinforced through various means until it becomes the nonconceptual ground of every moment of experience, and one's contracted sense of self and separation from the Whole is finally annihilated in the incandescent radiance of the complete expansion into perfect wholeness. Then one's perception fully encompasses the reality of a universe dancing ecstatically in the animation of its completely perfect divinity." *Tantra Illuminated*, Wallis.

[21] "Far away in the heavenly abode of the great god Indra, there is a wonderful net which has been hung by some cunning artificer in such a manner that it stretches out infinitely in all directions. In accordance with the extravagant tastes of deities, the artificer has hung a single glittering jewel in each 'eye' of the net, and since the net itself is infinite in dimension, the jewels are infinite in number. There hang the jewels, glittering like stars in the first magnitude, a wonderful sight to behold. If we now arbitrarily select one of these jewels for inspection and look closely at it, we will discover that in its polished surface there are reflected all the other jewels in the net, infinite in number. Not only that, but each of the jewels reflected in this one jewel is also reflecting all the other jewels, so that there is an infinite reflecting process occurring." *Hua-Yen Buddhism: The Jewel Net of Indra*, Cook.

[22] "No matter what the practice or teaching, ego loves to wait in ambush to appropriate spirituality for its own survival and gain."
Cutting Through Spiritual Materialism, Trungpa.

[23] "When transcendence of our personal history takes precedence over intimacy with our personal history, spiritual bypassing is inevitable. To not be intimate with our past - to not be deeply and thoroughly acquainted with our conditioning and its originating factors - keeps it undigested and unintegrated and therefore very much present." *Spiritual Bypassing*, Masters.

[24] *Ego Development: A Full-Spectrum Theory of Vertical Growth And Meaning Making.*

[25] *Nature and the Human Soul: Cultivating Wholeness and Community in a Fragmented World.*

[26] "It is a fact of life as a Construct-aware person [i.e.: high integral] that there are few other people like them. They may fear that almost nobody understands them in their complexity and sympathizes with their experience, and fearing this, they feel culpable of hubris, of feeling 'better' than others." *Ego Development: Nine Levels of Increasing Embrace*, Cook-Greuter.

[27] Maturana, *Autopoiesis and Cognition the Realization of the Living.*

[28] Adapted from "Maslow's hierarchy of needs", McLeod, and *A Theory of Human Motivation,* Maslow.

[29] "The Teaching of Sri Aurobindo."

[30] "The fruition of dzokchen is full realization of the enlightenment within. In practical terms, it involves the ability to rest in the innate state and not depart from it. Far from a state of dullness, lethargy, or apathy—as indeed it might seem from ego's standpoint—one rests in the natural state, or as the natural state, that is vivid, vibrant, and dynamic. The buddhas rest in the natural state and, as expressions of it, remain in that world, interact with others, teach the dharma, and express their compassion to sentient beings in myriad ways. Yet none of this is done based on conscious intention. It all unfolds as buddha activity that is always unpremeditated, spontaneous, and perfectly apt to the situation. The fruition of dzokchen produces men and women of extraordinary sanctity, compassion, and ability." *Secret of the Vajra World*, Ray.

[31] *Sex, Ecology, Spirituality.*

[32] *Process and Reality.*

| 10 |

Transpersonal Structure States

Figure 10.1 Kosmic Horizons[1]

High integral is the most advanced paradigm that humanity has evolved thus far. However, it is by no means the maximum of human potential. Mystics, saints, and sages throughout history and across cultures have explored the outer reaches of consciousness. Advancing beyond high integral, we leave paradigms behind and step into *transpersonal structure states.* The information presented here in Chapter 10 traces to the outer edges of the evolution of consciousness—and please know that this material is by no means necessary to understand in order to enjoy the following chapters of this workbook.

In order to understand structure states, I first need to spend some more time discussing *states* of consciousness and how they interact with *paradigms.* Individuals in every paradigm have access to the full range of states of consciousness (fig. 10.2).

States are the temporary experiences of the expansiveness of consciousness. A state of consciousness is my moment-to-moment experience of reality, for example, I'm awake, I'm dreaming, or I'm in deep dreamless sleep. States are transitory and can be accessed through spiritual practices like meditation and breathwork.

Paradigms are the stable interpretive lenses that mark the individual's maturation process. Paradigms are the place I spend most of my time translating reality through. Paradigms change on the scale of years, if at all.

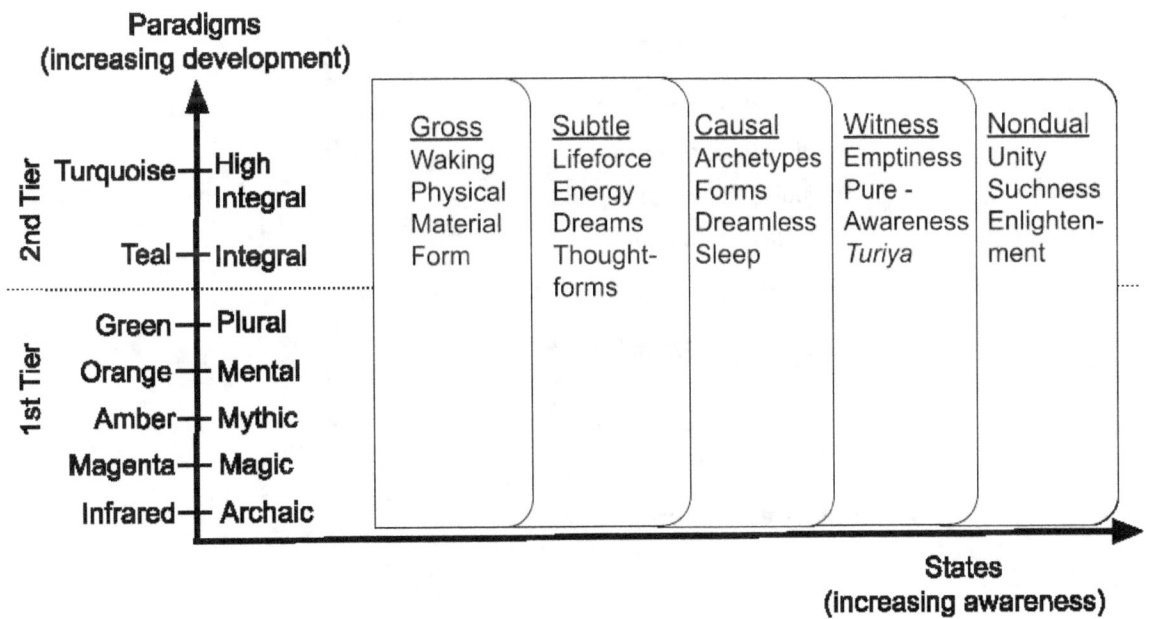

Figure 10.2 Paradigms and states of consciousness[2]

So, someone who's center of gravity is at magical could have a peak state experience into the pure witness realm, and then return to waking consciousness in the gross realm. In addition, someone at high integral can have an analogous state experience of the pure witness realm and then return to gross. The witness state, and indeed all states, are available to all humans across all paradigms.

However, because the high integral individual has grown through the iterative process of transcend and include, transcend and include, their experience of the world is much wider and deeper than the paradigms below it. Therefore, the high integral experience of the pure witness realm is actually more—they are able to receive and experience more of it through their wider lens. As the highest paradigm that is emerging in Western culture, the high integral paradigm has the most expansive and inclusive experience of the states of consciousness. The more one develops through the paradigms, the richer and deeper the states become.

Beyond high integral, the category of paradigms as organizing worldviews for culture and individuals no longer applies. Human culture has not yet developed the intersubjective morphic fields for these realms. However, mystics have traversed these higher realms. They have documented their subjective experiences and those reports have been tested and confirmed by other realized practitioners. While these higher levels of development are emergent and still forming, they are also well within the criteria for rigorous knowledge. I call these higher developmental levels *structure states*, which occupy a third tier.[3]

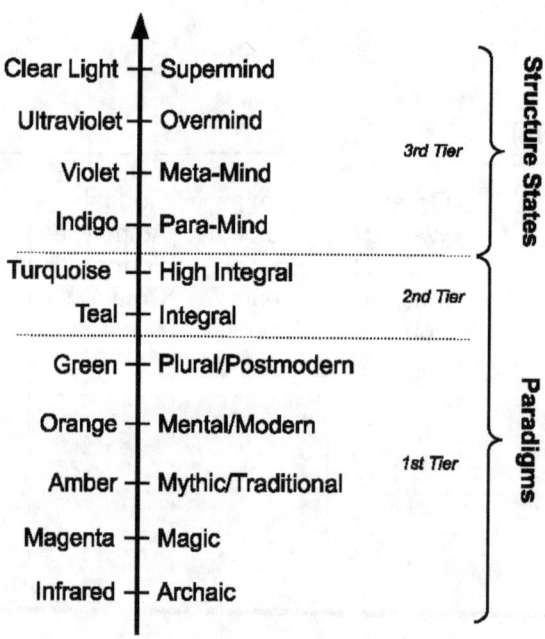

Figure 10.3 The holarchy of paradigms and structure states

Structure states each have a minimum *state of consciousness*. In the first and second tiers, I am free to hang out in the gross, waking state. I can have a peak experience into higher states through spiritual practice, but I generally land back in the gross state. Now at the third tier, a minimum expansion of awareness is required in order to occupy this developmental step, specifically, the trans-egoic gross state is required for Para-Mind, the subtle state is required for Meta-Mind, the causal state is required for Overmind, which can also include the witnessing state, and Supermind is the culmination of all structures together with all states including nonduality.

To put it another way, as humans evolve into more comprehensive steps in tier three, the stable experience of reality begins to embrace and enfold higher states of consciousness. Each successive structure state brings higher orders of awareness more fully into union with phenomenal reality. Para-Mind *sees* wholeness, Meta-Mind *feels* wholeness, Overmind *witnesses* wholeness, and Supermind is *being* whole. This progression moves up the structure states all the way to nondual suchness. Note that in each of the structure states below Supermind, I always have the ability to expand into even higher states.

Because structure states do not have any cultural basis, and because they conjoin a developmental lens with a state, I place them in a distinct category from the paradigms we've been discussing so far.

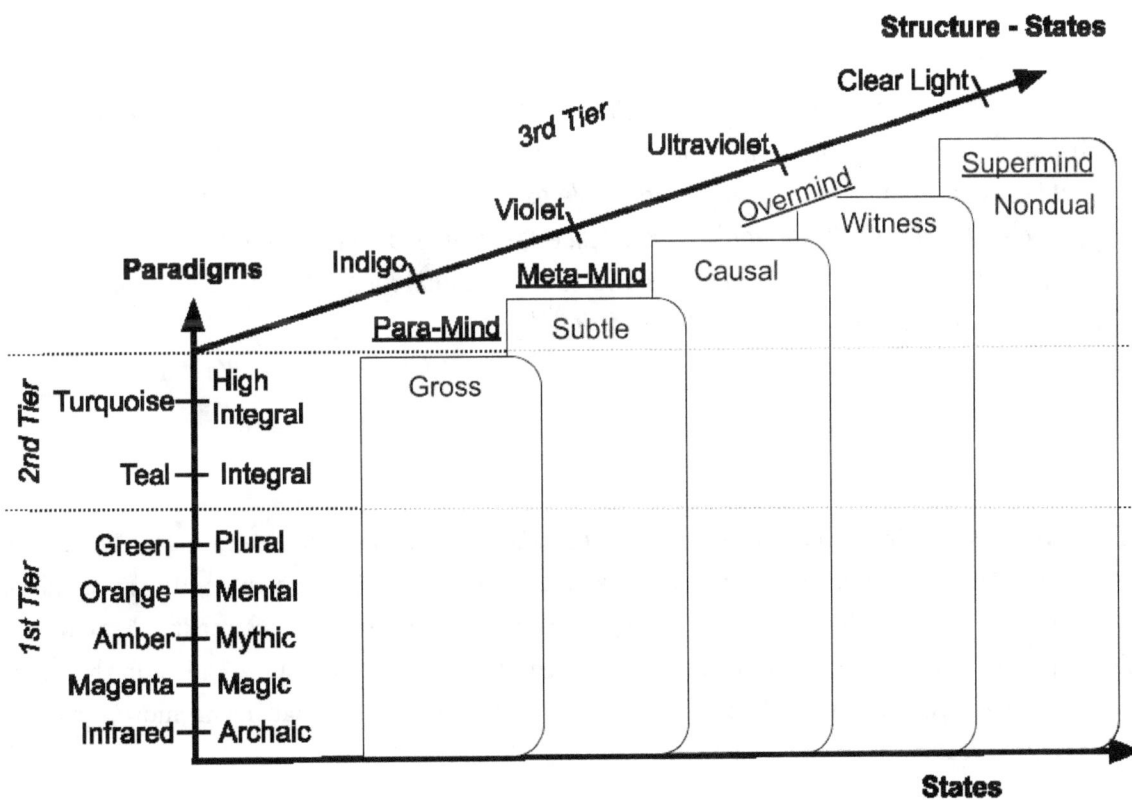

Figure 10.4 Paradigms, states, and structure states

The chart above illustrates the relationships between states, paradigms, and structure states— each of which have a distinct axis of progression. To unpack this a bit, the gross state extends up to Para-Mind and not above it. Para-Mind necessarily includes a transpersonal experience of the gross realm—a flow state is one example of this experience. At Para-Mind, I have full access to higher states all the way up to nonduality (moving right on the graph). But what separates Para-Mind from prior paradigms is that I must hold a stable baseline of trans-egoic consciousness of physical reality. This is why, in the graph above, the gross-state bubble extends up to Para-Mind, but not above it.

Meta-Mind holds a minimum stable experience of the subtle state. So, in order to be at Meta-Mind, I must have integrated the subtle realm into my waking awareness in an ongoing way—lucid dreaming is one example of this experience. Overmind holds a minimum integration of the causal state and Supermind integrates the nondual state. Let's take a closer look at these four structure states in turn.

The Para-Mind Structure State

Unless we go beyond the mechanistic process of the mind, real creativeness is obviously impossible, and what is necessary, surely, is a mind that is creative, so that it is able to deal with all these multiplying problems. To understand what is knowledge and go beyond the partial, the limited, to experience that which is creative, requires not just a moment of perception but a continuous awareness, a continuous state of inquiry in which there is no conclusion—and this, after all, is intelligence.

—J Krishnamurti[4]

Para-Mind is the first structure state to emerge and, thus, marks the beginning of tier three. For starters, Para-Mind occupies the next developmental step above high integral, transcending and including every paradigm that has come before it. High integral views reality through the high integral lens. Para-Mind has included high integral's subjective lens as an object in the more comprehensive Para-Mind lens. Thus, Para-Mind has internalized a broader and more inclusive *vantage point* of reality.

The new paradigm has a universal or cosmic perspective as an organizing principle and as a steady place from which meaning is derived. It is non-centered in the ego although the ego is available as a perspective when useful. Unlike state experiences that gave people glimpses of mystical or unitive experiences, now these are steadily available in the witnessing stance.

—Susan Cook-Greuter[5]

The second defining feature of Para-Mind is a stable, trans-egoic awareness of physical reality. Awareness conjoins with the gross state. In this structure state, the separation between mind and body falls away. High integral can understand this conceptually ("ego aware" and "construct aware"), but Para-Mind actually experiences this greater embrace with reality. At this level, I experience a seamless psychophysical reality.[6] The *psyche* is united with the *physical*: *psychophysical*.

Krishnamurti describes Para-Mind as *choiceless awareness*: a state of being beyond thinking and judging (see the quote above). Whitehead calls this *prehensive unity*, where the distinction between experiencing subject and experienced object unite into a seamless whole.[7] This unity is not a pasting together of two separate realms. Rather, I become conscious of the deeper nature of wholeness where perception and object are not separate.

Time in terms of minutes, weeks, and years is re-understood as a conceptual overlay on reality. Memories and thoughts of the past are simply an aspect of reality experienced as thoughtforms in the present. Projections and plans for the future are similarly re-experienced as a cognitive aspect of this moment now.[8] At Para-Mind, time becomes an experience of the ever-present nature of the kosmos.[9] Gebser describes an *aperspectival* world[10] in which consciousness is independent of the relative perspective of the observer—a state that moves beyond our normal conceptions of space and time. This departure from normal space and time is echoed by Csikszentmihalyi's study of *flow states*, which are described as a total immersion into experience together with a lack of anxiety about control and a letting go of time.[11]

The full realization of Para-Mind goes beyond the union of egoic perspective with its local object. It entails an experience of the interconnectedness of all of life:

What is actually occurring in [Para-Mind] is an infusion of consciousness with trans-personal elements that can be interpreted as multisystemic interconnections with virtu-ally all beings in existence, an experience of the Great Web of Life as being interwoven with one's own indigo Self as if it were the skin on one's expanded body, the realization that one is not merely an individual person but part of an incredibly extended system or network (or "Great Web") of life and being (which is thought at Turquoise [High Integral] but experienced at indigo [Para-Mind])– so that one begins to feel that way, as one's own expanded identity.

—Ken Wilber[12]

Sri Aurobindo describes the transpersonal awareness of Para-Mind as the *illumined mind* where immediate vision replaces normal cognition.[13] This greater awareness brings the recognition of the total interconnectedness of every object in the kosmos through this present moment. This has been described as the *process* nature of reality by Whitehead and as the universal movement of undivided wholeness, or *holomovement*, by physicist David Bohm.[14] Not only is the entire universe contained in each moment, but the totality of the physical universe is *seen* as a whole (i.e., a holon). This universal holon is evolving via Eros and experienced as a holarchy with layers and layers of nested evolutionary processes. The emphasis at Para-Mind is on how I *see* wholeness.

Prompts for Journaling and Discussion

How do the cognitive processes of thinking, judging, and managing separate the ego from phenomena?

Describe an experience of being in a flow state.

How does *flow* change your experience of subject, object, space, and time?

The Meta-Mind Structure State

> So the world, grounded in a timeless movement by the Soul which suffuses it with intelligence, becomes a living and blessed being.
>
> —Plotinus

Meta-Mind is the next developmental step after Para-Mind and, thus, sees through a bigger lens and experiences a new level of complexity. This more inclusive lens must be conjoined in a stable way with the subtle state. At Meta-Mind, physical matter and subtle energy are experienced as a unified whole. Again, this is not a pasting together of two realms, but represents an awakening to the more accurate level of perception where matter and subtle energy are a seamless continuum of phenomena.

Meta-Mind has its own form of understanding. Subtle energy is a felt sense, so at this point, awareness merges with feeling and reality is perceived through *feeling-awareness*.[15] Here at Meta-Mind, I am feeling the wholeness of reality, whereas in Para-Mind I was seeing wholeness. My awareness is coming into embodiment, which opens a direct, unmediated touching of reality. Aurobindo calls this type of perception *intuition*, which is an immediate understanding of truth that transcends and includes intellect, body, will, and emotion-based ways of knowing.[16]

The low subtle realm includes the expressions of life force, vitality, prana, chi, and biofield energy. At Meta-Mind, living beings are now kaleidoscopically felt. In this structure state, I am seeing or feeling chakras and auras immediately and naturally. Life becomes vibrantly alive. I experience the natural world not just as an interlocking life-system, but as a living, breathing, vital life-form. Nature's body and my body unite into a felt whole. Through this embodied awareness, I am touching aliveness all around me. In addition, I become aware of the energetic aspects of the earth, including ley lines, grids, and vortices.

The high subtle realm includes thoughtforms, visualizations, and dreams. The union of awareness and the high subtle realm means lucid dreaming becomes a stable experience. My capacity to visualize through meditation becomes every bit as real and immediate as 3-D reality. For example, the mandala of five Dhyani Buddhas (fig. 5.4) is experienced at Meta-Mind less as a picture of contemplation, but as a visual consciousness with depth and character. It becomes a realm unto itself that is vividly felt, seen, and experienced. Further, because this particular mandala depicts Buddhahood or enlightened consciousness, at Meta-Mind, meditating with this image becomes a doorway into even higher states of consciousness. In tantric spirituality, the image of the deity is not a representation—it *is* the deity in visual form. Similarly, speaking the mantra of the deity *is* the energetic form of the full deity.[17] In addition to mantras, music in all forms becomes a multisensory experiential realm at Meta-Mind.

Prompts for Journaling and Discussion

How do you experience aliveness?

What in your experience is not an aspect of aliveness?

What is your relationship with prayer, mantra, or chanting?

The Overmind Structure State

Overmind is the next developmental step above Meta-Mind. At a minimum, Overmind represents a union with the causal state, and then eventually conjoins the witness state. Overmind is a vast transpersonal consciousness in which the archetypes and deities are incorporated into consciousness, referred to as *deity mysticism*. When the pure I Am witness state stabilizes for an individual, the timeless, eternal, absolute state of consciousness conjoins with this staggeringly complex and inclusive developmental lens.[18] Overmind comprehends the unity of the kosmos from the vantage point of absolute consciousness—witnessing wholeness, which is a giant step beyond the feeling-awareness of Meta-Mind.

Very few humans have reached this structure state, and I am personally not there, so it's challenging to say much about it. In addition the ranges experienced within structure states tends to become more diverse as they progress.

That said, tune in to the awareness that you have while in deep, dreamless sleep. In the background, behind and beneath all content is a sense of I Am. This pure witnessing consciousness is always present, always empty, just being. There has never been a time when this I Am has not been with you. At the high end of this structure state, this I Am-ness or absolute consciousness, wakes up to itself within the individual. This has been described as the unborn Buddha-mind, "I Am that I Am" from Hebrew tradition, Jesus' claim "Before Abraham was born, I Am," *Aham brahma asmi* "I am Brahman" from the Upanishads, and Echkart Tolle, "I am the space in which things happen. I am consciousness. I am the now. I am."

This absolute consciousness stabilizes as one's lived experience and dances in primal duality with the relative world, which has been transcended and included, transcended and included across all states (except nonduality itself), all history, and all phenomena across the totality of the kosmos. This is the final way station before the nonduality of Supermind.

The Supermind Structure State

Supermind is the culmination of what we understand is possible for humans today. Supermind transcends the dualistic lens from Overmind. All phenomena, across all time and space, across all states of consciousness including the absolute, empty, I Am witness becomes one seamless tapestry.[19] Fully and truly, it is the human recognition of the whole kosmos.

It is the radical Freedom of the purest Emptiness plus the fullest of the fullest of the world of Form. It transcends absolutely ALL, in purest Freedom, and includes absolutely ALL, in the utter sum total Form of unmatched Fullness. Put bluntly, it transcends and includes the entire universe to date. That is, Supermind enfolds into its ongoing Consequent Nature the entire universe as it has unfolded till now, and then includes each future moment as a new and in some ways novel and creative moment.

—Ken Wilber[20]

One way to conceptualize the experience of nonduality at Supermind is to imagine becoming aware of the perceptions of all matter across all scales in the universe. The smallest particles have basic *prehension* of each other as they interact via the four primal forces. As arrangements of matter become more complex (ex: molecule, cell, organism), the depth and breadth of awareness becomes correspondingly fuller and richer. Nonduality is a simultaneous seeing through the eyes of all beings. It is a prehensive experience of all form, as all form, across every scale up to and including the unitive consciousness of the kosmos. This awareness is inclusive of gross sensory perception and ranges through the subtle, causal, and witness states of consciousness described above. All states of consciousness experienced together *with* and *as* all forms becomes unified into a seamless continuum: nonduality, enlightenment.

A handful of saints and sages throughout human history have realized Supermind. Recall that each state of consciousness is available to every step in the developmental staircase. Nonduality as a state can be accessed by individuals at magic, mythic, modern, and so on. However, the state of nondual unity is experienced differently by each paradigm and structure state. Higher levels have transcended and included more of the relative world, they have complexified their lenses and perceive a more holistic kosmos. Supermind represents the most expansive state of consciousness (nonduality) as experienced from the most complex and comprehensive worldview.

Summary

What we have here is a map for the process of growth and awakening of human consciousness. In my view, this is the best map humanity has produced thus far. Pieces of it have been developed and described by visionary philosophers, psychologists, and mystics over the course of Western civilization, and the full synthesis of this map was brought through by Ken Wilber—a profound gift to all of us.

It is worth noting that this map carries inherent biases toward Western adults, as it has been assembled and articulated by Westerners for Westerners. However, the underlying theories that create the meta-theory source from both science and spiritual traditions across many cultures. Ego Development Theory is a noteworthy inclusion in the meta-theory because it is an entirely empirical framework based on interviews with American and European adults. In this model, the paradigms of consciousness represent statistically significant groupings of respondents across class, gender, and race.[21]

While the integral map is descriptive of how healthy adults generally mature in our culture, it is not meant to be proscriptive, meaning each person traverses a unique path that will not fit these idealized labels. Put another way, the map is not the territory and it's only here as a guide.

With that in mind, we can now recap the general process for the evolution of consciousness:

- From the beginning, the kosmos has been in an ongoing process of change.
- This change exhibits a directionality toward complexity and wholeness. We call this evolutionary drive, *Eros*.
- The process of evolution is a three-part *dialectic of progress*: thesis-antithesis-synthesis, which has also been described as the *cosmogenetic principle*: differentiation-autopoiesis-communion.
- We observe three orders of evolution: the poiesis of physical systems (creating), the autopoiesis of living systems (self-creating), and the eleutheropoiesis of human systems (freedom-creating). Eleutheropoiesis can be further subdivided into three categories: freedom from- , freedom to- , and freedom as- , which exhibit an increasing embodiment of sovereignty.
- Further, human systems evolve through both an individual, subjective, psycho-spiritual dimension and a collective, intersubjective, cultural dimension. These two human dimensions are distinct, yet interdependent.
- Human consciousness evolves through a series of paradigms. These are organizing models we employ for self and kosmos. Each paradigm is a holon. It is a whole and valid worldview in itself and becomes part of the next, more complex paradigm.
- Paradigms must be sequentially grown through as a hierarchy. Thus, the organizing structure of paradigms is a growth holarchy that applies to both individuals and cultures. Later paradigms transcend and include earlier paradigms. This means they adopt a more complex lens on reality, while incorporating the prior paradigm as part of the new, larger whole.
- States of consciousness, which describe the moment-to-moment contents of awareness, are distinct from paradigms, which are the lenses we look through. States range from waking consciousness up to nondual suchness. Above the high integral paradigm, development requires ever-more-inclusive unions of states and paradigms, called structure states.
- Taken as a whole, this map describes the types of experiential realms in existence, together with the interweaving developmental pathways for evolution, representing the kosmos as an Erotic, self-liberating holon that is alive and conscious.

Prompts for Journaling and Discussion

Who am I?

What is consciousness?

Describe the kosmos and your place in it.

Notes

[1] Image by LongQuattro, 2024

[2] Adapted from the Wilber-Combs lattice.

[3] "These higher structures are simply potential worldspaces, pre-ontological worldspaces, that are given only as potentials, not as fate. But we do know that they are structural potentials of the human bodymind, because since its emergence in its present form (around fifty thousand years ago), that bodymind has indeed supported realizations across the spectrum (has supported the realizations of a Buddha, a Gaudapada, a Dame Julian, a Lady Tsogyal). In other words, that bodymind has already supported psychic, subtle, causal, and nondual realizations; and thus, by a reconstructive science, we know those potentials are already available." *Sex, Ecology, Spirituality*, Wilber.

[4] *Choiceless Awareness.*

[5] "Ego Development: A Full-Spectrum Theory of Vertical Growth and Meaning Making."

[6] "Para-Mind begins to display an understanding that the world is not just physical, it is psychophysical, whether that is understood in virtue of the role interpretation plays in all ontology, the inherent union of epistemology and ontology, the role concepts have in co-creating the perceived world, or the general understanding that every phenomenon in the world inherently possesses both interiors (consciousness) and exteriors (material form)—hence, it is psychophysical." *The Religion of Tomorrow.* Wilber.

[7] "In the first place, note that the idea of simple location has gone. The things which are grasped into a realised unity, here and now, are not the castle, the cloud, and the planet simply in themselves; but they are the castle, the cloud, and the planet from the standpoint, in space and time, of the prehensive unification. In other words, it is the perspective of the castle over there from the standpoint of the unification here. It is, therefore, aspects of the castle, the cloud, and the planet which are grasped into unity here…. We can be content with a provisional realism in which nature is conceived as a complex of prehensive unifications. Space and time exhibit the general scheme of interlocked relations of these prehensions. You cannot tear any one of them out of its context. Yet each one of them within its context has all the reality that attaches to the whole complex. Conversely, the totality has the same reality as each prehension; for each prehension unifies the modalities to be ascribed, from its standpoint, to every part of the whole. A prehension is a process of unifying. Accordingly, nature is a process of expansive development, necessarily transitional from prehension to prehension." *Science and the Modern World*, Whitehead.

[8] "Moreover, I do not say that past and future exist like the present. I say that the past, although vanished, is capable of producing a memory (smṛti) and of giving birth to a mind (citta) and mental events (caitasikadharma)…. It is the same for that which is things of the future. Although the present mind (pratyutpannacitta) is instantaneous (kṣaṇika) and without duration (asthitika), it re-arises in series (saṃtāna) and is able to recognize dharmas. Inwardly (adhyātmam) using the actual mind (manas) as cause (hetu) and outwardly using the dharmas as object (ālambana),

a mental consciousness (manovijñāna) takes up its job. This mental consciousness, which is sovereign (adhipati), cognizes (vijānāti) past, future and present dharmas." Sarvāstivādin-Sautrāntika Debate on Time, Nāgārjuna

[9] "So it is to live in the condition of eternity — not an escape into timelessness, but fulfillment in the wholeness of cyclic being, in the Eon. It is not merely living from moment to moment in a condition of open receptivity to changing influences and of availability in terms of ever-changing relationships, but rather living every moment consciously as well as openly as a particular phase of the process of existence, in as full an awareness as is possible of the function, meaning and purpose of that phase with reference to the whole cycle." *Planetarization of Consciousness*, Rudhyar.

[10] "Its four-dimensionality represents ultimately an integration of dimensions. It results in a space-and-time-free aperspectival world where the free (or freed) consciousness has at its disposal all latent as well as actual forms of space and time, without having either to deny them or to be fully subject to them." *Ever Present Origin*, Gebser.

[11] "Flow is a subjective state that people report when they are completely involved in something to the point of forgetting time, fatigue, and everything else but the activity itself.... The defining feature of flow is intense experiential involvement in moment-to-moment activity. Attention is fully invested in the task at hand, and the person functions at his or her fullest capacity." *Flow*, Csikszentmihalyi et al.

[12] *The Religion of Tomorrow.*

[13] "Illumined mind works not through thought but primarily through vision, which affects a powerful and dynamic integration by illumining thought-mind with inner vision, imbibing the heart with spiritual sight, and the emotions with spiritual light and energy.... The perceptual power of the inner sight is greater and more direct than the perceptual power of thought: it is a spiritual sense that seizes something of the substance of Truth." *The Divine Life*, Aurobindo.

[14] "Relativity and quantum theory agree, in that they both imply the need to look on the world as an undivided whole, in which all parts of the universe, including the observer and his instruments, merge and unite in one totality.... [T]here is a universal flux that cannot be defined explicitly but which can be known only implicitly, as indicated by the explicitly definable forms and shapes, some stable and some unstable, that can be abstracted from the universal flux. In this flow, mind and matter are not separate substances. Rather, they are different aspects of our whole and unbroken movement." *Wholeness and the Implicate Order*, Bohm.

[15] "Feeling-awareness is particularly a unity of intellect and feelings, knowing and being, in an unbroken, seamless conjunction, with epistemology and ontology so tightly bound as to rarely even be distinguished." *The Religion of Tomorrow*, Wilber.

[16] "Intuition has a fourfold power. A power of revelatory truth seeing, a power of inspiration or truth-hearing, a power of truth-touch or immediate seizing of significance, which is akin to the ordinary nature of its intervention in our mental intelligence, a power of true and automatic discrimination of the orderly and exact relation of truth to truth, - these are the fourfold potencies of Intuition. Intuition can therefore perform all the action of reason – including the function of logical intelligence, which is to work out the right relation of things and the right relation of idea

with idea, - but by its own superior process and with steps that do not fail or falter. It takes up also and transforms into its own substance not only the mind of thought, but the heart and life and the sense and physical consciousness: already all these have their own peculiar powers of intuition derivative from the hidden Light; the pure power descending from above can assume them all into itself and impart to these deeper heart perceptions and life-perceptions and the divinations of the body a greater integrality and perfection. It can thus change the whole consciousness into the stuff of intuition; for it brings its own greater radiant movement into the will, into the feelings and emotions, the life-impulses, the action of sense and sensation, the very workings of the body consciousness; it recasts them in the light and power of truth and illumines their knowledge and their ignorance." *The Divine Life*, Aurobindo.

[17] "For the Tantrik tradition, mantras are actually conscious beings, analogous to angels in the Western religions…. It is absolutely crucial to understand that in this tradition a mantra, a deity, and its goal are all one and the same. Thus, for example, Lakshmi's mantra *Om srim mahalaksmyai namah* is the Goddess Lakshmi in sound form; it is her sonic body. Nor is her mantra something separate from the goal for which it is repeated, i.e., to cultivate abundance, for it is the very vibration of abundance." *Tantra Illuminated*, Wallis.

[18] "When the overmind descends the predominance of the centralising ego-sense is entirely subordinated, lost in largeness of being and finally abolished; a wide cosmic perception and feeling of a boundless universal self and movement replaces it: many motions that were formerly ego-centric may still continue, but they occur as currents or ripples in the cosmic wideness. Thought, for the most part, no longer seems to originate individually in the body or the person but manifests from above or comes in upon the cosmic mindwaves: all inner individual sight or intelligence of things is now a revelation or illumination of what is seen or comprehended, but the source of the revelation is not in one's separate self but in the universal knowledge; the feelings, emotions, sensations are similarly felt as waves from the same cosmic immensity breaking upon the subtle and the gross body and responded to in kind by the individual centre of the universality; for the body is only a small support or even less, a point of relation, for the action of a vast cosmic in-strumentation. In this boundless largeness, not only the separate ego but all sense of individuality, even of a subordinated or instrumental individuality, may entirely disappear; the cosmic existence, the cosmic consciousness, the cosmic delight, the play of cosmic forces are alone left." *The Divine Life*, Sri Aurobindo.

[19] "At present we have arrived at an affirmation and some conception of the divine and creative Supermind in which all is one in being, consciousness, will and delight, yet with an infinite capacity of differentiation that deploys but does not destroy the unity, - in which Truth is the substance and Truth rises in the Idea and Truth comes out in the form and there is one truth of knowledge and will, one truth of self-fulfillment and therefore of delight; for all self-fulfillment is satisfaction of being. Therefore, always, in all mutations and combinations a self-existent and inalienable harmony. *The Divine Life*, Sri Aurobindo.

[20] *The Religion of Tomorrow.*

[21] "Ego Development Theory has been developed and refined over at least 40 years by empirical means unlike almost all other developmental approaches which first propose a theory, then find appropriate means to measure their constructs. Ego Development Theory is a grounded theory. It was derived solely based on evidence from responses to the sentence completion test or the MAP (Maturity Assessment Profile)." "Ego Development: A Full-Spectrum Theory of Vertical Growth and Meaning Making," Cook-Greuter.

| 11 |

The Masculinity Holarchy

Figure 11.1 The Evolving Masculine[1]

Masculinity is a developmental category that grows through each of the paradigms of consciousness described in the prior chapters. Integral philosophy recognizes multiple different lines of intelligence that each move through the holarchy, for example: cognitive intelligence, emotional intelligence, relational intelligence, sexual intelligence, and so on. Gender development is one such category. Not all of these developmental categories will necessarily have their center of gravity in the same paradigm, but they each grow through the same paradigmatic staircase. Using this model, I can locate my version of masculinity centered within one of the paradigms, explore how my masculinity has evolved over time, and look forward to what may be next.

Studying each paradigms and how masculinity progresses through them is useful because it shows me where I may have unintegrated shadow material. Whenever I judge an aspect of myself or my culture as unacceptable, unforgivable, or unlovable, I exile that place in my psyche and it enters my unconscious shadow. These psychological parts become wounded and distorted and the life force they carry becomes locked up. The exiled parts, or *complexes*, struggle with my ego for control, and when they take control—meaning, when I go unconscious—they will tend to wreak havoc on my life. At the end of the day, these parts are either wounded or misguided and what they ultimately need is for my adult self to give them love and acceptance. The challenge is that my ego is generally invested in repressing these parts and often the parts themselves are invested in hiding. I can use this holarchy as a tool to explore the shadow elements in my psyche. Once I encounter shadow parts, I meet them with kindness and offer them love to welcome them back home.

One of the jokes about integral philosophy is that it causes a sudden onset of proclaiming, "Look at me! I'm at integral!" At any rate, that's exactly what I did when I first discovered this theory. Learning how to see through the integral lens is probably the easiest part of the growth process. The real work is integrating the shadow. Recall that developmental growth takes a subjective lens and makes it an object of observation. Development doesn't happen by looking ahead so much as it's a process of *reaching down* to include more and more of what lies beneath. Aspects that I have pushed into my shadow are unconscious, meaning I can't see them. They can't be made into objects of awareness. Understood in this way, shadow work becomes perhaps my most powerful tool for growing through the holarchy. Growth is a *down-and-in* process more so than *up-and-out*. I can use this model of the paradigms to explore each level, find where I'm repressed, own that place, and receive the gifts more fully.

The most relevant paradigms for our exploration of masculinity will be mythic/traditional, mental/ modern, plural/postmodern, integral, and high integral. Each of these paradigms has a distinct set of values, identities, needs, and beliefs. Therefore, each structure will have a unique expression of masculinity. As a reminder, my purpose here is not to pigeonhole anyone. Rather, I'm using this tool to learn and grow.

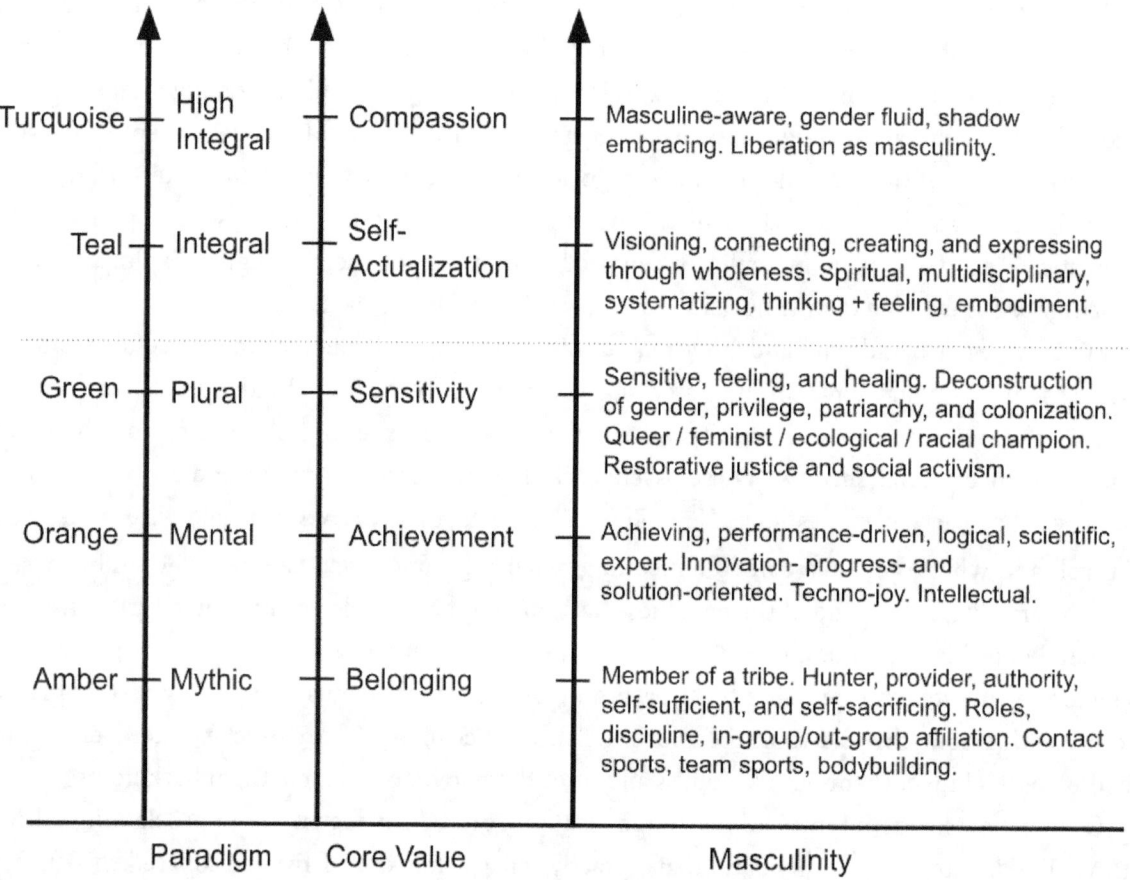

Figure 11.2 Paradigms of masculinity

The Amber Man

Mythic/Traditional, Belonging

I define who I am through my roles relative to groups and power structures. The myths and traditions about masculinity provide the masculine ideal. "Real" men, "manly" men, and "true" men follow the scripts and values of my chosen social group. I appeal to great men of the past for inspiration: heroes, fathers, leaders, kings, and patriarchs.

I am focused on my role within my affiliation group. Ideally, I'm a leader, but most important is the functioning of the group and my belonging within it. The tribe could be my family, friend group, coworkers, church, sports team, political party, or country. This masculinity is prone to be emotionally aloof, independent, and self-reliant in order to be a strong warrior, capable of making sacrifices for the tribe and engaging in conflict with hostile out-group members. As a man, weakness, and by extension vulnerability, is reason to be exiled or killed by the pack, so I hide my softness and develop a tough, aggressive, or powerful persona. Women, children, and the elderly are the vulnerable ones to be protected by my strength. Outsiders are threatening. I understand the use of power and force. I thrive in competition and hierarchical social structures. I may enjoy physically combative activities such as contact sports, martial arts, hunting, or bodybuilding. An important note at this point: moving up the developmental ladder *includes* the good parts of the lower rungs. I can enjoy bodybuilding, hunting, and so on from any paradigm.

The gifts of this masculine worldview include capacities as a leader, soldier, hunter, and provider. Here I learn skills including charisma, how to navigate group politics and power play, loyalty, teamwork, family values, generosity and self-sacrifice. I am strong, self-sufficient, disciplined, and virtuous. I am dedicated to my purpose and loved ones. I am faithful, dutiful, and honorable.

> *I'm talking about the kind of manhood lived by bold, caring, principled, passionate men. I'm talking about the kind of manhood that makes a family whole, a woman safe, a child confident, and a community strong. I'm talking about a manhood rooted in heritage and honor and devotion to tribe. It is often rowdy and eager for fun, but it is always on duty and never fails to mind the borders of the territory it is assigned.... Manly men live to the glory of God.*
>
> —Stephen Mansfield[2]

The shadows of this paradigm loom large in the world. The in-group/out-group dichotomy can become extreme and show up as fundamentalism (religious, political, etc.) and xenophobia of all flavors (sexism, racism, ableism, bigotry, solipsism, etc.). Military organizations and the masculine use of violence also reside here. The abuse of power and force extends into dominator hierarchies, bullying, and hegemonic masculinity. The tyrant, the sycophant, the outcast, and the terrorist are all pathologies in this paradigm.

> *Male dominance is restricted in this study to two general types. First, there is the exclusion of women from political and economic decision making. Second, there is male aggression against women, which is measured here by the following five traits: the expectation that males should be tough, brave, and aggressive; the presence of men's houses or specific places where only men may congregate; frequent quarreling, fighting, or wife-beating; the institutionalization or regular occurrence of rape; and raiding other groups for wives.*
>
> —Peggy Sanday[3]

In this paradigm, gender has an *essential* characteristic that is derived from biological sex. Masculinity is determined by the male sex, and femininity is determined by the female sex. There are many versions of the essentialist approach to gender, but I will simply sketch out a few here.

Biological determinism examines how gender developed due to biological asymmetry during the beginning of civilization when humans shifted from nomadic life into agriculture. The cultivation of crops required the operation of an animal-drawn plow in a field that is a larger distance from the home. Women who operate a plow during pregnancy suffer higher rates of miscarriage and cannot operate a plow while nursing. In addition, male bodies are generally stronger and larger. So, these emerging societies organized themselves with a division of labor where men focused on production and women on households. In addition, nursing women benefit from shelter, and so men became the more expendable sex for long-distance travel and dangerous activities like battle and hunting large game. The division of roles according to sexes is seen as an adaptation to environmental, physiological, and social conditions. This then forms the basis of the masculine and feminine genders and explains the asymmetry in economic and political power. The concentration of power into masculine actors is called a *patrifocal* social structure.

Other forms of gender essentialism appeal to human instincts by studying primate behavior, or by appeals to mythic, scriptural, or traditional sources that define how men and women were created within the divine order. In each culture, there is a singular interpretation for the "authentic" version of masculinity.

In addition to the patriarchal/patrifocal perspectives that claim that it is natural for men to wield power and authority, there are *feminist essentialist* perspectives, which are often included as a subset of *radical feminism*. In this view, because women gestate, give birth, and nurse children, femininity is superior or preferable to masculinity.[4] For example:

> It seems to me that the power of the new feminist culture, the powers which were attributed to the ancient matriarchies (considered either as historical or as mythic archetypes), and the inner power with which many women are beginning to feel in touch and which is the soul of feminist art, may all arise from the same source. That source is none other than female biology: the capacity to bear and nurture children.
>
> —Jane Alpert[5]

Whether the conclusion is pro-patriarchal or pro-feminist, the structure of the view (i.e., the organizing paradigm) is essentially the same: gender is either a naturally determined consequence of biology or a divinely determined creation. Gender essentialist views are typical of the mythic/traditional paradigm.

The Orange Man

Mental/Modern, Achievement

I am focused on performance and knowledge. For the Orange Man, competition is an individualistic endeavor to achieve, in contrast to the Amber Man, where competition is a natural mechanism for the organization of power structures. In this paradigm, I lead with my intellect. Logic, reason, philosophy, and science reign supreme. Information and technology are my tools and I view my life and the world as a series of problems to be fixed or solved. I can see a path of progress wherever I apply myself. I flourish in business, high tech, academia, science, engineering or any technical area. Because I am so strongly developed in my conceptual mind, I tend to be disconnected from emotions and devalue intuitive ways of knowing. I am highly motivated to climb the ladder and succeed. I am also motivated to be seen as successful by my peers. I have intellectual hobbies like strategy games, rhetoric, and literature. I define who I am and masculinity through achievement and knowledge.

This paradigm bestows the gifts of thinking logically and achieving success in the world. Roles may include the expert, strategist, scientist, savant, geek, policy wonk, or businessman. I excel at analyzing a situation and finding a solution. My tools are logic, reason, the scientific method, and access to detailed or obscure knowledge. I have access to motivation, innovation, and adaptability. I am progressive.

The values of the Age of Reason, democracy, and capitalism form the core ideology of this paradigm and the masculinity that it defines. Humans hold inalienable rights for "life, liberty, and the pursuit of happiness" and men are progressive agents of social change.

> *The only freedom which deserves the name is that of pursuing our own good in our own way, so long as we do not attempt to deprive others of theirs, or impede their efforts to obtain it. Each is the proper guardian of his own health, whether bodily, or mental or spiritual. Mankind are greater gainers by suffering each other to live as seems good to themselves, than by compelling each to live as seems good to the rest.*
>
> —John Stuart Mill[6]

The shadows of this paradigm are also taking a heavy toll on the world today. Materialism, consumerism, and wealth-hoarding behaviors are the outward signs of internal moral bankruptcy and ego inflation. The pathology of needing to be seen positively by others expresses as decadence, extravagance, and one-upmanship. As a man, I may be solely focused on my performance, success, and self-image. I may objectify those I'm sexually attracted to (another form of consumerism) and may use people as means to achieve my ends. The drive for performance shows up through workaholism, burnout, and obsessive behavior. Because I am so centered in rational thought, I may experience social anxiety, emotional immaturity, and physical or emotional fragility. This structure is home to the playboy and the know-it-all.

The mental/modern understanding of gender is rooted in *liberal feminism.* All humans are capable of rational thought, a stance that was not held in Western culture prior to the age of reason.

Therefore, all humans innately hold basic rights.[7] This infers legal, moral, and political freedoms. Thus, women are equally deserving of these fundamental rights and the role of government is to ensure these rights are provided.[8]

> *But we are assembled to protest against a form of government existing without the consent of the governed—to declare our right to be free as man is free, to be represented in the government which we are taxed to support, to have such disgraceful laws as give man the power to chastise and imprison his wife, to take the wages which she earns, the property which she inherits, and, in case of separation, the children of her love; laws which make her the mere dependent on his bounty. It is to protest against such unjust laws as these that we are assembled today, and to have them, if possible, forever erased from our statute books, deeming them a shame and a disgrace to a Christian republic in the nineteenth century. We have met to uplift woman's fallen divinity upon an even pedestal with man's. And, strange as it may seem to many, we now demand our right to vote according to the declaration of the government under which we live.*
>
> —Elizabeth Cady Stanton[9]

Liberal feminism is also known as first-wave feminism or mainstream feminism. The securing of freedoms and rights has largely, though not entirely, been accomplished in the Western world. Liberal feminism aims at creating equal access to opportunities. However, it will require a further complexification of world view, in order to *see* the ways that privilege and cultural bias subtly warp the ideal meritocracy of the mental/rational paradigm. These themes of privilege and bias will be the work of the plural/postmodern paradigm.

In addition to liberal feminism, which seeks to secure women's equality within capitalism, Marxist feminism identifies the inherent incentives toward sexism that arise from the system of capitalism itself. In this view, capitalism and the male elite benefit from the subordination of women.[10]

Individual men further benefit when their wives do housework by freeing up more time for education and productive labor. The system is invested in the nuclear family unit, in part because married men are less likely to revolt. And finally, capitalism profits by the exploitation of the feminine as sex objects.

Whether the stance is pro-capitalism or anti-capitalism, the understanding of gender in this paradigm is essentially a rational one that advocates for equal rights and equal opportunity.

The Green Man

Plural/Postmodern, Sensitivity

I am focused on activism and feeling my inner landscape. At this paradigm, I awaken to the previously invisible privilege that I hold, and I work to dismantle it in myself and in my society. I am deconstructing social conditioning across gender, race, and class. I am actively dismantling the power structures from the prior two paradigms (including hegemonic masculinity, colonization, racism, sexism, ableism, ageism, etc.) in order to create a more equitable world. Feminism, ecology, and political activism all may become personally relevant to me. I may delve into psychotherapy, nonviolent communication, restorative justice, grassroots organizing, and advocacy. If I identify with the dominant in-group of society, I may become an ally for marginalized groups. Or, if I identify with a marginalized group, this is where I find my voice and my identification becomes a strength instead of a stigma. I care about reconciliation, restoration, right-relationships, civil rights, and equality. I define myself through how I am making a difference in the world.

The gifts of this masculine worldview include capacities as a facilitator, mediator, healer, activist, and organizer. I learn how to see systems and think on a systemic level. My core value is sensitivity. With my new focus on depth of inner-life, I learn how to communicate, feel my emotions, and be vulnerable. This new inward focus brings me into psychotherapy and emotional or spiritual healing modalities. I become both deeper and broader as a man. I learn how to listen (finally!), and I gain multicultural awareness, passion to make a change, and an understanding of marginalization and discrimination. I can identify my roles within hegemonic systems (more on this below). As a man, I am doing serious work to heal gender, sexual, and relational wounding, and to embody nonviolence as a way of life.

> *I have argued for the rejection of masculine spirituality due to its patriarchal nature and restrictive treatment of gender. But this does not close down in any way men discussing religion and spirituality in terms which resonate with being a man. It opens up a conversation which resonates with any number of ways of being a man (or masculine) that rejects patriarchy. It is a pro-man conversation because it is pro-person, which by necessity must involve the liberation of all people. Feminist and queer theories and theologies have done most of the work in making way for such a conversation. What is needed now is for predominantly straight men to step up and play their part in a process which will benefit the vast majority of people.*
>
> —Joseph Gelfer[11]

The shadows of this paradigm include oversensitivity, sentimentalism, paralysis through emotional processing, and believing I'm guilty, broken, or traumatized forever. Moral relativism (i.e., all truth arises within cultural context) may lead me to nihilism (there is no truth). Deconstruction may lead into fragmentation, chaos, or oblivion.

I may enroll strongly in the *drama triangle*.[12] I may see myself as a victim to my trauma, or I may take on the unforgivable weight of being a perpetrator. Alternately, I may see myself as a safe masculine savior. Whichever role I identify with carries assumptions of blame and disempowerment.

I may disown my cultural heritage, gender, or any trait that carries privilege—throwing the baby out with the bathwater. I spoke in the introduction about the *sensitive new age guy* (lovingly abbreviated as SNAG) and *disaffected masculinity*. Typical of the plural/postmodern paradigm, these approaches to masculinity recognize the harm that has been caused by men in the world and bring a much-needed step beyond the cycles of violence. However, they also source in judgment and reaction against other forms of masculinity. Within disaffected masculinity, I will never be sourcing my masculinity internally from an experience of wholeness. These are necessarily partial expressions of the masculine in reaction against other types of masculinity.

While each paradigm carries pathology and shadow, the pathologies of the earlier paradigms have had more time to develop and carry more power within society. Thus, we feel them more. In addition, each paradigm initially arises in response to the problems created by the prior paradigms and then proceeds to define itself. Plural/postmodernism is still growing and defining itself beyond dismantling the problems from the prior two paradigms.

At plural/postmodern, gender is largely understood as a social construction. Different societies and cultures hold diverse definitions of gender, and therefore, there is no singular or universal masculine and feminine. Gender only exists because everyone in society agrees and acts as if it exists. There is no absolute truth because gender is always relative to social context. The plural/postmodern paradigm employs a systems view of gender, known as *intersectionality*. Gender does not exist as a silo within culture, rather it *intersects* other social constructs including race and class. Gender norms are implicitly taught to each individual and then unconsciously and systemically reinforced through our interactions and relationships. We are therefore "doing gender."

Poststructuralism is most often associated with a rejection, or at least a critique, of humanist logic and aspirations. It therefore involves a rethinking of concepts such as 'meaning', 'truth', 'subjectivity', 'freedom', 'power', and so on. Poststructuralist theorists such as Foucault argue that there are no objective and universal truths, but that particular forms of knowledge, and the ways of being that they engender, become 'naturalised', in culturally and historically specific ways. For example, Judith Butler, and Monique Wittig argue (in slightly different ways) that heterosexuality is a complex matrix of discourses, institutions, and so on, that has become normalised in our culture, thus making particular relationships, lifestyles, and identities, seem natural, ahistorical, and universal. In short, heterosexuality, as it is currently understood and experienced, is a (historically and culturally specific) truth-effect of systems of power/knowledge. Given this, its dominant position and current configuration are contestable and open to change.

—Nikki Sullivan[13]

Within the postmodern/plural paradigm, the social construction of gender creates limits or constraints on each individual's capacity to exist in society by imposing an artificial mask upon them. Each of us identifies with and is viewed through the conditioned overlays of gender. In addition, these social "systems of power/knowledge" both subtly and overtly discriminate throughout social institutions. The great work of this paradigm is to deconstruct this false conditioning in order to liberate individuals and create a more just society beyond privilege and bias. The queering of gender aims to subvert cultural norms and liberate proscriptive and limiting gender roles.

Engaging in social equity work is a journey. In my experience, there is no fixed marker for success or arrival. It is an ongoing process of learning—both as new layers within myself become accessible and because the field as a whole continues to evolve. The work itself is largely about sitting in discomfort. By all accounts, it's not easy.

A proposal that has been very helpful in my process is that both dominant and subordinate groups benefit from social equity work. As a privilege-holder, part of my work is to voluntarily relinquish power, authority, and the social benefits that accrue through holding a dominant position. On the other side of this work is the promise of freedom from the false scripts and conditioning that imbue my beliefs and behaviors. I gain the ability to meet people authentically: human to human, and the gift of living in a more inclusive, compassionate, society. Raising the well-being of all people is of immeasurable benefit to me personally through the countless positive feedback loops that percolate through society. Finding my personal benefits within anti-oppression work has been a key for me to continue engaging in this challenging field. With this in mind, change begins with awareness and awareness is exactly where the Magician excels.

Being a man has multiple socially constructed components, including sex, gender, and orientation, each with shades of meaning. Being a *male* includes the genes, genitals, hormones, and physiology that I hold. There is no bright line demarcating any of these biological categories where maleness begins or ends. Rather, it's a normative social category. Being *masculine* refers to gender identity (how I perceive myself) and expression (how socially communicate my gender). *Cisgender* means the gender identity and expression I hold today is the same as what was presumed at birth. Personally, I identify as masculine today, which is the same as when I was born, making me cisgendered (in contrast to transgendered). Both categories combine into the social identity of *man-ness*.

Queer theory argues for the dismantling of all binaries (straight/gay, man/woman, cis/trans, etc.). Third gender posits a distinct third category and agender posits an absence of gender (both of which I include in the androgyne morphic field).

Social Category	Dominant Group	Subordinate Groups
Sex	Male	Female, Intersex
Gender	Masculine, Cisgendered	Feminine, third-gender, a-gender, gender-queer, trans-gender, etc.
Sexual Orientation	Heterosexual	Lesbian, gay, bisexual, queer, asexual, pansexual, etc.

Figure 11.3 Sex and gender social identity categories

In addition, there is a related but distinct social identity category of sexual orientation. Heterosexual defines the preference of "men" being attracted to "women" for sexual partners, mates, and romantic bonding. Some of these categories (heterosexual, lesbian, gay, and bisexual) rely on the social constructions of man-ness and woman-ness across sex and gender and often presume a binary of men and women.

Each of these three social identity categories contains a dominant group and some number of subordinate groups (fig. 11.3). The dominant groups in today's culture are male, cisgendered masculine, and heterosexual.

Dominant groups operate in a number of influential ways in society. Members of these groups define knowledge, set the standard for what is normal or normalized, and model the assumed perspective through which the world is viewed and interpreted. For instance, historically, the vast majority of school textbooks have been written by men. The definition of knowledge includes biases and prejudices which tend to be negative toward subordinate groups and positive toward the dominant group.

Second, dominant groups benefit from privilege. This privilege is conveyed between individuals (for example, a man being promoted in the workplace by men at the top of the company), and impersonally by institutions (for example, the gender pay gap across the workforce).

Third, dominant groups wield power. There are many interpretations of what power means, but for a starting approximation, power is the capacity to mobilize resources and influence or coerce the behavior of others. The dominant group holds power over the subordinate groups. For example, as of today, 110 of the total 116 Supreme Court justices of the United States have been men, meaning the country's national laws have overwhelmingly been adjudicated by men. These laws determine which set of behaviors is acceptable in society.

The system where men define knowledge, benefit from privilege, and wield power is what is meant by the term *hegemonic masculinity*. This structure is not held by any individual, but rather exists within collective identity groups and institutions of our society. Individuals in the dominant groups benefit, while individuals in the subordinate groups are suppressed. A crucial component of *men's work* today is to engage in the process of recognizing how I fit into these social structures and then changing how I participate within them.

At plural/postmodern, the systems–view of society comes online. Here, I can see my individual self positioned in complex relationships with collective group identities and societal institutions (fig. 11.4). The four parts of the psyche (being, thinking, acting, and feeling) both influence and are influenced by the other two collective entities. These connections are both overt and subtle. In addition, social groups are continuously interacting with social institutions. Dominant groups wield more influence over individuals (whether in-group or out-group) and institutions than subordinated groups, as is indicated by the darker arrows in the diagram.

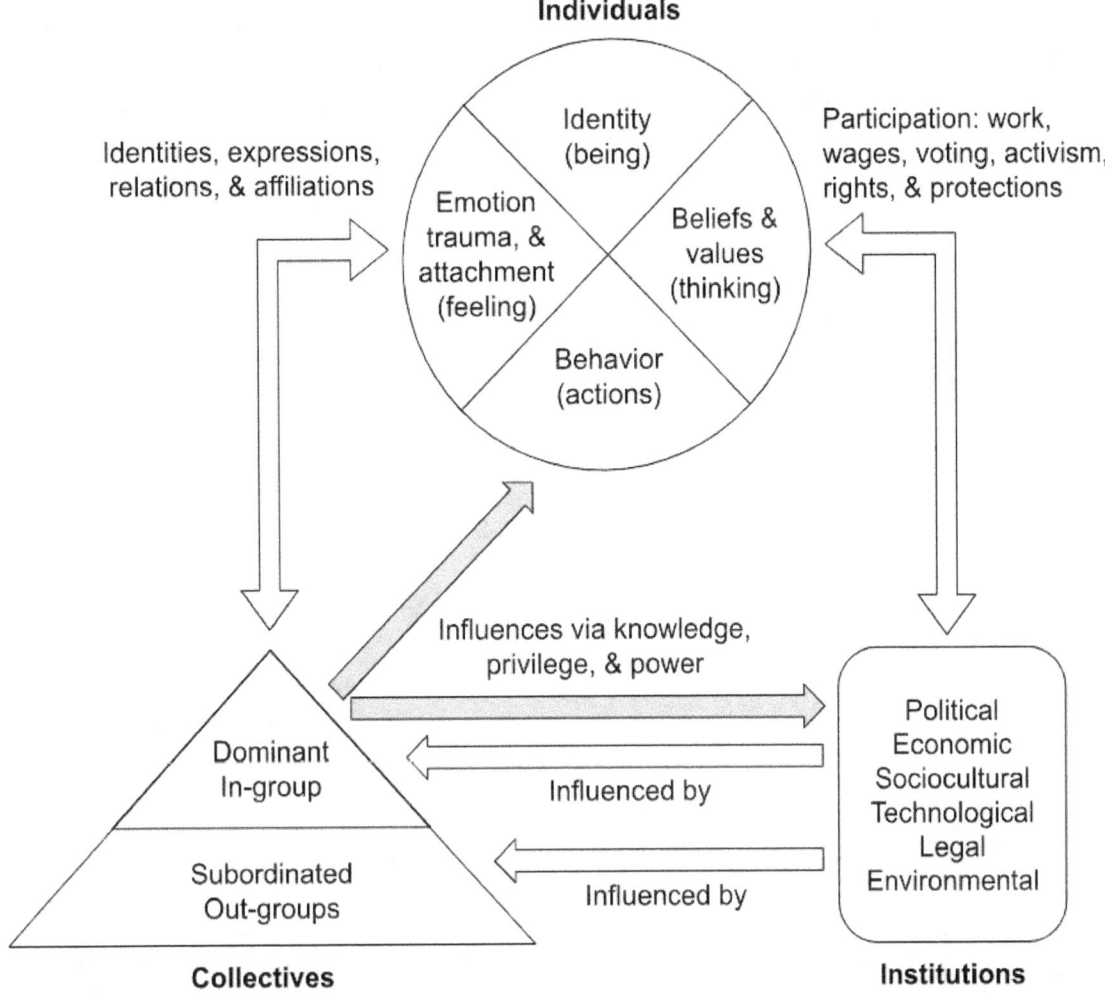

Figure 11.4 Social categories woven through identity, collectives, and institutions

In addition, the three categories of sex, gender, and sexual orientation *intersect* with other major social categories in complex ways (fig. 11.5). Each social category has both in-group and out-group affiliations. These categories are interwoven, overlapping, and cannot be understood in isolation from all other social categories. At plural/postmodern, the social system begins to reveal itself as an emergent, chaotic *Gordian knot*, which can make social activism a slow, confusing, and laborious process.

Each of these systems is connected to all other systems, though not hierarchically in relationship to one another and where no single form of oppression (or triad, for that matter) is first or foremost. Together, these systems create an intricate network of structures and self-perpetuating processes that, in effect, constitute an all encompassing matrix of domination.

—Raúl Rosado[14]

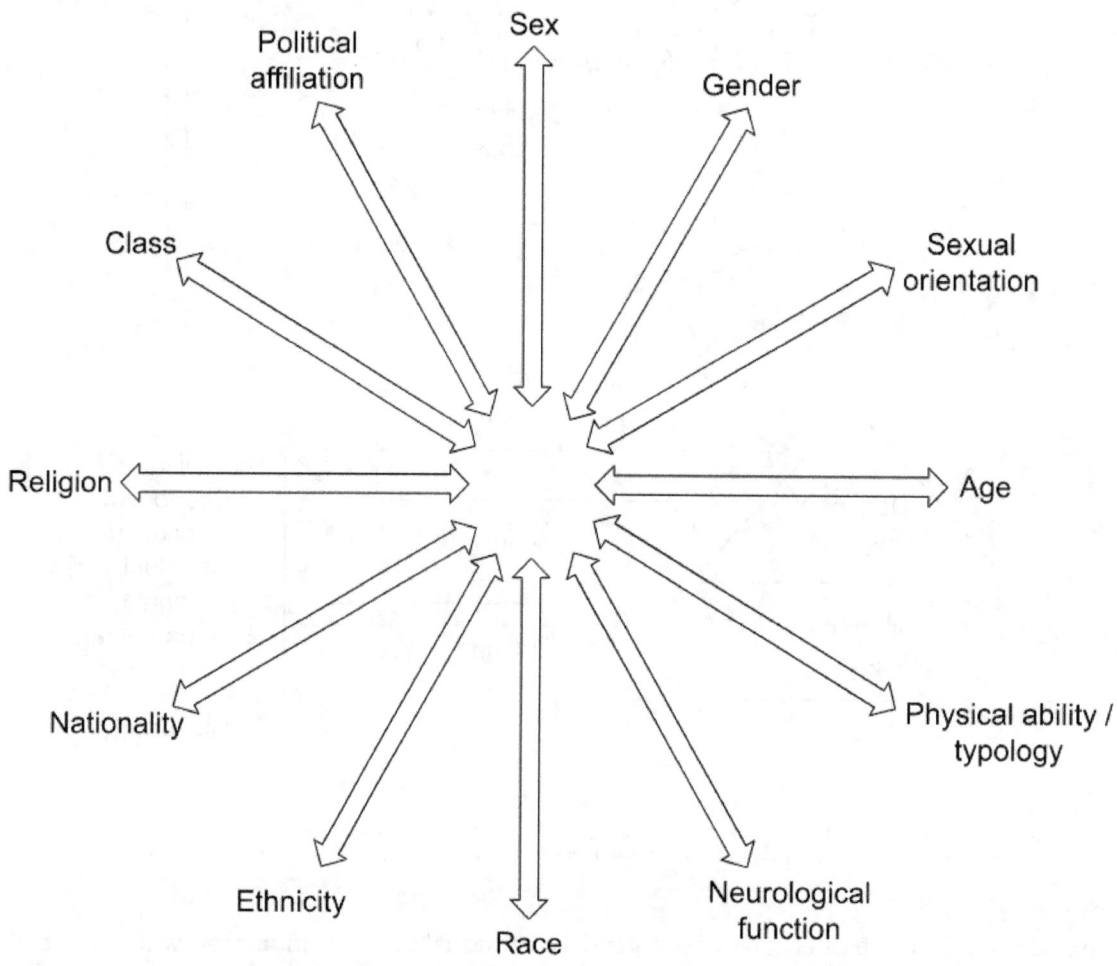

Figure 11.5 Intersectionality of social categories

For any of the categories where I inhabit the dominant in-group, I want to bring awareness to my dominant biases, privileges, and power, and then dismantle those modes within my personal psyche and work to create more balanced and liberating social systems. As an in-group member, working for the benefit of out-groups is known as *allyship*. For any of the categories where I inhabit a subordinated out-group, I want to bring awareness to the *internalization of oppression* that I may have taken on through distorted identities, limiting beliefs, collusion, and emotional or nervous system impairment. As I heal my internal landscape, I find my voice and step into empowerment to begin working on collective-level changes.

It is important for me to stress that while this workbook presents integral as the exciting and sexy step in consciousness, there remains a massive amount of work to be done (at least for myself as a man) here at the plural/postmodern paradigm. In *Lore Book II: The Warrior*, I will offer more depth on how to take *action* in anti-oppression work.

The Teal Man

Integral, Self-Actualization

I am focused on interconnection, holism, and self-expression. Having taken the giant leap to arrive at tier two, I am connecting with life, consciousness, and spirituality. This new awareness arises first as an intellectual recognition, followed by more and more immersion into direct experience. I learn how to enroll my conceptual mind in service to the creativity, wisdom, and love of life. By stepping aside, I learn to embody these transcendent qualities: I am creativity, I am wisdom, and I am love. Through all of the healing, shadow-work, and personal-growth, I tap into an incredible reservoir of energy that aligns me ever more fully to my purpose. I am a synthesizing, visionary, multidisciplinary, embodied man. I own my masculinity, cultural heritage, and privilege by re-defining, reincorporating, and reimagining these traits in wholeness. I am cultivating myself in abundance, fertility, and prosperity to become the full measure of human across all developmental lines. I balance growth with presence, becoming with being.

The gifts of this paradigm include *level five leadership*,[15] the capacity to work deeply with self and others, and a meta-systemic view that reveals holistic solutions. At integral, I begin to access core experiences of belonging to this universe, spiritual truth, and worthiness. I become a purpose-driven man. I am able to access these qualities as the basis of my lived reality instead of fleeting peak experiences. I show up as a man from wholeness, rather than woundedness, isolation, or scarcity. And with the beginning footholds in a transpersonal identity, I do not need to *identify with* or *believe in* my masculinity. Rather, masculinity becomes an aspect of consciousness that I willingly participate in and play with.

Integral is still emerging in our culture so the shadows have not been fully defined. However, pathologies of the Teal Man include an arrogance at having *figured it out* and an impatience for folks at lower levels. The wholeness I find in myself, may lead me to complacency or denial toward ongoing shadow work. The spiritual realms that begin to open can be so enticing that I *ascend* into bliss realms and disconnect from the *default world*. The masculine version of escaping real-world issues into spiritual "nirvana" is one form of *Peter Pan syndrome*. Another version of integral masculinity's bypassing is the tendency at integral to view challenging anti-oppression work as too mired in the victim mentality of postmodernism. For example:

I want to integrate thoroughly the lessons that healthy [Postmodern] liberation traditions offer, so that a healthy [Integral] is actually emancipatory, and not transcending "isms" to the point of disengaging from the messy needed political anti-oppression work. Menness is a signature of "going up" called progress; it doesn't like to "go down." That's what Western civilization, at least, has given us as a hegemonic meta-narrative and mythos.

—R. Michael Fisher[16]

As an emerging paradigm, integral does not yet hold a coherent theory of gender in the collective consensus. In addition, academia and gender studies are largely centered in the plural/postmodern paradigm and have not made the monumental leap of consciousness into tier two. What this means is that our deepest subject experts on gender are not yet looking through the integral lens, and therefore, integral theorists and gender studies folks are largely speaking different languages.

Academia takes a critical inquiry into the social construction and intersectional nature of gender. Postmodernism views gender within systems of human society. An integral approach to gender will include these insights while transcending the postmodern view, moving into meta-systemic and holistic frameworks. Integral is able to locate the systems of socialized gender within even larger frameworks including the four-quadrant model, the states of consciousness, and the holarchy of paradigms discussed in previous chapters.

The four-quadrants model from the end of chapter 7 maps how holons exist throughout the experiential realms. The holon of masculinity constellates throughout these four quadrants. The individual interior holds my gender identity (how I see myself as a gendered being), sexual identity (how I see my biological sex), and sexual preference (what type of sexual partner I see myself as). The individual exterior holds my biological sex (male, female, intersex) as well as my sexual embodiment (inclusive of transsexuality and sexual bodily modifications via surgery or hormones). This quadrant includes sexual anatomy, hormones, chromosomes, and physiology. The collective interior and exterior (lower quadrants) together hold my gender expression and include any historical and cultural contextualization of gender. How my gender-symbols are collectively understood occupies the interior collective quadrant. The outward expressions of gender through visual presentation and behavior are held in the exterior collective quadrant. This quadrant also includes the ways that social institutions (schools, workplaces, government, law, etc.) interpret and define gender.

Upper Left Interior-Individual	Upper Right Exterior-Individual
Gender identity, Sexual identity, Sexual orientation	Biological sex, Sexual embodiment
Lower Left Interior-Collective	Lower Right Exterior-Collective
Group affiliations. Gender expression through language & meaning	Gendered & sexual behaviors, social institutions

Figure 11.6 Gender and sex in the four-quadrants

There are three notable aspects of the integral view that influence the understanding and experience of gender in this paradigm. These are (1) the integrated multiparadigmatic inclusivity of integral, (2) the sourcing of truth and rigorous knowledge claims contextually, and beyond the moral relativism of postmodernity, and (3) the recognition of ongoing evolution, which leads to a learning-perspective on gender instead of focusing on a fixed definition.

First, integral uniquely recognizes the validity of all other paradigms and is therefore able to include the truths from all other vantage points. So, to make this concrete, I can welcome the ways that biology and instinct contribute to masculinities (essentialism from mythic/traditional), while also advocating for equal human rights for all (liberal feminism from mental/modern), and simultaneously recognizing the social conditioning of gender embedded in my culture (social construction and intersectionality from plural/postmodern). All of these perspectives contribute kernels of truth that I'm able to integrate into a holistic tapestry for the meanings of masculinities.

Integral Theory offers feminist thought the capacity to acknowledge each domain: the operation of structural systems; socialization, gender roles, and history in the culture; the effects of biology; the hurdles of psychology in development; and manner in which the coarising process through which all of these define Woman. Importantly, this framework also engages with spiritual subjectivity, yet is not in any way bound to a singular religious framework or patriarchal lineage. It also gives feminism a way to identify the stages of development of itself as a movement, and the limitations of isolated perspectives emerging from specific schools, and a way to integrate these parts into a whole.

—Sarah E. Nicholson[17]

Any claim about gender that is made within an integral framework is situated within its context. Integral makes definite claims about reality (including gender) and positions those claims within the paradigmatic lens as well as the contexts of relative versus absolute truth via the states of consciousness. Integral holds flexibility and adaptability with regards to truth claims. This is known as *vision logic*.

The second shift that integral brings is even more profound. At integral, I source truth from the experience of wholeness within myself. Other gender theories that I've covered here begin with gender oppression (i.e., hegemonic masculinity) and then argue for a solution. Any theory that takes oppression as its core assumption is going to be unable to move beyond that oppression. Integral, in contrast, sources in wholeness. I find the experience of the sacred, life-affirming masculine within myself. From this foundation, I am able to recognize the sacred core of masculinity woven throughout the kosmos. This experience of masculinity has the explanatory power to account for the suffering, distortions, and oppressions of hegemonic masculinity, without being defined by and, thus, beholden to that suffering. Integral aims to *transcend* into wholeness while *including* the anti-oppression work of postmodernity.

Here is what I mean when I say integral masculinity sources in wholeness. I am able to more fully recognize the cultural conditioning, stereotypes, mythologies, and biases inherent to thinking in gendered language. Beyond all of these, I am able to find a core experience of self. This is not *thinking about myself*, it is the *experience of being myself*. This *organic self* provides a compass for how I know truth. Whatever is happening for me is true because I experience it. In addition, by integral, I have integrated enough of my fragmented psychological parts, that I am less seducible to my conflicting inner agendas. Centering in my *adult self*, my experience is trustable. This is the place of wholeness. I must experience my wholeness directly—no amount of wishful thinking will take me there. From this inner center, I have an experience of the masculine. These experiences are not necessarily mystical or profound. Today, when I took out the trash, I was in my masculine. The reasons why, or critical interpretations, or whether this would be true for anyone else is secondary. I had an experience of the masculine within myself. In fact, once I learn how to trust this level of feeling, I'm able to experience the masculine regularly both in myself and in others. This masculinity is naturally life-affirming: *organic*. At integral, each of us is able to reference our inner compass for truth foremost, which arises from the wholeness of the self. My experience of masculinity (and femininity and androgyny) from the wholeness of my organic self provides the core of gender at integral.

Third, integral recognizes and deeply values the evolutionary process. Any position on gender is understood at integral to be the current interpretation within an ongoing process of discovery, enrichment, and unfolding. This process focus undermines the dogmatic and static positionality of first-tier understandings of gender. I am not looking for the singular correct answer. Instead, I am cross-referencing as many theories as I can get my hands on to discover commonalities and trends, and to synthesize new holistic concepts. Whatever conclusions I make about gender today become the foundations for tomorrow's more complex and holistic synthesis.

Having laid out the elements of gender at integral, now, here is my understanding of masculinity through the integral lens. As described above, my holistic self has a natural and innate capacity to recognize masculinity, which provides the true and trustable experience of the masculine.

The masculinities that proliferate throughout gender identity and expression are one layer of the masculine morphic field. This field imbues all realms of the kosmos below unity consciousness including biology, subtle energy, evolutionary archetypes, and the high archetypes. At the high causal layer, the primal, divine, sacred masculine forms a trinity together with the primal, divine, sacred feminine and the primal, divine, sacred androgyne. The masculine and feminine fields define themselves contextually through polarity with each other. Thus, there is no *singular* or *universal* masculine trait, only specific instances of polarity. Definition only happens contextually. And yet, my heart feels and recognizes the masculine, beyond theories or concepts, in the immediacy of experience. Whatever traits or context the masculine is holding in that moment *is* the true masculine here and now. I know the masculine when I feel him. The morphic field of masculinity is simultaneously singular and infinitely diverse. This field manifests uniquely within each individual and is continuously evolving throughout individuals, cultures, and humanity.

The morphic field for masculinity also constellates throughout the archetypes in the causal realm. As I will cover in chapter 13 on archetypes, individuals and collectives have a need to *mature* through the masculine morphic field. This is accomplished by identifying oneself through a succession of archetypal roles. For the masculine in Western culture, these archetypal roles are the boy, the hero, the man, and the elder. Each successive role bestows greater power and carries more responsibility. We graduate through archetypal roles by the process of initiation.

Including the archetypes into our theory of gender offers a more holistic interpretation of hegemonic masculinity along with potential new solutions. When an individual or culture becomes stuck and is unable to advance through the archetypal roles via initiation, then the living-system becomes diseased, pathologic, and begins to drive toward death in order to renew the flow of the life cycle. Western civilization has lost initiations, rites of passage, and access to sacred space. Over the course of our advancement through the paradigms of (1) monotheism and tradition, (2) secularization and modernization, and (3) postmodern deconstruction, the initiatory rites from our tribal past have been eradicated. Because of this, individuals and our society are stuck primarily in the heroic adolescent archetypal role. As adolescent heroes, we are egocentric, achievement-focused, and consumerist. We are living in a pathologic, diseased civilization that is advancing toward death while simultaneously clinging to comfort and security. It is through a reintegration of initiatory rites that we are able to *re-member* ourselves into the organic masculine, organic feminine, and organic androgyne. We must enter back into the archetypal death-and-rebirth cycles of life in order to find the sacred in ourselves and all of life. This is how the more holistic integral perspective, which includes archetypes and the life-affirming core of gender, is able to recontextualize hegemonic masculinity in a way that is not embedded within the system of suffering. We are thus able to offer novel solutions out of the dysfunctional crisis.

The Turquoise Man

High Integral, Compassion

I am aware of masculinity, how it weaves through myself and culture, and how its morphic field traverses realms of consciousness. This level of awareness goes beyond the social deconditioning of the plural paradigm. At high integral, I am seeing how masculinity, femininity, and androgyny, in their myriad forms and expressions constellate throughout reality itself. I am letting go of my attachment and identification with gendered archetypes, the process Jung called *individuation*. The result is that I become freer to play, create, and explore gender. Gender fluidity largely emerges at postmodern as I learn to play with my gender presentation and choose my gender scripts intentionally. By high integral, the play is with the forms and fields of the archetypes themselves through deities, myths, and increasingly direct access to the causal realm.

I recognize that the masculine, feminine, and androgyne hold some of my deepest wounds and obscurations. At the same time, I recognize the eleutheropoietic nature of these archetypes, meaning: I experience masculinity as a facet of the creative self-liberation of the kosmos.

> *Our embodiment as women or men in culture becomes the vehicle by which we engage the evolutionary process.*
>
> —Elizabeth Debold[18]

Creative liberation through masculinity means giving myself fully into this archetype, wielding it through my human form, and expressing myself through its morphic field. Whereas Integral tends to idealize an image of "conscious" or "sacred" masculinity, at high integral the current, lived experience of masculinity *is the fruition* itself. In essence, I am choosing to be the masculinity I want to embody, and I am meeting my masculinity with ever-increasing kindness.

At this level, there is an even deeper reaching down to embrace shadow elements within myself. When asked about her selfless humanitarian work, Mother Teresa replied she began "on the day I discovered I had a Hitler inside me." This *shadow embrace* means learning to see myself in all aspects of humanity beyond the value judgements. Another example:

I am the child in Uganda, all skin and bones,
my legs as thin as bamboo sticks.
And I am the arms merchant,
selling deadly weapons to Uganda.

I am the twelve-year-old girl,

refugee on a small boat,
who throws herself into the ocean
after being raped by a sea pirate.

And I am also the pirate,
my heart not yet capable
of seeing and loving.

—Thich Nhat Hanh[19]

High integral masculinity brings online the tools to explore the darkest, most maligned parts of the masculine archetypes. I am finding the killer, the rapist, the nihilist, the tyrant, the victim and many other shadow aspects within my psyche and welcoming them to be loved and integrated. This process opens me naturally to the core value at high integral, which is compassion. Thich Nhat Hanh's poem, quoted above, concludes like this:

Please call me by my true names,
so I can hear all my cries and my laughter at once,
so I can see that my joy and pain are one.

Please call me by my true names,
so I can wake up,
and so the door of my heart can be left open,
the door of compassion.

By integrating the shadows of my psyche, I become more accepting of the outer world exactly as it is. I enter into equanimity. Layer by layer, I am owning and loving the cruelties and judgments within myself. As the places of separation fall away, I experience myself more interwoven with all of life. This is eleutheropoiesis at high integral.

In addition to a deeper embrace of gender as a doorway to compassion, at high integral I am more fully witnessing the core mechanisms in gender that obscure reality as it is. Language is gendered, and I think in language so the nature of my thinking and communication is imbued with the assumptions and limitations of my language. I become increasingly *construct aware* of gender. In moving beyond attachment to concepts through language, I open myself to experience reality on reality's terms. It is not that gender ceases to exist, it's that the inherent limits in naming, categorizing, and defining an experience become increasingly inadequate and, thus, irrelevant. The richness, creativity, and nuance of direct experience takes ever-more precedent over conceptual filtering and processing. At high integral, the ineffable mystery unfolds itself more and more nakedly.

Contextual Definitions of Masculine and Feminine Traits

Throughout this workbook, I have made the claim that there are no universal masculine traits. Now, having outlined my integral approach to gender, I'd like to cover why I make this claim and why I think it's important. Personally, I continually catch myself collecting various traits to define masculinity. My mind wants to have a solid definition to hold onto. In my framework for sexual polarity, I use the traits of *presence* and *penetration* as one option for a masculine partner to inhabit, which polarize with *power* and *surrender* for the person in the feminine role.[20] These traits work together and make sense in a particular context. But can the feminine hold presence? For sure. Can a drag queen be penetrating? Absolutely! For any term I apply to the masculine, numerous counter examples immediately present themselves. Furthermore, at integral the self-referential experience of masculinity takes priority within each individual. If I experience an act of surrender as masculine, that takes precedence over any external theory about surrender as a feminine trait.

But still within integral theory there persists a story—a mythology—of an essential masculinity and femininity. Here is Ken Wilber:

> *Many feminists agree with the extensive research that suggests that men tend to emphasize agency (or the autonomous self) and women communion (or "connection" and the "permeable" self).… We saw that men and women both develop through the same gender-neutral basic structures or expanding spheres of consciousness, but men tend to develop through these expanding spheres with an emphasis on agency, rights, justice, and autonomy, whereas women tend to develop through the same holarchical spheres based more on communion, responsibility, relationship, care, and connection.[21]*

Again, we do not have to look far to find counter examples: women's rights activists prioritizing agency, rights, justice, and autonomy; and male psychotherapists focusing on communion, responsibility, relationship, care, and connection. At best, qualifying masculinity as *agency* and femininity as *communion* are generalizations that miss many individuals, including the entire gender-queer population.

Beyond the inaccuracies, there is another issue with this characterization, which is raised by Elizabeth Debold:

Wilber draws a neat parallel between masculine and feminine, Eros and Agape, ascent and descent, transcend and include, freedom and fullness. The parallels that he draws that equate (or at least deeply associate) the masculine, [with] Eros, [and] ascent, [are] aesthetically pleasing in their symmetry, and appear to grant equal importance to the masculine and feminine (and implicitly to men and women). But in an evolutionary context, connecting Eros, transcendence, and freedom with the masculine—by which we primarily mean men and their capacity for agency—means that we leave women out of the evolution equation.[22]

Whenever we assign a normative trait to masculinity, that carries with it all of the positive and negative biases of that word. It also implicitly excludes folks who do not identify as masculine from holding that trait. This is exactly the mechanism of social conditioning that the plural/postmodern paradigm is so adamant to deconstruct.

Essentialist, universal, objective claims about masculine traits do not and cannot represent the whole truth. When I hold a normative stance on gender, that creates biases that miss the ineffable mystery of the humans that inhabit gender. When a group of people carry these biases, our culture becomes distorted, and when the group wielding power within society carries biases, it becomes oppression that weaves into our economic and governing institutions. This recognition is the gift of the plural/postmodern worldview. The pitfall at postmodern is to conclude that masculinity is not real (or only as real as we construct it to be) and therefore to conclude that a gender-free society would be more liberated. Personally, I spent years of my life holding this view.

The next step, at integral, is a return to gender from a more holistic worldview. Even though there are no universal gender traits, there are universal morphic fields that underlie sex, gender, and archetype (i.e., masculine, feminine, and androgyne). While normative beliefs about gender are inaccurate and contribute to social oppression, there are infinitely diverse individual expressions of gender that are contextually true. In a given situation, for a given person or group, a specific description of maleness, masculinity, and what it means to be an archetypal man can all be true. These contextually descriptive traits are true insofar as the individuals within this context align to that experience. Diverse individuals within a shared experience can simultaneously hold differing truth claims. And the specific truth claim of masculinity for any given instance makes no claim or implication for any other instance. At integral, I know what is true in this moment, inclusive of gender, through my direct experience. The gift of integral is to understand that *gender traits* can be described by contextually specific truths, but cannot be described by universal, normative claims.

The more practice I have looking through the integral lens, the more natural and centralized it becomes as my paradigm. So with that in mind, here is one more pass on this topic, zoomed a bit farther out. Plural/postmodernity recognizes the social construction of gender, and then goes on to claim that *all truths about gender are relative*. Taking the giant step into integral, I can see that "all truths about gender are relative" is itself a universal, objective truth claim. Integral recognizes that relativism is not a valid metaphysical stance. Even the position, "there is no truth" is itself a truth claim. Beyond that, integral recognizes how plural/postmodern consciousness uses relativism to privilege its own views, methods, and values. So then at integral, I now accept that universal truth claims are unavoidable, and I am able to *see* where it is appropriate for relative truth claims and where it is appropriate for universal truth claims. "There is an underlying masculine essence in primal polarity with the feminine essence of the kosmos" is a universal truth claim—one that more accurately describes a more complex and holistic kosmos. "This singular masculine morphic field expresses in unbounded variety through each individual and cultural instance of sex, gender, and archetype" is another universal truth claim. Finally, "masculine traits are contextually descriptive and validated through individual experience" places the relative truth claims for masculinity where they belong, within the sovereignty of each human.

Locating the Organic Masculine

Recall that I define the organic masculine as life-affirming. This means I show up with authenticity, respect, and kindness. When I reside here, I flow with the cycles of birth and death, creation and destruction, transformation and rebirth. I hold life precious and I honor the great mystery.

If you were to ask me where on the developmental ladder of masculinity the organic masculine resides, I would answer, "Everywhere." Each paradigm represents a completely valid expression of masculinity and is fully capable of affirming life. Our task is not to evolve ourselves to the top of the staircase in order to finally arrive at the organic masculine. Rather, the organic masculine is available right here and now. My task is to realize the organic core of masculinity throughout every paradigm I am able to access.

If you were to ask me where on the graph, *toxic masculinity* lives, again I would answer, "Everywhere." Each paradigm has its shadows, wounds, and demons. The shadows of the mythic/ traditional paradigm have had millennia to establish themselves. The shadows of the modern/ mental paradigm are embedded within the most powerful institutions on the globe today. We feel these wounds most acutely and they have the largest impact. The shadows of the integral paradigm are still being discovered—these grooves in consciousness are not fully formed yet. Nevertheless, each paradigm contains shadow and that means there is shadow work for me to do at every level that I have access to.

One of the roles of the Magician is to guide me into my shadows. It is my natural response to push away that which harms, disgusts, or denigrates. However, my work as a growth-oriented human is to recognize the shadows of each paradigm and to move toward that place in myself. This arises from the understanding that pushing anything away empowers it further. What I condemn, condemns me back. Instead of scapegoating "those men" as the problem, my task is to find those wounds and shadows within myself. When I find these parts, I welcome them with love and acceptance.

This map of the paradigms of masculine consciousness invites me to become intimate with all of masculinity: every paradigm, in darkness and in light. It is through this embrace that I evolve ever-greater wholeness in masculinity within myself and on behalf of the collective. This is how men's work will transform the world.

Prompts for Journaling and Discussion

Fill out the table below with the shadow and light of your expression of masculinity in each paradigm.

	My Masculine Gifts	My Masculine Judgments and Shadows
High Integral		
Integral		
Plural		
Mental		
Mythic		

Notes

[1] Image: DALL.E-3, 2024.

[2] *Mansfield's Book of Manly Men.*

[3] *Female Power and Male Dominance: On the Origins of Sexual Inequality.*

[4] "Feminist essentialism says that female attributes and activities, especially parenting, are not only intrinsically valuable but should be models for the betterment of society in general. If adopted, such a stance would call for radical social change. Regarding sex difference, then, feminist essentialists are not saying 'vive la difference,' as biological determinists usually do, nor are they saying that women should be more like men (which is what many antibiological determinists say). Rather they are posing a new question - why can't men be more like women? - one that implicitly values women and devalues men." *Sex and Gender in Society: Perspectives on Stratification*, Nielsen.

[5] "Mother Right: A New Feminist Theory."

[6] *On Liberty.*

[7] "Right is defined by the decision of conscience in accord with self-chosen *ethical principles* appealing to logical comprehensiveness, universality, and consistency. These principles are abstract and ethical (the Golden Rule, the categorical imperative); they are not concrete moral rules like the Ten Commandments. At heart, these are universal principles of *justice*, of the *reciprocity* and *equality* of human *rights*, and of respect for the dignity of human beings as *individual persons.*" *Communication and the Evolution of Society*, Habermass.

[8] "Liberal feminism might be characterized most simply as the application to women of the policy that all men are equal. Early liberals are strong advocates of individual rights in general define a good society as one in which there is freedom from state interference and as one in which the state (e.g., law, police, judicial systems) protects individual rights (for example, the right to vote) from infringement and generally endorses a policy of individuals' having the right to pursue happiness.... The liberals acknowledge psychological sex differences but see them as the result of different life experience. Their interest in showing that psychological or personality differences between the sexes are due primarily to social conditioning is necessary to back the claim that women are as rational as men and therefore deserving of full and equal human rights." *Sex and Gender in Society: Perspectives on Stratification*, Nielsen.

[9] Seneca Falls Keynote Address.

[10] "Marxist-feminists argue that female oppression in the contemporary world is sustaining by (1) the power of capitalists to protect and enhance their interest, which include low wages for women and unpaid domestic and familial work by women; (2) a patriarchal ideology, developed, supported, and disseminated by capitalists; and (3) the support of male members of the working class for the system of capitalist patriarchy because of the relative advantages - at home and in the labor force - that accrue to them. For Marxist-feminists, the elimination of female oppression

requires the demise of both capitalism and patriarchy, as an ideology and as a form of husband-wife relationship. It requires that maintenance/social-reproduction work cease to be the specific province of women, and the women share equally with men the labor involved in production for exchange." *Gender Equity: an Integrated Theory of Stability and Change*, Chafetz.

[11] *Numen, Old Men.*

[12] Discussed in Chapter 8.

[13] *A Critical Introduction to Queer Theory.*

[14] *Consciousness-in-Action.*

[15] "Level 5 leaders embody a paradoxical mix of personal humility and professional will. They are ambitious, to be sure, but ambitious first and foremost for the company, not themselves. • Level 5 leaders set up their successors for even greater success in the next generation, whereas egocentric Level 4 leaders often set up their successors for failure. • Level 5 leaders display a compelling modesty, are self-effacing and understated. In contrast, two thirds of the comparison companies had leaders with gargantuan personal egos that contributed to the demise or continued mediocrity of the company. • Level 5 leaders are fanatically driven, infected with an incurable need to produce sustained results. They are resolved to do whatever it takes to make the company great, no matter how big or hard the decisions. • Level 5 leaders display a workmanlike diligence—more plow horse than show horse. • Level 5 leaders look out the window to attribute success to factors other than themselves. When things go poorly, however, they look in the mirror and blame themselves, taking full responsibility. The comparison CEOs often did just the opposite—they looked in the mirror to take credit for success, but out the window to assign blame for disappointing results." *Good to Great*, Collins.

[16] Quoted in Nicholson, *Integral Voices on Sex, Gender, and Sexuality.*

[17] *Integral Voices on Sex, Gender, and Sexuality.*

[18] "A Deep Integral View on the Future of Gender" from *Integral Voices on Sex, Gender, and Sexuality*, Nicholson.

[19] From "Please Call Me By My True Names."

[20] To be covered in *Lore Book III: The Lover.*

[21] *The Eye of Spirit.* Wilber

[22] "A Deep Integral View on the Future of Gender." From *Integral Voices on Sex, Gender, and Sexuality*, Nicholson.

| 12 |

Relationship and Sex Holarchies

Figure 12.1 The Evolution of Relationships[1]

In the prior chapter, we explored the developmental line of masculinity through the paradigms of consciousness. In this chapter, we'll explore how relationships and sex each evolve through the paradigmatic holarchy. Relational intelligence and sexual intelligence both follow their own developmental ladders that share common deep features as they progress through the paradigms.

The descriptions I'm offering here are my *interpretations* of relationships and sex at each altitude. They are biased by the subcultures I inhabit, so I don't hold them as definitive. Rather, I share this qualitative roadmap as a starting place for you to create the interpretations that are accurate and relevant for your lived experience.

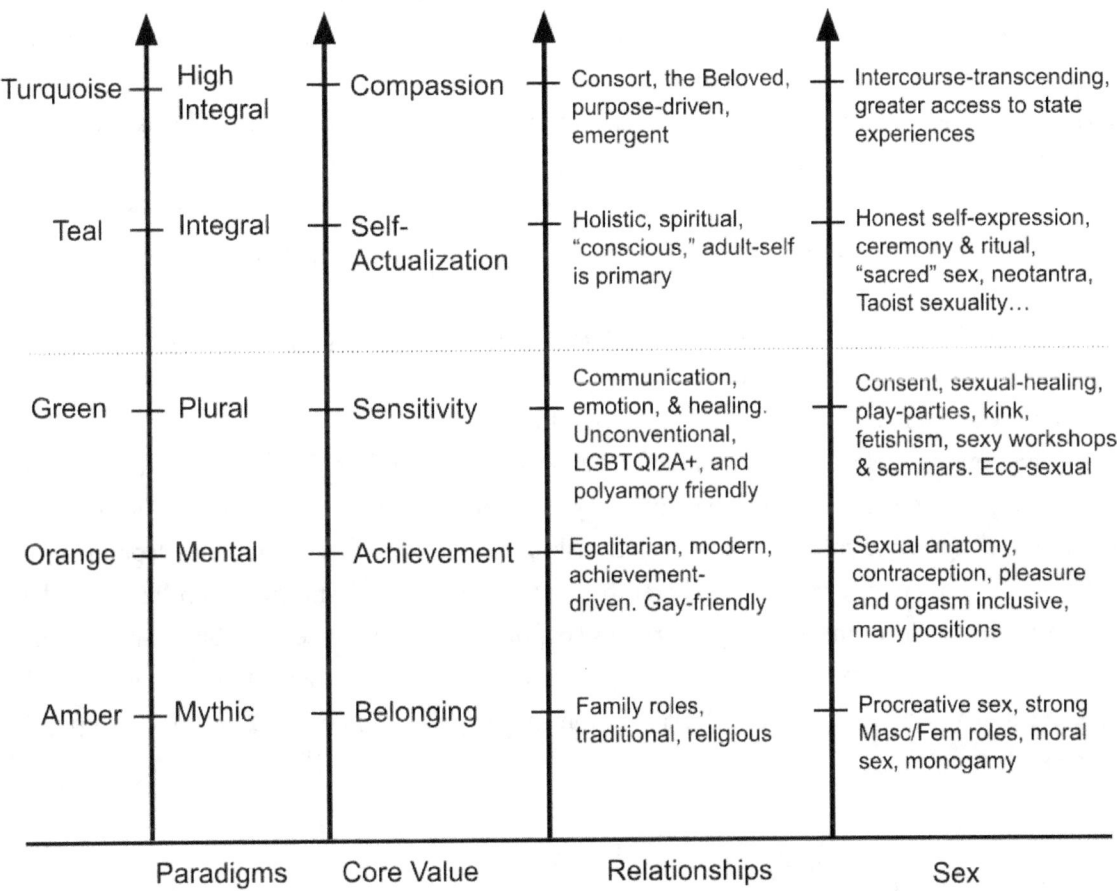

Figure 12.2 Paradigms of relationships and sex

Amber Relationships and Sex

Mythic/Traditional, Belonging

My relationship is focused on the unit of the couple, how I belong within that unit, and how that unit belongs within the larger social group. Social norms will have a heavy influence on how we relate. Because the core need at this paradigm is belonging, I have a strong sense of loyalty to my partner. My relationship is most likely monogamous and *till death do us part*—at least in intention, if not in fruition. This kind of relationship is often in service to raising a family with strong ties to my extended family, community, and religious institution. Traditional Western gender roles place the man as the dominant provider and the woman as the submissive caretaker. My relationship ascribes to chivalry, which is devotion steeped in gender roles at this paradigm (the postmodern deconstruction of chivalry relabels it *benevolent sexism*).[2] More generally, my relationship may be heavily influenced by morals and norms, for example being a "good husband," being a "good father," and so on.

My sex life may be primal and passionate. I have not disembodied into my intellect like the mental/ modern paradigm, so I may have a strong sex drive, though that can be mitigated by repressive sexual norms. Sex in this paradigm will likely have minimal variation: mostly missionary style. My partner and I participate in traditional masculine/directive and feminine/submissive polarity during sex. I adhere to social and moral taboos around sex. We may have sex with the lights off. I may adhere to sexual abstinence outside of marriage. Because of the sexual taboos, I don't talk about sex much with my partner or my peers. This may be accompanied by shame, dysfunctional sexual dynamics, and extramarital affairs. I may pursue partners and sex as an act of hunting or conquest.

The gifts of this paradigm include faithfulness, passion, commitment, and the stability to raise a family. My relationship is connected to ancestry, heritage, and culture. In this paradigm, I have full permission to inhabit a strong sexual expression of masculinity.

The shadows of this paradigm include repression, shame, and/or feeling trapped and stuck in a relationship. There may be minimal intimacy and little space for an authentic me to express. Because adhering to the role within my relationship is so strong, there may be codependence as I put the needs of my partner or the partnership ahead of my own. In American families, the relative isolation of the nuclear family unit perpetuates corporal punishment, sexual abuse, and trauma. A pathology of this paradigm is repression and phobia of nonnormative sexualities and genders. Due to the cultural restrictions on sexual exploration and expression, committed partnerships often become sexless.

Orange Relationships and Sex

Mental/Modern, Achievement

My relationship is focused on achievement and success. The careers of one or both partners may take up significant space in the relationship. The partnership may be adventure-focused, travel-focused, or centered on the success of the children. My relationship embraces modernity and liberal values. We hold the ideal of equality of power between me and my partner, even if this is not perfectly executed. Whereas relationships in the Mythic paradigm tend to be repressive of homosexuality, the Mental paradigm is inclusive of gay relationships and has more space for alternative relationship styles.

My sex life is a meaningful, but potentially minor part of my life. I enjoy good sex, and yet my life tends to be busy to the point where my partner and I rarely make time to invest and grow through sex. Alternatively, sex is a pleasurable hobby or pastime. The scientific focus of this paradigm means I have likely learned sexual anatomy and am pro-contraception. I am not bound by the same moral imperatives as the mythic paradigm so I am more likely to engage in casual sex and dating. Sex for pleasure and orgasm is more common and I am curious to experiment with many sexual positions and scripts.

The gifts of this paradigm include pragmatism, material prosperity, and permission to be myself and follow my life goals and dreams. The focus on equality in power, duties, and earnings between partners offers greater individual liberty and creativity to both partners in relationship—meaning less adherence to gender roles.

The shadows of this paradigm include emotional disconnection, lack of intimacy, shallowness, and relationships of convenience. Because achieving other goals may overshadow the relational and sexual connection, and because this structure is centered in the conceptual mind, there may be little or no sex in long-term relationships.

Green Relationships and Sex

Plural/Postmodern, Sensitivity

I recognize that I have inherited invisible privileges and biases through my cultural affiliations. I am doing my work to deconstruct the social conditioning and old paradigms of relating. This liberates me to explore new relationship models. My love life may be quite unconventional. I may have multiple partners. I may explore polyamory, relationship anarchy, open relationships, and sex parties—though these are by no means necessary. The more holistic perspective of this level opens up *compersion*, meaning happiness for my partner's happiness. Whereas the mental paradigm is gay friendly, plural welcomes the full LGBTQI2A+ rainbow.[3] At this level, I am focused on healing through relationships. I may be pursuing psychotherapy or coaching. I am likely studying trauma healing, attachment theory, and communication techniques like nonviolent communication.[4]

Sexually, I am likely exploring all my options. I may be into BDSM, kink, and fetishism. Play parties, sex toys, and fantasy roleplaying are all on the table. I am likely learning how to have consent and STI conversations.[5] Feminist sex, eco-sexuality, sexology, and sex work may enter my repertoire. This exploration will take me to workshops, seminars, and retreats to learn more about sex. I am likely to engage in sex as an act of healing. This paradigm undergoes a massive overhaul and redefinition of sex and relationship.

The gifts of this paradigm include personal and collective healing, improved communication, and broadening of sexual and relational frontiers. In addition, the new core value of sensitivity brings me deeper into my emotions, makes space for my partner's emotions, and opens the door for much deeper intimacy.

The pathologies of the plural paradigm generally stem from too much deconstruction or too much sensitivity. In deconstructing harmful sexual scripts, I may conclude that sex itself is harmful.

In deconstructing stereotypical genders, I may disconnect from gender entirely. There may be so many parts of myself that I can't locate a core self or my true desires. This can be profoundly disorienting and ungrounding. I may explore so many sexual options that I lose my authentic sexual self. While sexual liberation brings more diversity and frequency of sex, it often does so at the cost of intimacy. I may become deeply enrolled in the drama triangle.[6] I may become overly sensitive, fragile, or addicted to processing emotions. The cost of oversensitivity is that I lose my resilience and disconnect from strong passions because they're overwhelming or unsafe.

Teal Relationships and Sex

Integral, Self-Actualization

At integral, relationships and sexuality are powerful crucibles for self-actualization. Somewhere between plural and integral, I do the work to break free of codependent relating habits, and I become an individual in partnership. I learn how to be unapologetically myself. I speak my truth with kindness, even if it hurts my partner, even if it is uncomfortable for me. My relationships become tools for my growth and creative self-expression. Every encounter is an opportunity to expand into more of me. Relationship becomes an avenue for my core focus on self-actualization.

Integral is the first level where my *adult self* and my partner's *adult self* are both the primary psychological parts that we relate through. While individuals in earlier paradigms may relate from the adult self, it becomes a necessary step to arrive at integral in the relational developmental line. The adult self is the centered place within me that is capable, resourced, and mature. From here, I am able to stay connected to my love and the love I feel for my partner. I am responsive instead of reactive. Tier one relationships are characterized by adherence to roles and socialization or rebellion against those roles. In these earlier relationship paradigms, much of the turmoil and drama stems from my reenactment of past wounding by fragmented parts of the self (ex: I turn my partner into my mother). At integral, my adult self is directing my behavior most of the time. I am able to see the system that my fragmented parts create with my partner's fragmented parts, and together we're able to *step outside of the dysfunctional system.* I learn to take responsibility for my emotional triggers. As I do my healing work, my wounded parts transform into allies in my internal psychological system. My psyche becomes more whole. In the process of moving from plural to integral, I actively engage in trauma healing, attachment healing, and unwinding my limiting core beliefs. Beneath all of these distortions is the experience of *wholeness*, which now becomes the anchor of who I am and where I relate from.

Additionally, I now recognize *the organism* of my relationship. I experience my relationship as its own living entity with needs and desires, which itself can move into actualization and wholeness. My relationship becomes a container to share spirituality, embodiment, and earth connection: the relationship becomes a vehicle for ongoing evolution and awakening. Integral relationships are likely to move through cycles of death, birth, and transmutation, as the individual partners align to growth and change.

It is worth noting that transitioning a long-term relationship from first to second tier is every bit as monumental as for an individual to make the leap. When I find wholeness within myself and no longer source that in my partner, the historical reason for the relationship may die. If I have been using my partner as my therapist, parental figure, or savior and then I step beyond needing those roles, then my relationship will either dissolve or find a new mode of engagement. Similarly, if my fear of being alone has been keeping me in my relationship and then I heal that wound, I will either find a new reason to relate or become free to move on.

Generally, one partner makes the leap to integral first, and their increasing invitations for intimacy, growth, and actualization will present a crisis for the relationship. Either we grow together, or we grow apart. Crucially, the second partner must find their authentic desire to *self-actualize*. They cannot do it to save the relationship or please their partner—these motivations miss the very essence of self-actualization. At integral, I understand that my primary commitment within relationship is to my well-being and growth. I then work to craft my relationship in service to my and my partner's self-actualization.

Sex at integral spans a much vaster realm of experience. I learn the distinction between intimacy and closeness. True intimacy means sharing myself exactly as I am, across the full spectrum of emotions and internal parts. Lovemaking may bring me to grief, anger, pain, silliness, or joy—all of which are increasingly included from a place of ownership, not reaction or reenactment. I am now able to own my emotions without blaming or projecting them onto my partner. Sex is about getting real and bringing all of myself into it. The focus on orgasm, which is so strongly celebrated at plural (particularly female orgasms), may subside as we explore more subtle sexual realms. Sex now includes a spiritual dimension as higher states of consciousness become increasingly accessible. We may practice ceremony or ritual around sex. We may explore neo-tantra, Taoist sexual practices, or other forms of "sacred" sexuality.

> *Transcendent episodes during sex, however bizarre, resemble those recognized in the world's major spiritual traditions. In fact, except for the context (making love as opposed to meditating, praying, ingesting sacred medicine, or participating in ritual ceremonies), transcendent sexual experiences have exact counterparts in the shamanism of indigenous religions as well as in the mysticism of Christianity, Judaism, Islam, Hinduism, Buddhism, and Taoism.*
>
> —Jenny Wade[7]

As a sidenote, I am choosing to put quotes around "sacred" sexuality and "conscious" relationships, which are typical labels used at the integral level. In my view, all sex is sacred, and all relating is an expression of consciousness. Here at integral, however, I am beginning to recognize this sacredness and label my experience with these terms.

The gifts of this paradigm include the freedom to expand into my authentic self through partnership. I recognize more and more of my inherent wholeness and belonging, which releases my partner from filling those needs for me and enables me to relate from sovereignty. When both partners are aligned at this level, the relationship becomes a rapid growth and evolution dynamo.

The primary relational shadows of this paradigm are spiritual bypassing and spiritual materialism. I may identify so strongly with the light, joy, and pleasure that there is a repression of the darkness or wounds. I may develop a spiritual identity that places myself or my relationship above others. I may use my intense focus on evolution to turn my partner into a project for growth. As noted in the prior chapters, the emergent nature of integral means we are still discovering the pathologies and shadows of this paradigm.

Turquoise Relationships and Sex

High Integral, Compassion

The consort relationship is a form of partnership that prioritizes truth and realization over comfort and security. In this relationship, each partner functions as a sacred mirror to reveal the wounds,

withholds, and attachments of the other. I hold my partner with a level of devotion that I would hold toward a divine being—for, in truth, my partner is a divine being. The consort is my *other half* in the way that Buddhist deities are often pictured as a pair in embrace. The consort relationship may come online as early as plural/postmodern, and by high integral, it will be the primary focus of partnership. Here are the main agreements of the consort relationship:

Commitments for the Consort Relationship

1. I am taking care of myself.
2. I am showing up.
3. I am loving you exactly as you are.
4. I am aligning to truth.

At high integral, also called *ego aware*, I am dissolving the last vestiges of a separate egoic self. In relationship, this opens me to play with the duality of Self and other. I may experience the relationship as a transcendent third, which is known as *hieros gamos* or the Beloved. Surrendering into the organism of my relationship opens me into a larger realm of existence. Because so many of the constructs have been dissolved—not just socially, but psychologically and linguistically—relationships at high integral may defy definition and be highly emergent.

The devotional quality of a conscious relationship allows us to see the other not as other but as self. Then to open to that "other self" as beloved. In the devotional aspect of relationship, one sees one's beloved as the very essence of being.... When one sees in this manner, one sees that the other person doesn't have to be perfect in order to be perfect for you. And the nightmare of perfection that warps the pulchritude of another's exquisite heart drops away. One sees the other as a divine gift, a co-conspirator on the path toward the unspeakable enormity. More than just mind, greater than even the heart are lovers who care for each other without reservation, yet care for the Beloved even more.

—Stephen and Ondrea Levine[8]

Just as individuals in second tier tend to move into transformational professions, partnerships also orient toward making a difference in the world. This may happen either naturally or intentionally as an outpouring of the goodness that is being sourced through the relationship. First-tier relationships tend to be karmic, meaning they offer a crucible for each individual to do their healing work. At second tier, and especially by high integral, relationships are now both dharmic and karmic. A dharmic relationship is in active service to the liberation of others. The integral level recognizes the organism of the relationship as its own entity. Now at high integral, the relationship becomes purpose driven. Examples of this range from high-visibility couples who co-lead spiritual communities to the less public-facing couples whose thriving becomes a natural support and example for other couples and community members.

I think of sex at high integral as intercourse transcending. Lovemaking begins the moment I become present with my partner. It includes cooking our meal together, the dinner conversation, and the sunset walk. By the time we actually begin to physically touch each other, the eros has been flowing and evolving for hours. Intercourse is one beautiful and direct mode of entering into our shared experience. And the lovemaking doesn't end when intercourse ends—it carries through into dreamtime and picks up again the next morning. Sex ends when I disconnect my energy and consciousness from the shared space that my partner and I inhabit together. Intercourse is merely the physical expression of sex.

There is nothing like making love with the Beloved. Nothing like the boundaryless heart to make us edgeless and agile. The Beloved embraces old fears and strategies, dissolving lovers into oneness. In the shared body two aspects of the identical primal energy intertwine like a double helix. Our lovemaking decoding the genetics of form—meeting at the boundary of formlessness, love becomes the catalyst for creation. When the formless makes love in form, we are present at the Creation.

—Stephen and Ondrea Levine[9]

With even more access to higher realms and a truly transpersonal experience of reality looming on the horizon, sex becomes a spiritual doorway that I explore with my partner. Sex is neither higher nor lower than meditation, yoga, and breathwork. Rather, sex finds its place as a tool in the eleutheropoietic unfolding of self. I learn to experience the full range of state experiences through sex, from energy-body activation to full nondual union as the heart of the kosmos.

Prompts for Journaling and Discussion

For each romantic relationship in your past, which paradigm held that relationship?

In your friendships and family relationships, which paradigm holds that relationship?

For the sexual connections in your past and present, which paradigm holds that connection?

Notes

[1] Image: DALL.E-3, 2024.

[2] "Benevolent sexism is when someone advances a favorable attitude toward women, but it's actually rooted in sexism. In the world of dating it shows up when a man orders for a woman, refuses to ever let her pay, insists on walking on the side nearer the street, must lead when they walk in a crowded place, et cetera. This may seem normal, perhaps even justified, but the reason is never rooted in equality. The logic is rooted in an inequality that women require protection from men, but the result appears to be preferential treatment for women. Benevolent sexism is like misogyny with a wink. It may seem inoffensive, but it replenishes the well of sexism every time we do it." *For the Love of Men*, Plank.

[3] Lesbian, Gay, Bisexual, Transgender/Transsexual, Questioning/Queer, Intersex, Two-Spirited, Allied/Asexual/Aromantic/Agender.

[4] *Nonviolent Communication: A Language of Life*, Rosenburg.

[5] The terms *sexually transmitted diseases* (STDs) and *sexually transmitted infections* (STIs) may be used interchangeably. The conversation basics: The last time I was tested was . I was tested for , , and . The results of those tests was (positive/ negative). Since that test, I have had sexual partners that included the following activities . I (did/did not) have this STI conversation with each partner, and their status was .

[6] See chapter 8.

[7] *Transcendent Sex: When Lovemaking Opens the Veil*

[8] *Embracing the Beloved.*

[9] *Embracing the Beloved.*

| 13 |

The Archetypes

Figure 13.1 Minotaur in the labyrinth[1]

From the unconscious there emanate determining influences which, independently of tradition, guarantee in every single individual a similarity and even a sameness of experience, and also of the way it is represented imaginatively. One of the main proofs of this is the almost universal parallelism between mythological motifs, which, on account of their quality as primordial images, I have called archetypes.

—Carl Jung[2]

In the prior chapters, I covered states of consciousness and paradigms of consciousness, largely following the approach of integral philosophy. In this chapter, I'll examine the archetypes in depth. I'll begin by acknowledging the pitfalls of working with archetypes, which will then provide the foundation to understand why we care about the archetypes and indeed why they are essential for a well-functioning civilization. Along the way, I'll explore how to utilize the archetypes, their relationship with initiation and sacred space, and the specific archetypal forms of the psyche that constitute the structure of this workbook series.

The archetypes are morphic fields embedded in the causal realm of consciousness. By *morphic field*, I mean an organizing pattern of influence that remembers all past instances and evolves by accretion. These are grooves in the fabric of consciousness. The causal realm exists above the subtle realm of thoughtforms and biofield energy, and below the pure witness realm of unitary consciousness. The causal realm holds the basic building blocks and formative structures of the kosmos, including the archetypes.

There are actually two categories of archetypes: *causal* and *evolutionary*. The causal archetypes are the structures that were required at the moment of the big bang in order for the kosmos to blossom forth in this specific form. These include forms, ideals, colors, and numbers. These causal archetypes are not the topic of this chapter.

The evolutionary archetypes are what we more commonly associate with the word *archetype*, and it is these I will be focusing on. Evolutionary archetypes are the patterns of meaning and identity that developed together with humans over time. They are universal, undefinable, and unbounded aspects of consciousness that live in our collective. These archetypes are also called symbols, and I'll use both words interchangeably.

Carl Jung noticed that the same symbols arise in individuals across all cultures and times. These symbols share the same deep meanings as those found in myth and religion, again across all cultures and times. Therefore, we have reason to believe that there is a universal repository of symbols that all humans are able to access. The symbols are not held solely within any individual's psyche or even in any one culture. They exist in the collective unconscious. Whereas underlying symbols are universal, the myths and deities are specific. Individuals and cultures interpret and name these symbols through their unique contexts, languages, and cultural lenses as myths.

Pitfalls of Myths and Archetypes

1. Myth as Social Power

For starters, it is important to recognize that myths and archetypes provide the socially order-ing and power structure of the mythic/traditional paradigm of consciousness, outlined in Chapter 8. In this paradigm, the myths describe the one transcendent truth. Myths are the carriers of that truth, and they explain morality and salvation. Crucially, it is the shared mythology that unifies me with others in my in-group as a chosen people. The use of myths in this way is a developmentally appropriate tool to move beyond the limits of the magical/tribal paradigm. Myths enable humans to organize in large groups harmoniously by instilling a moral and social order.

For a large segment of people in the mythic/traditional paradigm, myths convey literal truths about reality. For example, God literally created the world, animals, and humans in seven days. Because these myths are taken concretely to convey a unique path to salvation beyond this life, they have historically led to some of humanity's darkest conflicts. If we look across all paradigms today, both in Western civilization and throughout the globe, the mythic/traditional paradigm holds the largest number of people.

This means, if I am going to adopt archetypes and their culture-specific myths on my path of personal growth, I need to be responsible with how I share them and how they may be interpreted through the lenses of other paradigms. If I adopt a mythology that appears to be at odds with or threatening to the mythology of *true believers* in other systems, I have every reason to expect hostility coming my way.

Moreover, myth-holders wield power. By becoming the sole conduit for access to this salvation-giving mythology, those who carry the myths make themselves an indispensable authority. Operat-ing without accountability from external sources, myth-holders predictably insert their individual agendas into the social system. History has shown time and again that myth-holders concentrate power and misuse it. This is a legitimate concern particularly for men's movements operating today within the mythic/traditional paradigm, like Promise Keepers, for example.

However, all levels beyond the mythic/traditional paradigm access truth and social ordering from more complex and holistic sources than myths. Approaching men's work from the integral paradigm, as is the case in this workbook, welcomes the value of archetypes from an internal determination of truth. Centering in the wholeness of self, I am interconnecting my truths with the myriad of social and religious truths throughout human history. At integral, both morality and truth are sourced from within and then interwoven out into culture. So the danger of myths and power abuse at this level is drastically reduced.

2. Myths Support Hegemonic Masculinity

Another argument that is essential for any approach to men's work to address is whether the organizing mythology is either subtly or overtly perpetuating hegemonic masculinity. There is a valid argument that if the archetypes are accessed through myths that emerged from misogynistic religions and societies, then aligning ourselves with those myths perpetuates these misogynistic values in us. In his book, *Numen, Old Men*, Joseph Gelfer makes the following observation:

> *Instead of innocently bearing witness to the experiences of men in what might otherwise be perceived as an overly feminine spiritual economy, masculine spirituality actually promotes an all-too-familiar patriarchal spirituality. This patriarchal spirituality encourages a certain type of hegemonic masculinity that dominates women and subordinate masculinities; it does this chiefly by defining masculinity by archetypes, revising the definition of and depoliticising patriarchy, and encouraging what it perceives to be an authentic masculinity via the adoption of sex role theory.*
>
> —Joseph Gelfer[3]

In particular, the archetypes of the King and the Warrior can be adopted by men as the impetus to wield power over others and act violently. Even if the *intent* is to access masculine power and wield it for good, Gelfer points out that the *effect* can be a strengthening of hegemonic masculinity. Sylvia Walby identifies six relational realms where patriarchy is enacted: housework, paid work, the state, violence, sexuality, and culture.[4] If, for example, a man claiming his Warrior increases inequality within any of these spheres, then he is contributing to hegemonic masculinity. Again, Gelfer:

> *Members of the mythopoetic and various Christian men's movements can be puzzled when they are charged with being patriarchal because it is not necessarily their intention for their projects to manifest any of those six aspects of patriarchy. However, the net effect of building masculinity around, for example, archetypes or servant leadership is a tendency towards those six aspects of patriarchy. We are asked by these men, in all sincerity, to accept their warrior identification and claims to servant leadership with the gentlemanliness with which it is intended, not the despotism to which it can succumb.*
>
> —Joseph Gelfer[5]

This is an argument that I wish every leader in men's work would sit with and digest. If the myths that we use are violent, oppressive, and misogynistic, then the culture we are creating is perpetuating hegemonic masculinity.

Gelfer's conclusion is that archetypes are domineering and simplistic and therefore must be avoided by any worthy version of masculine spirituality. In contrast, when I contemplate this risk, I feel *more compelled* to understand the use of archetypes in men's work.

In the self-worldview that I am inviting you into throughout this workbook, the archetypes are universal patterns of meaning. They constellate throughout all layers and levels of consciousness. Archetypes hold the core symbolic meanings of masculinities, and therefore, robust men's work and masculine spirituality *must* engage with them. To deny the archetypes is to relegate them into the shadow of the unconscious. This would create more separation and further empower the wounded, violent, and oppressive expressions of them.

Granted: men's work to date has failed to fully integrate the archetypes in life-affirming ways. But this is exactly what the emerging *integral* paradigm does best. Integral has the capacity to *include* the valuable wisdom from mythic/traditional spiritualities while *transcending* the oppressive social structures of hegemonic masculinity. It does this by digesting postmodernist arguments like Gelfer's. But instead of deconstructing into oblivion, integral sources in wholeness. As I shared in the introduction, our heart's natural and innate experience of masculinity comes first. The fact that I have direct, nonconceptual experiences of masculinity signifies that it is something real. Because it arises in my heart, it is sacred just as all of life is sacred. Integral re-members us into the sacred world. From this sacred core within each of us, the true aspects of masculinity distill away from the wounds and distortions. Similarly, the archetypes are inherently morally neutral. They carry the potential for both darkness and light. At core, the archetypes are sources of unconditioned power and their effect is determined by how we humans are able to channel them into our lives. According to Jungian psychology, when we are unconscious of the archetypes, they rule us. As we *individuate*, we liberate ourselves by entering into conscious relationships with these powerful energies.

> *For whatever the source of masculine abuse of power, it is our responsibility as contemporary men to understand it and to develop the emotional and spiritual resources to end it. The issue should never be how to get rid of the urge for power, masculine or feminine. The real issue is how to steward it, and how to channel our other instincts along with it into life-giving and world-building activities.*
>
> —Moore and Gillette[6]

Let's make this experiential and immediate. Look within yourself to see whether there are four parts to the psyche: thinking, acting, feeling, and being. My claim is that these broad categories cover most of our experience. Now, when you are experiencing gender, either the masculine, feminine, or androgyne, look to see whether you are inhabiting one of these four quadrants: Magician, Warrior, Lover, and Monarch. I often pose this question at the beginning of a men's retreat: When is your masculinity *not* expressing through one of these four archetypes? They're not perfect, but they do cover a majority of the psychic landscape. I use these archetypes because they represent universal patterns of meaning that we all can access. I use them because when I speak to other men through these symbols, it resonates. Archetypes give us the language of gender.

Yes, there is shadow and distortion in the culture-specific myths humans use to interpret the underlying universal archetypes. The fact that myths and archetypes are so pervasive and influential therefore becomes a call to action. It is up to us to engage with them, to heal through them, and to integrate them. Through this process of *individuation* we come into balance where we are able to center in the Self, while receiving the powerful life-giving and ordering energies of the archetypes. This understanding is a call to embrace the archetypes. It levies on us the responsibility to meet our shadows through the archetypes. Again, Robert Moore:

> *When we talk about the sacred masculine and the masculine spirituality that's related to it, there are two components we need to discuss. The first component is for a man to get connected to the power, to the great power that he needs for life, that his family needs him to have, that his community needs him to have, that the world needs him to have. And second, masculine spirituality is about what a man needs to do to keep his power from turning demonic and destructive in his personality and life, in his family, in his community, and in the world. That's what masculine spirituality is about, two parts: A man has to connect to the power and then figure out how to keep that power from destroying him and his world.[7]*

Working with masculine archetypes personally landed for me in my experiences at retreats that shepherded initiation within a container of sacred space. In these contexts, I was able to tap into the powerful currents of the archetypes and feel them for myself. Having gone through the initiation experience, the potency of archetypes is a lived reality. This is how my approach separates from the academic perspective. Academically, this Jungian school of thought has issues around perpetuating misogyny. Therefore, let's look for a more socially cleaned-up gender theory to align to. This makes sense from the academic lens. Experientially however, the archetypes are here whether we like them or not, and as I will discuss below, they are key ingredients for a healthy, well-functioning civilization. *Denying* them is irresponsible, at best.

3. The Pre/Trans Fallacy

The next pitfall is known as the *pre/trans fallacy*. Here is the basic idea: from my rational perspective, when I encounter nonrational practices, I must distinguish whether that material emerges from a more basic prerational paradigm, or whether it constellates a more advanced transrational paradigm. Reductionism is the tendency to dismiss advanced spiritual practices as meaningless superstition. Elevationism, on the other hand, is the tendency to place basic spiritual practices on a high pedestal. In his book, *Sex, Ecology, Spirituality*, Ken Wilber spends a chapter debunking both Joseph Cambell and Carl Jung's positions, arguing that myths and archetypes are not, in fact, useful for transrational spiritual development. "Beyond mythology is reason," Wilber states, "and beyond both is Spirit." In his view, myths are prerational and should not be elevated to transrational spirituality. Here is Wilber:

> *The Jungian archetypes are for the most part the magico-mythic motifs and "archaic images"– they should really be called "prototypes"–collectively inherited by you and by me from past stages of development, archaic holons now forming part of our own compound individuality (they come from below up, not from above down). And coming to terms with these archaic holons—befriending and making conscious and differentiating/ integrating these prototypes—is a useful endeavor, not because they are our transrational future, but because they are our prerational past. I agree entirely with Jung on the necessity of differentiating and integrating this archaic heritage; I do not believe that this has much to do with genuine mystical spirituality.*

—Ken Wilber[8]

Myths are stories we use to understand self and kosmos. As an interpretive lens for reality, they are more basic than logic and reason. The rational mind has a more complex, more holistic method to understand self and kosmos, namely, logic and the scientific method. Advancing into the integral paradigm brings *vision logic*, which is a transrational lens for reality.[9]

Given that myths and archetypes arose from our archaic past, is there a meaningful place for them at the cutting edge of consciousness? Wilber, and integral philosophers in general, have said no.[10] My answer is yes. In order to address this criticism, I will first need to lay out my understanding of the archetypes. At the end of this chapter, I'll circle back around to how the archetypes offer benefits for "genuine mystical spirituality."

***

Before moving on, there are two related pitfalls to acknowledge. The first is that most myths and archetypes refer to common experiences, not experiences of realization. The archetypes are, by their nature, the footprints of humanity. Most humans, most of the time are not accessing nonduality or primary religious experiences. Thus, most of our myths and symbols are common ones, not spiritual ones. Consider the majority of the material in *Grimm's Fairy Tales* or *Aesop's Fables*. These are moral stories for everyday life. The second related pitfall is that simply because the archetypes are *collective* does not mean they are enlightened or enlightening. The collective unconscious is indeed vast and powerful, but the archetypes include both darkness and light. Myths carry our collective shadows, suffering, and distortions. There is nothing inherently *more spiritual* about them simply because they are collective. These two pitfalls point to a need for skillful use with archetypes. There are indeed myths about spiritual realization that I can use if that is my aim. Which myths I use and how I employ them matters.

That said, now let's take a look at why I think we should care about archetypes.

Archetypal Maturation

So far, I've explored two distinct developmental pathways: *awakening* through states of consciousness, and *evolving* through the paradigms. Now I'll introduce the third distinct pathway, which is *maturing* through the archetypal roles. On the first pathway, accessing higher states of consciousness entails an expansion of awareness. On the second pathway, I evolve through paradigms by developing more sophisticated and comprehensive worldviews. Here on the third path, I mature through archetypes by integrating higher orders of sovereignty. From child to adolescent, to adult, to elder, we develop through increasingly more sovereign archetypes as humans.

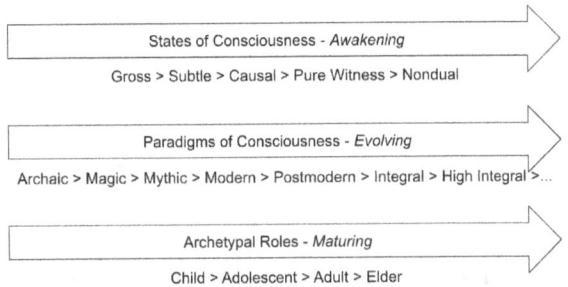

Figure 13.2 Three axes of development in consciousness

The *archetypal role* is the pattern of meaning that identifies me and my place in the human life cycle. Each role carries an identity, empowerments, and a set of responsibilities for my function within my society and ecosystem. I move from one archetypal role to the next via the process of initiation. Within rites of passage, I am able to access sacred space and transform my identity from one archetypal role to the next.

The maturation process is linked to physical age, but not determined by it. I do not automatically advance archetypes as I get older. Aging unlocks the possibility to progress but is not sufficient in itself to provide the transition. Looking around, I observe many adults today who have personalities that are still primarily children or adolescents. Arrested maturation can happen when either I don't receive initiation into the next phase, or my current phase becomes so stunted or wounded that it cannot provide the foundation for the next phase to build upon. Like the paradigms, these archetypal phases of maturation form a growth holarchy—a staircase of progression where higher levels transcend and include those below.

In Western culture, these roles are gendered into either masculine or feminine archetypes. Masculinity uses the archetypal progression from the boy to the hero, to the man, and the old man. Women progress through the girl, the maiden/heroine, the woman, and the crone. As far as I'm aware, trans and queer folks do not have distinct archetypal pathways. Rather, the androgyne uses both pathways, or sometimes one and sometimes the other, or neither. From my perspective, the lack of a unique archetypal progression is part of the struggle of invisibility for these folks in our culture. We don't have language, roles, and archetypes for the androgyne established collectively—though one could make the case that these pathways have been slowly emerging over the last forty years in the West. Other cultures including Hawaiian, the Dagara of West Africa, and the Lakota, Quechan, and Navajo, all include roles and symbols for the androgyne in their collectives.

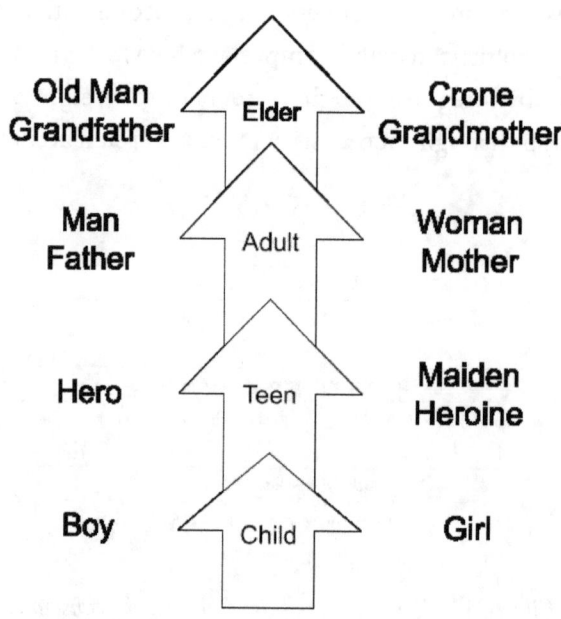

Figure 13.3 Masculine and feminine maturation

It is worth noting that all archetypes are available to all people, and just because there is a normative pathway does not mean it will be every individual's path. As morphic fields that have been laid down by our culture over thousands of years, these are best understood as the maturation habits of individuals in Western civilization, not immutable laws.

Let's consider the roles, powers, and responsibilities of this developmental ladder. The child grows through pre-egoic stages of development, and their identity is very much in formation throughout childhood. The role of the child is to play, explore, learn, and grow. The powers bestowed to children are limited, and the responsibilities are equally minimal.

In adolescence, the heroic ego or emerging ego grants the first true autonomy. The ego naturally works for its own growth and self-becoming. Here is what it means to have a healthy ego: I know who I am, I am in relationship with my shadows and younger parts, I am able to set clear boundaries and ask for what I want, I take care of myself, and I have agency to follow my desires and dreams. There is so much focus within spiritual circles on ego transcendence or ego death, and often it comes at the expense of cultivating a healthy ego. In my view, the ego is a required foundation for higher levels of development, so the growth process entails investing in the well-being and balancing of my ego.

The initiation into adulthood happens through *the willing sacrifice*. It is the arrival of the Monarch (i.e., the King or Queen). On the masculine path, the hero becomes a man and on the feminine path, the maiden/heroine becomes a woman. We may initially think that the rational mind, the ego, is what rules adulthood. This is a confusion we hold from living in an immature, adolescent society. When examining cultures with intact rites of passage, adulthood represents a step into trans-egoic identity. In true adulthood, I mature into an understanding of self as an interdependent member of society, ecosystem, and spirit. Initiation bestows recognition of my soul-identity, together with my service, or dharma, for this life. Bill Plotkin calls this the *Soul Initiation*:

> *Your personal development is no longer your primary concern – at least not the way it was when you were a child or student, as an Explorer, Thespian, or Wanderer. Now, every day, you are keenly mindful that you live on the same boat as all other Earth creatures; you all float or sink together. The evolving life of the collective – the more-than-human community – matters as much to you now as your individual trajectory because, after all, they are inseparable. You are now more an agent for the Mystery—for soul and spirit —than for your narrowly defined self.*
> —Bill Plotkin[11]

The transition from the heroic ego of adolescence into the soul identity of adulthood is a profound shift that needs to be understood. As I move into the soul self, the ego remains operational as the organizer and manager of sensory inputs and tasks. What shifts is the seat of sovereignty. When my ego is sovereign, my actions prioritize the growth and well-being of my egoic identity foremost.

At this transition, I recognize a larger, more expansive self: my soul self. This is the me that existed before I was born and will continue after I die. This is the me that intuitively knows my life path. It is the voice that tells me, "If I don't take this leap, I'll regret it for the rest of my life." As my ego comes to recognize my soul self, I choose to braid my egoic will into the larger will of my soul. I put my narrow ego interests aside and work toward something larger. I begin to act from my soul's intuitive knowing—and this is what I mean by shifting the seat of sovereignty.

Most men who have matured into manhood know when and how they became a man. I'll share two stories here. The moment I became a man was a sexual encounter in my early thirties. I had been dating a new woman for two months and was falling deeply in love with her. At this time, we had been having sex for about two weeks—it was still very new and exciting. She joined me at a festival where I was presenting. I had just facilitated a breathwork ceremony for a large group of participants. Happy to be complete with my commitments, my new love and I hiked back into the woods where we found a secluded stream. We went skinny dipping. One thing led to another and we were about to make love. However, I wasn't able to have an erection. Whatever the reasons, my body wasn't available for sex. Normally, I would have hidden this by shifting the focus onto pleasuring her. But not this time. I slowed down and shared what was happening for me. Instead of shaming myself, I chose kindness. Instead of performing, I chose vulnerability. I have a very clear memory where I am laying on my back in the mud by the stream and my lover is kneeling between my legs. She is holding my soft cock with both hands and gazing into my eyes with unconditional love. In this moment, the adolescent within me who would try to prove himself and win over the pretty girl gave way to a grander, more mature aspect of my adult self to step into sovereignty. This is the moment I became a man.

The second story is about a friend of mine. He's a remarkable human. He was a successful businessman, married, had kids, retired, and became a grandfather. In his free time, he enrolled in an intensive psychotherapy training, which is how I met him. This man decided to attend a men's retreat that I was facilitating. Over the course of the retreat, he connected with brotherhood and an authentic version of masculinity that had always been missing. In the integration circle at the end of the retreat, he was proclaiming through tears of joy, "I finally became a man." Despite all the achievements, life passages, and healing work he had done, it wasn't until he entered an initiatory container with other men that he was able to receive the archetypal upgrade into manhood.

After adulthood comes initiation into elderhood and the sovereign center of the Self. I call this initiation *succession* because here the adult Monarch steps back from active leadership to focus on mentorship of the younger generations as an elder. On the ladder of sovereignty, the heroic-ego emerges from a pre-egoic childhood. The ego, in turn, forms the foundation for the soul self in adulthood, which eventually becomes the foundation for the Self as the next sovereign center in elderhood.

The Self is the totality of the psyche, which includes the ego, the shadows, the archetypes, and everything in the collective unconscious. The Self represents the experience of wholeness within the psyche across higher consciousness, waking consciousness, and subconsciousness. Individuating into the Self is, by all accounts, a very difficult process. Few people make the journey. All of my exiled shadows need to feel safe enough to come into the light to be loved and integrated. My egoic self needs to enter into service to the larger entity of the Self—this involves layers and layers of letting go of control. The forces of the unconscious are vastly more powerful than the ego. In meeting these forces, I get humbled. The individuation process advances not because my ego wants or directs it. Rather, it happens to the degree that my ego surrenders into the larger intelligence of the Self, which individuates in its own time, and in its own way.

In addition to a larger identification with the Self, initiation into elderhood brings with it empowerment and responsibilities. Elders act as a repository of cultural wisdom, they are the bridges to the unseen realms and the ancestors, and they administer the rites of passages for younger members of the community.

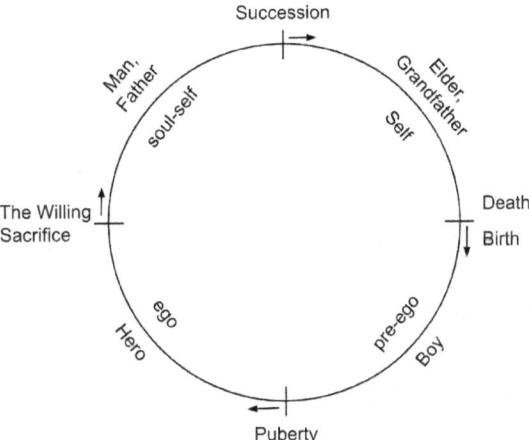

Figure 13.4 The masculine life cycle with archetypal roles and initiations

In summary, the masculine path moves through the archetypal roles of the Boy, the Hero, the Man, and the Elder. These archetypal roles position me on the human life cycle. Each archetypal role carries its own identity, empowerment, and set of responsibilities within society and ecosystem. Each transition is marked by an initiation, and it is to this initiatory process that we will now turn.

Prompts for Journaling and Discussion

When did you become an adolescent—an archetypal hero? What marked that occasion?

When did you become an adult—an archetypal man? What marked that occasion?

How do you recognize your soul self?

How do you understand your dharma, or path, in this life?

Sacred Space and Initiation

Figure 13.5, Rosa Celeste: Beatrice and Dante gaze upon the highest heaven.[12]

It is impossible to overemphasize the paradox represented by every hierophany [i.e., sacred revelation], even the most elementary. By manifesting the sacred, any object becomes something else, yet it continues to remain itself, for it continues to participate in its surrounding cosmic milieu. A sacred stone remains a stone; apparently (or, more precisely, from the profane point of view), nothing distinguishes it from all other stones. But for those to whom a stone reveals itself as sacred, its immediate reality is transmuted into a supernatural reality. In other words, for those who have a religious experience all nature is capable of revealing itself as cosmic sacrality. The cosmos in its entirety can become a hierophany.

—Mircea Eliade[13]

Humans experience two distinct modes of reality: *ordinary space* and *sacred space.* Ordinary space corresponds to waking consciousness where objects are permanent, time moves linearly, and the universe is understandable through rational thought. In sacred space, all bets are off. Reality is highly mutable, time may collapse into a timeless now or we may visit the past or future, and logic no longer applies. The Greeks distinguished two types of time: *chronos* is ordinary time, and *kairos* is significant time. Ordinary space/time is where we carry out the relative, relational aspects of our lives: we work, we eat, we run errands, and so on. Sacred space/time is transcendent, absolute, and transformational. It is where we experience noetic truth and unconditional love.

To understand how sacred space is formed in human consciousness, let's take a detour to consider how living systems emerge from physical systems. The second law of thermodynamics states that entropy is always increasing. What this means is that each closed system will naturally move toward increasing disorder until it reaches a state of thermal equilibrium. In more technical language, thermal equilibrium is an "attractor" for nonequilibrium states.

But when we look at living systems, they maintain themselves in an ordered state far from equilibrium. This is called homeostasis. There is a different attractor at play. Living systems are dynamic (they resist equilibrium) and they are self-ordering (they circumvent entropy). This dynamic self-ordering has been formally described by systems theorists in what are called *dissipative structures*.[14] In sufficiently complex systems, far from equilibrium, there are sources of stability and order and it is in these places that biological systems emerge from purely physical systems.

Returning now to our primary topic, in ordinary space, psychic entropy is always increasing. The ordinary world is in a constant process of running itself down and deconstructing itself. It is moving toward the psychic equivalent of thermal equilibrium. Sacred spaces, on the other hand, are the regenerative, ordering, meaning-giving structures that exist far from equilibrium. Sacred space is a dissipative structure in human consciousness.

In sacred space, we access *the center*, which is the fixed point upon which the kosmos is created. Systems theorists would call the center an *attractor*. The center is absolute. It is the source of meaning and purpose in life. It is through the center that we access the life-giving and ordering qualities of higher consciousness. From the center, the collective power of the archetypes radiates, the grace of Spirit descends, and the abundance of Source pours through.

Ordinary space has no access to the center. Instead, ordinary space naturally moves toward disorientation, meaninglessness, chaos, and confusion: maximum entropy.

> *When human beings cannot find the center, they fall into Chaos. That chaos has different forms. It can be a cold chaos. You've all been depressed. You've all been without energy, a cold chaos of the wasteland. Or if you don't know where the Center is, you can have a hot chaos, where you've got a lot of energy banging off the walls and lighting you up like a Christmas tree, but it's making your life crazy. It's destroying your world. Before you find that Center, you either have cold or hot chaos in some way, and there's no space in the world that is habitable.*
>
> —Robert Moore[15]

In Jungian terms, the center is the Self, which is the organizing psychic totality beyond the ego. This is symbolized as the center point of a circle in mandalas and religious art.

Figure 13.6 The Wheel of Fortune, Rider-Waite tarot

In sacred space, the full spectrum of states of consciousness becomes accessible.[16] It is here that I encounter primary religious experience—generally reported as the most meaningful and important experiences of our lives. Research has shown that more time clocked in higher states accelerates one's growth through paradigms and into structure states of consciousness.[17] Through sacred space, I enter into naked contact with the archetypes. Because the archetypes are transpersonal, unbounded morphic fields, they offer a limitless supply of vitality and wisdom for me to tap into. Finally, by touching the center of sacred space, I locate and connect to my center, both within myself and in the kosmos.

In order to access sacred space, I must move away from the equilibrium of normal life and into nonlinear mystical realms. I undergo a journey to access the sacred. In this journey, I am stripped of

my normal identities and personalities. I enter into a dangerous and unfamiliar world where I have very little power or control. As I surrender and offer myself to these larger forces, I am transformed. This frequently takes the form of a psychological death and rebirth. I emerge on the other side of this experience elevated to a new level of empowerment. I mature. Eventually, I journey back to my familiar landscape and reenter ordinary time. This process of transformation though sacred space is called *initiation*.

Initiation is also known as the rite of passage or the hero's journey. The process of initiation follows a similar structure across all human societies and is familiar to all of us through our myths and stories. The process of initiation is a universal symbol. There are three phases to the process: the call, the ordeal, and the return.

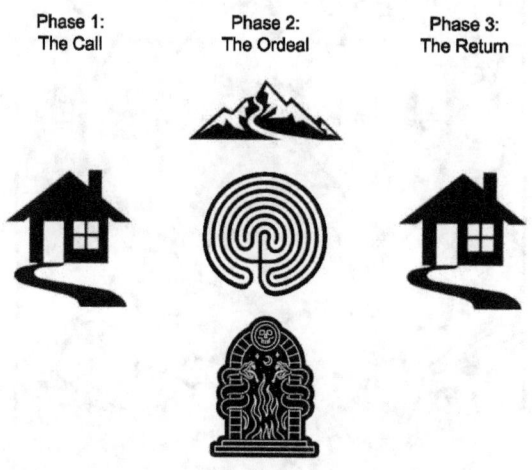

Figure 13.7 Phases of initiation

The first phase is *the call*. I begin in ordinary time and with my normal identity. I inhabit my *life-world*. Then I hear *the call*. I have come to a place where my psyche needs to die, dissolve, or re-organize itself in order to continue growing. The Self is calling the ego to its next phase. Whatever I've been doing with my life has become stale and old and it's time for something new. This need for change may present itself as a crisis, depression, anxiety, or dissatisfaction.

The call is always scary because the call is always into the unknown. It requires me to give up my comfy, secure life-world. Initiations lead into the death of identities, so we have good cause to fear them:

> *It is actually very scary once you get into this process, as if it is Good Friday and you don't know about the Resurrection. We like to think that Jesus knew about the resurrection in advance, and all the disciples too, but the fact is, the archetypal nature of this process is, that before a needed transformation no one knows how it will turn out.*
>
> —Robert Moore[18]

Sometimes I am thrust into the initiation without a choice—for example, the sudden death of a family member. Other times I hear the call and am free to choose. Because the call is scary and I tend to resist change, I may avoid this calling. Joseph Campbell termed this *the tyrant holdfast,* in which my ego clings to safety and instead drives for self-aggrandizement.[19] The imperatives of the call then become louder and stronger.

In the biblical myth of Jonah and the whale, the Lord calls Jonah to preach his message. Jonah refuses and instead flees by booking passage on a boat. The Lord causes a storm to rise up so violently that the ship is likely to be destroyed. At this point, Jonah confesses to the crew that the storm is due to his avoidance. Jonah ran from the call until it became utterly unavoidable. Crucially, at this point he surrenders to his fate. In order to save the ship, Jonah is cast overboard into the sea. He is swallowed by a whale where he enters his initiation. Jumping from the known into the unknown takes us into the second phase of initiation: *the ordeal.*

In order to move from ordinary space into sacred space, I must cross a threshold. Crossing over is no small feat. I must undergo a process of *disenchantment* where I am stripped of my possessions, identities, and familiar environment. I am put into a state of submission and humiliation before vastly larger forces. Jonah being thrown into the ocean during a violent storm is an appropriate image. Dismemberment and death (psychological or otherwise) are often the price we pay to enter sacred space. In many cultures this process involves physical wounding or scarring.

There are three archetypal pathways in the ordeal of initiation, which correspond to the three gendered high archetypes. The masculine path leads to the apex above, the feminine path leads to the void below, and the androgynous path leads to the horizon outward (fig. 13.7). Paradoxically, each of these extremes provides access to the center. Take another look at *figure x* in the introduction for an illustration of these three pathways in relationship to the center. An important point: even though the pathway is connected to a high gendered archetype, individuals of any gender can traverse each path. Continuing with our example of Jonah, he is thrown from the familiar human structure of the boat, down into the sea. Water is a symbol of the unconscious. From there he is swallowed by a whale and taken down into the depths of the ocean for three days. Eventually, the whale rises again and spits Jonah back onto land. This initiatory path is the feminine journey downward into the void.

Let's consider a few more examples. On the masculine path, Moses and Mohammed meet the Divine on the mountain top, Sleeping Beauty meets the witch and pricks her finger in the highest room of the tower, and Black Elk ascends into the heavens for his vision. On the feminine path, Inanna and Persephone descend into the underworld, Little Red Riding Hood is eaten by a wolf, and Dante's *Descent* is led by Virgil into the hell realms. The androgynous path is accessed laterally (neither ascending nor descending) through a process of disorientation. Theseus enters the labyrinth and Hansel and Gretel get lost in the woods. This initiation is also physically symbolized by dismemberment, as with Dionysus and Osiris. One may also cross the androgyne's threshold through a mirror or portal—Narcissus dives into his reflection in a pool, and Alice enters sacred space *through the looking glass.*

Sacred space cannot be located on any map. It is heaven, hell, or limbo. It is the mountain peak, the womb/tomb/cocoon, and the labyrinth. Strange characters inhabit this space. Time is warped. It is a liminal realm of magic, myth, and legend. In psychological terms, sacred space is a *secured-symbolizing field* in which I am held in a strong container, I meet symbols and archetypes directly, and I am able to be transformed.[20] Within sacred space, I journey to the center of the kosmos, known as the *axis mundi*.[21] This is the organizing, life-giving, center point.

At the center, I meet my unconscious directly. The normal repression and control of my ego have been taken offline. Neurologically, we can say that the *default-mode network* in the brain deactivates within sacred space.[22] As an interconnected network in the brain, the default-mode network interprets reality into a coherent picture and holds my identity. With this function greatly diminished, other parts of my psyche open up. In order for this to happen, "me" in the ordinary sense enters into a state of submission. In sacred space, my shadows become unrepressed and look to integrate into waking consciousness. It is here that I encounter the *epiphany*, the Self, the mystical, and the Divine.

At the center, two things happen: I am remade and the world is re-created. After death, dismemberment, or total humiliation, I enter the process of rebirth, resurrection, and remembering (literally: re + member). In the return to life, I am elevated to a more mature, powerful, and expansive station. I advance to a new archetypal role. My identity changes to something new.

The outer landscape is similarly transformed. After destruction, dissolution, or engulfment in chaos, the creation myth of the kosmos is reenacted and the realm is restored to glory. This is known as the *eternal return*.[23] It represents a reestablishment of the divine order. Mythologically, the hero saves the world from destruction.

The third phase of initiation is *the return*, where I make the journey home. Here, I must cross the threshold from sacred space back to ordinary space. Exiting sacred space can be every bit as perilous and challenging as entering it. For example, Inanna is pursued by demons on her ascent out of the underworld. In this phase, the egoic self comes back online. My focus is on integrating my new empowerments and identity. I return with more maturity, agency, and wholeness. At the end of the journey, the hero returns with the *healing salve* to the village so that all may benefit.

These three phases form a universal pattern. The process of initiation follows these phases across cultures and religions. In this sense, initiation is itself a universal archetype. This illustrates the collective intelligence of human consciousness to undergo transformation. Robert Moore has argued that there is a "universal human need for sacred space." Without sacred space, we disconnect from life itself and the result is suffering and death.

> *Our species has evolved to the point where we either must continue to provide conscious, creative, and responsible rituals of life that serve the maturation and healing of all its people, or face the alternative of unconscious and destructive participation in rituals of personal, social, and global death.*
>
> —Robert Moore[24]

Each paradigm of consciousness has its own relationship with sacred space. Take a moment and turn back to figure 9.6 where I illustrated how each paradigm experiences the sacred. For folks living in the magical paradigm, the sacred world is reality. In indigenous villages, rituals are part of the daily rhythm of life.[25] In the mythic/traditional paradigm, access to the sacred becomes the domain of the religious caste within the organized religion. Lay people generally have no direct access to the sacred. The mental/modern paradigm refuses the sacred on principle. Plural/postmodernism is largely focused on humanitarian and cultural aspects of religion. So while the sacred is acknowledged, it is not centered. And then at integral, we have the *monumental leap* that ushers in a return of the sacred as a primary value.

The vast majority of Western culture lives within the traditional, modern, and postmodern paradigms. This means the vast majority of our culture has little or no access to meaningful rites of initiation or sacred spaces. The primary mechanisms that individuals and cultures have used throughout human history to mature through the phases of life and connect to the transcendent sacredness of reality are largely unavailable for us today.

Consider the aspects of the crisis that Western civilization faces today: ecological collapse and mass extinction, consumerism, wealth disparity, social unrest, and physical and mental health degradation—just to name the more salient issues. These are the symptoms, not the causes, of a broken civilization. In my perspective, there are two root causes of dysfunction in our society. The first is trauma. Pervasive individual and collective trauma is unrecognized and untreated. This trauma is passed down from adults to children generationally. Until we heal and transform this cycle, our civilization will necessarily continue to be broken.

The second cause is our lack of initiation and the disappearance of sacred space. In a healthy civilization, individuals are evenly distributed between the archetypal roles of child, adolescent, adult, and elder. Each individual is able to transition to their culturally appropriate role as they age. They transition through social structures of initiation. In Western civilization and more generally in the globalized world today, most humans only have access to the child and adolescent archetypal roles.

Our wheel is stuck. It isn't turning. Our individuals remain psychologically immature and thus become diseased and drive toward death. Without a rotating wheel where members flow through the full cycles of human life, our culture will remain fundamentally immature and broken.

We live in a largely adolescent world. And it is, in great measure, a pathological adolescence. There is absolutely nothing wrong with (healthy) adolescence, but our cultural resources have been so degraded over the centuries that the majority of humans in "developed" societies now never reach true adulthood. An adolescent world, being unnatural and unbalanced, inevitably spawns a variety of cultural pathologies, resulting in contemporary societies that are materialistic, greed-based, hostilely competitive, violent, racist, sexist, ageist, and ultimately self-destructive. These societal symptoms of patho-adolescence, which we see everywhere in the industrialized world today, are not at the root of our human nature, but rather are an effect of egocentrism on our humanity.

—Bill Plotkin[26]

Figure 13.8 Death, Builders of the Adytum tarot

Let's consider a few of the ways that our lack of sacred spaces is warping Western civilization, starting with our relationship with death. We tend to view death as the end of life, which is to be avoided at all costs. In general, Westerners live in a cognitive dissonance around death where we intellectually understand that we will die, but generally avoid facing that fact. Our culture is choosing to spend untold resources to prolong life through situations of terrible suffering and disease rather than succumb to death. Within the context of initiation, death is neither the opposite of life or the end of life. Death is the opposite of birth, and both are fundamental aspects of the cycle of life. Death conquers birth just as surely as rebirth conquers death. Dying is not only one of the most profound and therefore precious experiences for humans, it also happens psychologically and socially many times in the course of our biological lives if we allow it. In many spiritual traditions, to die before one dies is a major initiation into eternal life. Because we have largely disowned this wisdom in favor of the modern ego's project of self-perfection, our culture is choosing a slow degeneration into prolonged stasis instead of the radically regenerative powers that death bestows. In the Qabalistic Tarot, the Death card (fig. 13.8) corresponds to the Hebrew letter *nun,* נ, which is attributed to *the fish* as a symbol of regeneration.[27] The deeper revelation of death is life's power of regeneration.

Now turning to hegemonic masculinity. The postmodern paradigm is calling this *toxic masculinity* and is actively doing its best to dismantle it. The context of initiations offers a wholly different perspective and approach. The healthy masculine psyche follows a natural maturation, or progression through distinct phases over the course of his life cycle (fig. 13.4). The toxicity is a symptom of masculine psyches that are not able to transition into adulthood via initiation.

Without initiations, our bodies age but our identities do not mature. Individuals and cultures get stuck in immature stages. When I get stuck, I succumb to the *tyrant holdfast,* attempting to hoard resources for my egoic self-interest. Hegemonic masculinity is properly understood as a pathological form of immature masculinity. Today, within both individuals and our collective culture, hegemonic masculinity is ready to undergo a psychological death. While doing no physical harm to self or others, it is entirely possible (indeed strongly advisable), to undergo a psychic death. Go ahead and die—just don't hurt yourself in the process. This death and rebirth can be most effectively shepherded through the framework of initiation, just like humans have done for the vast majority of our history.

Moore and Gillette are worth quoting at length on this point:

> Oppressive 'macho' societies deny men their mature masculinity as certainly as they degrade women and feminine attributes. Typically a small minority of underdeveloped males at the top of the social pyramid will control power and wealth to the exclusion of all others, male and female. They rank these others in a descending order of their usefulness to themselves and defend against them with all the force of their inflated self-regard. Patriarchy is therefore a manifestation of the infantile grandiosity suffered by its leaders.
>
> Patriarchy is set up and run not for men as a gender or for masculinity in its fullness or in its mature expressions, but rather by men who are fundamentally immature. It is really the rule of boys, often cruel and abusive boys. For the most part, we believe human societies have always consisted of boys and girls more or less unconsciously acting out their immature and grandiose fantasies. Our planetary home more often than not has resembled the island world of William Golding's Lord of the Flies. Thus our societies have, on the whole, opposed the realization and expression of both mature feminine and masculine psyches.[28]

How this initiatory process will unfold for civilization is an open question. Collectively, political revolutions and wars have generally been the mechanisms of social death and rebirth. It is my hope that through Modernity's recognition of the inalienable rights of individuals and post-modernity's strong adherence to nonviolence, that our global village will find a less bloody, less species-threatening process in order to die and be reborn.

The gift of the plural/postmodern paradigm is that it clearly and directly illuminates the problems in the mythic and mental paradigms. One of the challenges for postmodernity has been its limited capacity to effect the sweeping changes that society needs. Hegemonic masculinity is one such example. The optimistic promise of the emerging integral paradigm is an innovative wave of practical solutions to the problem areas that postmodernism highlights. Initiation and the rediscovery of sacred space offers a new solution for earlier paradigms, one that works together with their members instead of fighting against them. As all members of society undergo initiation, the selfish, pathologic, death-seeking parts of the ego (i.e., the unhealthy aspects of the psyche) are able to die and transform. Then a new, life-affirming identity takes its place. Initiation gives me optimism for the transformation of hegemonic masculinity into the organic masculine.

While there are many topics that could be addressed through the framework of sacred space and initiation, I'll simply mention one more: our connection to nature. During ordinary time, the world deteriorates. As a whole, Western civilization has been without meaningful sacred space since the Eleusinian mysteries in Greece were halted in 392 CE. Even more far-reaching, mystical traditions on the fringe of Western culture were actively burned out with the rise of the rational mind in the

Renaissance and Enlightenment periods. As a civilization, we have not accessed sacred space in a very long time. The wasteland that we are rapidly transforming the Earth into is an effect of the absence of sacred spaces in our collective. Through this lens, we can understand mass extinctions, biodiversity loss, and climate change as psycho-spiritual problems foremost. Today, we have the technology, the policy levers, and economic tools to live regeneratively. What is missing is collective will—we are caught in the *tyrant holdfast*, refusing *the call* of initiation.

Recall that two things happen at the center: we are reborn, and the world is recreated. *As without, so within.* Again, the optimistic promise of the integral paradigm is that we will reintroduce sacred spaces into our culture. Integral does not proceed from an authoritarian or traditionalist approach, but from the cutting edge of the evolution of consciousness. On a civilization level, when the collective reawakens to sacred space, we will also recreate the world. We will enact the *eternal return* and renew life in the world.

At the still point of the turning world. Neither flesh nor fleshless;
Neither from nor towards; at the still point, there the dance is,
But neither arrest nor movement. And do not call it fixity,
Where past and future are gathered. Neither movement from nor towards,
Neither ascent nor decline. Except for the point, the still point,
There would be no dance, and there is only the dance.
I can only say, there we have been: but I cannot say where.
And I cannot say, how long, for that is to place it in time.
The inner freedom from the practical desire,
The release from action and suffering, release from the inner
And the outer compulsion, yet surrounded
By a grace of sense, a white light still and moving,
Erhebung without motion, concentration
Without elimination, both a new world
And the old made explicit, understood
In the completion of its partial ecstasy,
The resolution of its partial horror.
—T. S. Eliot

Prompts for Journaling and Discussion

When and how have you experienced sacred space?

What initiations are you missing or needing in your life?

In what ways are you avoiding *the call* in your life?

What is your relationship with death?

Spirit and Archetypes

Returning now to the question posed early in this chapter about whether archetypes have a role in *genuine mystical spirituality*. In addition to the archetypal roles that position me on the human life cycle, the archetypes have long-standing uses in spiritual traditions that have every right to be included in the canons of integral spiritual practice. Simply because the process of initiation originated in the magic/tribal paradigm does not mean it holds no value for us today. The same is true of the myths and deities arising from the mythic/traditional paradigm. The genius of integral is the capacity to harvest truths throughout all earlier paradigms.

One of the goals on my pathway toward realization is to move into identification with broader and more encompassing experiences of the kosmos, and the archetypes help me do that. Archetypes are patterns of meaning. Each of the major functions of the kosmos has a symbol that represents it, as examples: creation, destruction, karma, and temperance. When I touch an archetype, I'm not simply gaining a cognitive understanding of that symbol. Archetypes are intuitive, immediate, and experiential. The symbol acts as a stepping stone into the symbolized process itself. For example, going through a ritual enactment of *letting go* opens me to the embodied experience of letting go.

The tarot deck can be understood as a book of archetypes for Western consciousness. In my perspective, using the tarot (or other oracles) to predict the future does not constitute rigorous spiritual practice. However, there is a long-standing history of the tarot symbols being used as a series of initiations into the full range and expression of the kosmos.

> *Imagine the Tarot deck as a pocket-size symbolic universe that exists within the infinite symbolic universe in which we live. The Tarot deck can be viewed as a set of flashcards encoding thousands of symbolic data bits that contain and apply to our larger universe. When properly understood, each card offers guidance for understanding and constructing our symbolic universe, within and without.*
>
> —Pamela Eakins[29]

Archetypes act as a bridge between the conceptual mind and direct experience. Understanding this function, I can utilize them as tools for the expansion of my consciousness. To take this even a step farther, let's consider symbols and myths for enlightenment and the Divine. Across many mystical traditions, contemplation of the divine symbol has been used as a rigorous spiritual practice—one that has been honed by generations of practitioners. I'll share just two examples here.

In the Christian practice of contemplating the stations of the cross, the practitioner follows a series of depictions of the trials of Jesus culminating in his death and resurrection (fig. 13.9). The practitioner recites prayers at each station and the imagery invites the practitioner to identify with this archetypal initiation through the ordeal, surrender, death, and rebirth.

Figure 13.9 Stations of the cross[30]

In the Tibetan Buddhist practice of deity yoga, the practitioner visualizes a deity in exquisite detail. Every digit of every finger and the specifics of each garland is brought into the visual field. The practitioner then imagines that they are the deity. Through this identification process, using the mythic representation as the stepping stone, the practitioner opens into the enlightened state of being.

Through visualizing ourselves as an enlightened buddha, even at the level of imitation, we are accomplishing two things. First, we are temporarily taking our concept of ego "off-line" and rendering it inactive. This disruption of our normal, habitual egoic visualizing makes room for something deeper and more genuine to emerge. Second, we are engaging in seeing ourselves as a selfless, compassionate being, and in the long term we find ourselves beginning to identify with this enlightened image. These two effects of visualization are referred to, in traditional terms, as the accumulation of merit.

—Reggie Ray[31]

Figure 13.10 Vajrayogini[32]

In both of these examples, the culturally specific myth is the focus of contemplation. That myth (Jesus on the cross, or Vajrayogini) is the interpretation laid over the universal symbol for the pure witness realm of consciousness. In these cases, we call it Christ consciousness or Buddha-mind. Contemplation of the symbol grants access to the experience.

I've outlined three modes for how I utilize the archetypes. First, I identify myself with a gendered role within the human life cycle. These roles advance through the process of maturation, bestowing increasingly greater empowerment and responsibility. The second mode is to identify with an archetypal power or function of the kosmos, for instance, using a tarot deck, to understand a particular aspect of life, consciousness, and the universe. The third is to identify with an enlightened being, deity, or mandala, which leads into transpersonal experiences of unity, wholeness, realization, and liberation.

1. Gendered role within the life cycle (*maturation*): child, adolescent, adult, and elder.
2. Understanding the functions of the kosmos, such as creation, destruction, temperance, karma, etc.
3. Identification with a deity or symbol of wholeness granting species-identification, deity-identification, life-identification, or kosmos-identification.

Beyond the ways that I, as an egoic personality, may choose to use the archetypes on my path of realization, I would like to suggest a complementary and equally powerful use of the archetypes. Recall that Carl Jung theorized the existence of an organizing center of the total psyche, which he called the Self. We could call the Self the Christ, Buddha nature, Atman, or in integral terms, the unitary consciousness of the pure witness realm.

The Self has its own agenda. It works toward the wholeness and integration of all parts of the psyche including the ego. The process of the whole reaching downward to embrace the parts is called *Agape.* Just as it is the nature of parts to reach upward, like a plant growing toward the sun, it is the nature of the whole to reach downward, like the sun shining its light upon the plant. As an individual, I follow my spiritual practices to evolve toward greater wholeness. This is *Eros* moving through me. Simultaneously, the Self reaches down in equal measure to embrace me through compassion and grace—*Agape.*

Consider for a moment how you have felt Spirit, or the Self, communicating to you in your life. What is the mechanism that you receive this guidance through? For me, Spirit communicates primarily through intuition, dreams, and serendipity. Symbols, (i.e., the archetypes) are the language that Spirit uses. These patterns of meaning emerge from the unconscious and then need to be interpreted by my conscious mind.

When I look at the ordering of the states of consciousness, the pure witness realm of the Self sits directly above the causal realm of the archetypes. In order for the Self to communicate down to the gross realm of my physical reality, it must reach through the causal realm. In other words, the archetypes are the units of meaning that exist closest to the Self.

So, on any given day, my personality-self spends time doing my spiritual practices—meditation, yoga, and the like—to open into higher states of consciousness and evolve toward wholeness. Then, I go to sleep and my personality takes a break while the Self performs its practices of sending me messages through dream symbols. Archetypes are the language of Spirit's compassionate embrace. Understood in this way, receiving and interpreting the archetypes becomes every bit as essential to *genuine mystical spirituality* as rigorous meditation.

There is a potentially unbroken continuity of experience stretching from the ordinary, limited awareness of "me" (my seemingly small and separate waking "self"), all the way to a transcendent awareness of completeness and oneness and self-identification with the ALL—the Divine. In my experience, all dreams are ultimately aimed at this transcendent, direct, conscious, creative participation in the collective, archetypal, divine energies that are given shape in the cosmic dance of all life.

—Jeremy Taylor[33]

In summary, these evolutionary archetypes serve a wide range of functions in our lives. Yes, they hold the potential to be used to promote fundamentalism and violence. Yes, the myths carry cultural shadows and are often nothing more than simple moralistic stories for children. But in addition, the archetypes connect us to our roles within the human life cycle and thus form a necessary foundation for a well-functioning civilization. Archetypes empower and instruct us to engage with life generatively. They open us to experience the full diversity of the powers of the kosmos. And with skillful use, they can be harnessed to enter experiences of spiritual realization. Finally, whether we choose to utilize the archetypes or not, Spirit is undoubtedly employing the archetypes to speak to us. This universal symbolic language comes in service of love and compassion. It is the Self's benevolent wish to integrate all illusions of separation, and the archetypes are the messengers of this grace.

Prompts for Journaling and Discussion

What messages have you received from Self/Spirit recently? How did you receive them?

What are the most prevalent cultural or religious myths in your life? What symbols lie beneath them?

Notes

[1] Photo by Derick D Miller, Conimbriga Roman ruins, Portugal.

[2] *Collected Works of C. G. Jung, Volume 9 (Part 1)*.

[3] *Numen, Old Men: (Gender, Theology and Spirituality)*.

[4] "Patriarchy needs to be conceptualized at different levels of abstraction. At the most abstract level, it exists as a system of social relations.… At a less abstract level patriarchy is composed of six structures: the patriarchal mode of production, patriarchal relations in paid work, patriarchal relations in the state, male violence, patriarchal relations in sexuality, and patriarchal relations in cultural institutions. More concretely, in relation to each of the structures, it is possible to identify sets of patriarchal practices which are less deeply sedimented. Structures are emergent properties of practices." *Theorizing Patriarchy*, Walby.

[5] *Numen, Old Men: (Gender, Theology and Spirituality)*.

[6] *The King Within*.

[7] *The Archetype of Initiation*.

[8] *Sex, Ecology, Spirituality*.

[9] "Vision-logic cognizes wholes, connections, and unity-in-diversities (metaparadigmatic and cross-paradigmatic)." *The Religion of Tomorrow*, Wilber.

[10] One exception is Dr. Sarah Nicholson in her book, *The Evolutionary Journey of Woman*, which inter-weaves the myth of Inanna with integral feminism.

[11] *Nature and the Human Soul*.

[12] Gustave Doré, 1892, Canto XXXI in *The Divine Comedy*.

[13] *The Sacred and the Profane*.

[14] "It is shown that non-equilibrium may become a source of order and that irreversible processes may lead to a new type of dynamic states of matter called 'dissipative structures.'" *Time, Structure, and Fluctuations*, Prigogine.

[15] *The Archetype of Initiation*.

[16] See chapter 6.

[17] "Research suggests that the net effect of altered states or peak experiences is that they accelerate development through various stages of growth. There is no evidence that altered states will allow one to skip stages of growth, but they do accelerate their unfolding. The upshot of all that research is simply that the more often one is dunked into the Divine via altered states, the more likely one will grow and evolve to a point where one can maintain that awareness of the Divine in a more permanent and enduring fashion. Combine states with stages and you are on the fast path to Spirit." Ken Wilber in the introduction to *Transcendent Sex*, Wade.

[18] *The Archetype of Initiation*.

[19] "The inflated ego of the tyrant is a curse to himself and his world—no matter how his affairs may seem to prosper. Self-terrorized, fear-haunted, alert at every hand to meet and battle back the anticipated aggressions of his environment, which are primarily the reflections of the uncontrollable impulses to acquisition within himself, the giant of self-achieved independence is the world's messenger of disaster, even though, in his mind, he may entertain himself with humane intentions." *The Hero with a Thousand Faces*, Campbell.

[20] C.f. "Theory of Analytic Interaction," Goodheart.

[21] "The cry of the Kwakiutl neophyte, 'I am at the Center of the World!' at once reveals one of the deepest meanings of sacred space. Where the break-through from plane to plane has been effected by a hierophany, there too an opening has been made, either upward (the divine world) or downward (the underworld, the world of the dead). The three cosmic levels - earth, heaven, underworld - have been put in communication. As we just saw, this communication is sometimes expressed through the image of a universal pillar, *axis mundi*, which at once connects and supports heaven and earth and whose base is fixed in the world below (the infernal-regions). Such a cosmic pillar can be only at the very center of the universe, for the whole of the habitable world extends around it." *The Sacred and the Profane,* Eliade.

[22] "We believe the DMN is the part of our brain that is responsible for judgment, tolerance, reality testing, and a sense of self. Freud called this the 'ego.' Author, Journalist, and experiential researcher Michael Pollan, in his book How to Change Your Mind (2018), referred to this area of the brain as the 'me' network. This area lights up when given a list of adjectives relative to one's self-identity. It also reacts similarly during daydreams, magical thinking, self-reflection, and when we receive Facebook likes (Pollan, 2018). Subsequently, the Default Mode Network activates 'by default' when there is no task at hand." "Default Mode Network: Ego Vs. Mindfulness," Husum.

[23] "For religious man of the primitive and archaic societies, the eternal repetition of para-digmatic gestures and the eternal recovery of the same mythical time of origin, sanctified by the gods, in no sense implies a pessimistic vision of life. On the contrary, for him it is by virtue of this *eternal return* to the sources of the sacred and the real that human existence appears to be saved from nothingness and death." *The Sacred and the Profane*, Eliade.

[24] *The Archetype of Initiation.*

[25] Anthropologist Victor Turner on the pervasiveness of ritual, "For I was constantly aware of the thudding of ritual drums in the vicinity of my camp, and the people I knew would often take their leave of me to spend days at a time attending such exotically named rites as *Nkula, Wubwang'u,* and *Wubinda." The Ritual Process.*

[26] *Nature and the Human Soul: Cultivating Wholeness and Community in a Fragmented World.*

[27] "Mystery School teachers of old assigned the symbol 'fish' to Nun. The fish is associated with regeneration. The fish indicates that whenever things go wrong we can begin again and that death will always be accompanied by new life." *Kabbalah and Tarot of the Spirit*, Eakins.

[28] *The King Within.*

[29] *Kabbalah and Tarot of the Spirit.*

[30] Portuguese Church, Kolkata. Source: Rangan Datta Wiki, CC BY-SA 3.0.

[31] *Secret of the Vajra World.*

[32] Nāropa's Ḍākinī photograph from a Thanka.

[33] *The Wisdom of Your Dreams*, Taylor.

| 14 |

Magician, Warrior, Lover, Monarch

Figure 14.1 The four archetypal parts from the Rider-Waite tarot

Now let's examine the four archetypal parts of the psyche in more detail. Take a moment to look at *figure ix* in the introduction, where I illustrate *The Archetypal Masculine Psyche*. The Magician, Warrior, Lover, and Monarch describe psychological and social aspects that we draw upon to form our personalities. These could also be called characters. They are the roles that we play, with unique gifts as well as shadows. The three gendered high archetypes of the masculine, feminine, and androgyne each have full access to these four quadrants of the psyche.

Each of these archetypes is holonic—it is a whole character in our personality and it works together with the rest of the psyche to support the overall gendered-archetypal maturation process outlined above. The Lover is the first archetype to come online in childhood (for example, lover boy, daddy's girl, and so on). The Warrior emerges with the word "No!" in toddlers, and the Magician is discovered through creative play and imagination. With the onset of puberty, the Lover's interest transitions away from the parental figures. Around this age, the rational mind emerges for the Magician and the Warrior finds their place within the tribe of peers. These shifts herald the transition from the Child into the Hero, Heroine, and Maiden archetypes of adolescence. During the adolescent phase, these three archetypes support the emergence and development of the egoic self. Prior to the initiation into adulthood, the Warrior and the Hero are generally fused as a single archetype (fig. 14.2).

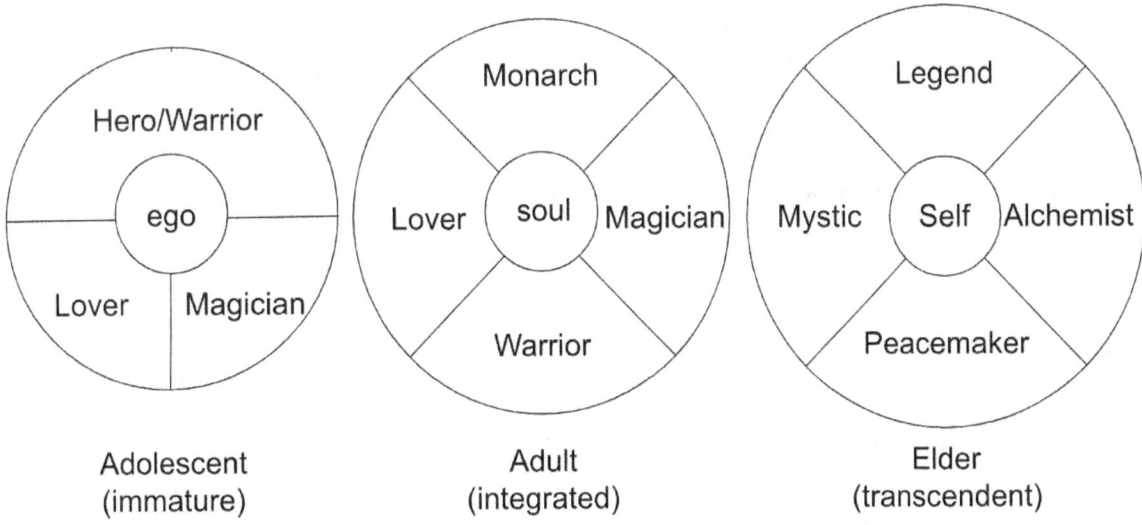

Figure 14.2 Developmental progression of the archetypes

When we transition into the archetypal role of the adult, the Warrior becomes a distinct archetype occupying one quadrant of the psyche, and the Monarch emerges from the Hero, Heroine, or Maiden. The Monarch, in the form of the King or the Queen, holds a higher order of sovereignty, which supports the transition into the soul self. While this initiation into adulthood can happen naturally by becoming a parent or other life experiences, there is no formal initiatory rite of passage that is held in our culture to shepherd the death of the Hero into the birth of the Monarch and soul self. This initiation is called *the willing sacrifice*. Parents learn to put their children first, and the Monarch becomes a servant of their realm.

> *The process in a boy's childhood of incarnating his mythic potential in the actual world of hurly-burly and competition is made possible by the Ego-Hero configuration. The Hero is the culminating archetypal influence of boyhood. Where the boy's Ego is appropriately accessing the Hero, he is empowered to differentiate himself from the universe, from the complexes and archetypal energies within him, and finally and especially from his mother and father. It enables the boy to "slay" the internalized parental opinions, values, and controls, and break free of their domination. Once this is done, the Ego must pass beyond the heroic stage, the last stage of legitimate grandiosity, to a condition of true humility. It must offer its loyalty to the Transpersonal Other in its form as the archetypal King and Queen. The entire process, if all goes well, consolidates an emergent Ego-King axis and leads to mature selfhood.*
>
> —Moore and Gillette[1]

These archetypes are available at every paradigm of consciousness. However, the experience of the archetype is different at each paradigm because higher paradigms have more complex world-views. In figure 14.3, below, I sketch out some of the professional roles that the four archetypes inhabit across the paradigms. Please note that this table is descriptive, not definitive—my interpretations are here to give you a feel of the terrain. Also, each of the lower roles is included by higher paradigms. So, for example, the Magician as a mechanic in the traditional paradigm is also available as a modern mechanic, postmodern mechanic, and integral mechanic—all the way up.

Integral	Personal Coach, Neo-Shaman	Holistic Health Coach	Cultural Creative, Sound Healer	Leader of Change Institute
Plural/ Post-modern	Academic, Therapist	Activist, Perma-culturist	Sex Educator, Bodyworker	NGO/Nonprofit Head
Mental/ Modern	Doctor, Scientist, Tech Expert	Lawyer, Politician, Athlete	Digital Artist, DJ	CEO
Mythic/ Traditional	Mechanic, Technician	Hunter, Soldier, Farmer	Sculptor, Dancer, Singer-Songwriter	Pastor, Family-Business Owner
	Magician	**Warrior**	**Lover**	**Monarch**

Figure 14.3 Professional roles typified across archetypes and paradigms

As my archetypal role advances from child, to adolescent, to adult, to elder, the archetypal parts of the psyche also change (Fig 14.1). The four archetypal parts move from immature, to integrated, to transcendent expressions. Note that even though the Monarch does not emerge until adulthood, the psychic space of the Monarch is latent for children and adolescents.

Now, let's look at the qualities of the four archetypes in the immature phases through early childhood and into adolescence. As a child, I have many needs for love, belonging, nourishment, and learning. Necessarily, my family, friends, and environment will not be able to meet these needs. Because I don't have agency as a child to meet my own needs, I must rely on others to take care of me. I develop strategies in order to get my needs met. Each of the four archetypes, or characters, has its own strategies—what are called *character strategies*. These represent intelligent solutions to challenging situations we encounter as children that become baked into our personalities as traits. My character strategies stick with me into adulthood and show up to help me meet my needs when I'm challenged or triggered. While they were an intelligent response for me as a child with little agency, today, they show up as immature habits. Each of the four archetypal parts contains two character strategies—an outwardly expressive distortion and an inwardly collapsed distortion (also known as the *bipolar shadow*). Most folks will adopt one of these strategies as their primary character trait, but we all have access to all strategies.

As I grow older, my strategic characters then weave into the tapestry of my personality. Ideally, as I continue to mature in adulthood, I learn how to meet my own needs and reparent my internal child parts. I dethrone the immature character strategies, and my mature soul self takes the reins. This process leads to an integrated Magician, Warrior, Lover, and Monarch. It's important to understand that our younger parts never leave us and this process is not about removing them. Rather, the younger parts learn to give up their reactive control so that my adult can be responsive. Instead of being ruled by child and teenage parts, the adult becomes sovereign. The child parts then take a seat at my inner council, each with their own gifts. As I accept and love these parts, they weave more and more seamlessly into my whole self.

If I continue my maturation process to trans-egoic levels, then an even higher, transcendent archetype comes online who is governed by the Self. It's worth stating again that while the maturation process is influenced by age, it advances by creating healthy foundations at each stage and then transitioning via initiation. Thus, the transcendent archetype becomes available once the adult soul self reaches sufficient development and balance to open to the Self beyond. The transcendent archetypes are the Alchemist, Peacemaker, Mystic, and Legend.

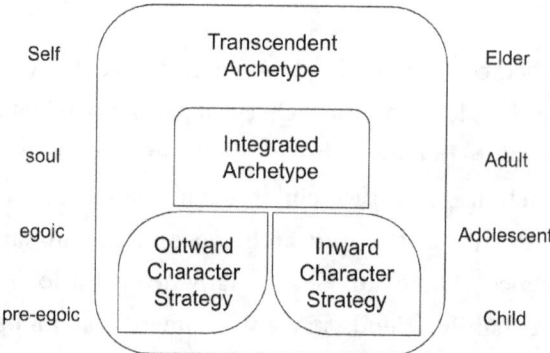

Figure 14.4 Structures of archetypal maturation

You will find a detailed description of this archetypal maturation structure for each of the four archetypes in their respective Lore Book. The character strategies for all archetypes are drawn from the Hakomi method of psychotherapy, and the transcendent archetypes are being newly introduced in this text.

Archetypal Progression of the Magician

Now let's take a look at how these pieces fit together for the Magician. The two immature character strategies for the Magician are *performing* and *sensitive/withdrawn*. The transcendent form of the Magician is the *Alchemist*.

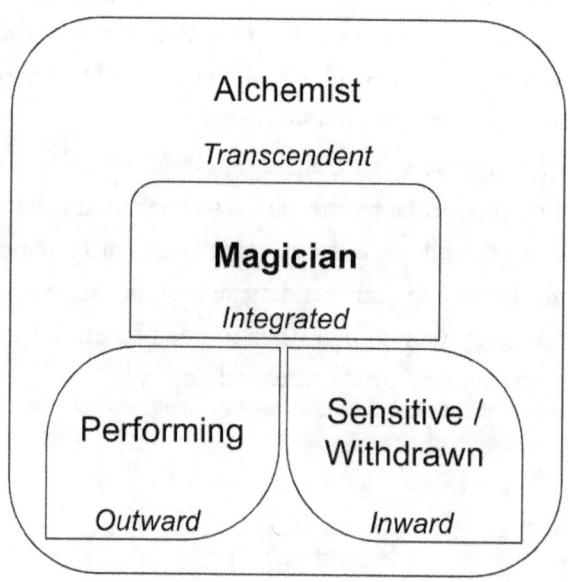

Figure 14.5 Archetypal structures of the Magician

Performing

When I am the performing character, I am soliciting attention from others through performance, drama, or neediness. I feel unseen, unrecognized, or unappreciated and my strategy is either to become helpless or make a fuss to attract attention. I want to be chosen and I want to feel special. I fear being uninteresting enough to be loved and so I compensate with a colorful personality. Often, this presents as a younger, childlike part that just wants to be adored, protected, and cared for. Whether conscious or unconscious, I am engaging in some degree of manipulation to secure help or attention.

Almost always, these strategies are accompanied by *limiting beliefs*, which are simple statements that I accept as true about the world or myself. My limiting beliefs reinforce the need for my character strategy. These are called "limiting" beliefs because they are generally no longer true as an adult, though they may have been true during childhood. By holding onto them, I limit my growth and capacity for intimacy in relationships. For the performing character, limiting beliefs include, "I'm too much for other people," "I'm not interesting enough," "My specialness isn't appreciated," "Being an adult is boring," and "If I don't entertain you, you'll lose interest in me."

The emotion that motivates me as the performing character is a feeling of insecurity in relationships with others. I project that other people will not find me interesting. In secret, I don't find myself interesting. I judge myself as boring, normal, or underdeveloped. My outward performance is to receive admiration from others, but I cannot really take in their praise because at core, I'm not interested in myself.

The first step in working with this pattern is to find the place of self-judgment and to own that *I habitually judge myself.* Then, I can explore how my judgment functions to suppress my natural innocence, creativity, and playfulness. By constantly performing, I don't make room for the authentic me. The next step is to feel the pain that my self-judgment causes, meaning, to feel my own cruelty. Feeling the pain of what I do to myself provides the needed impetus to change my pattern.

Sensitive/Withdrawn

As the sensitive/withdrawn character, I believe myself to be fragile or weak. My strategy is to contain my strong emotions and to withdraw from an overwhelming world. This strategy may be an adaptation to trauma, attachment wounding, or trouble regulating my nervous system. Alternatively, it may stem from a fragmented or shallow sense of self. As the name suggests, I am highly sensitive and withdrawn. I am shy, reserved, and hold others at a distance. I either resist my emotions or am cut off from them—often this leads me to be overly intellectual and mechanical.

Limiting beliefs typical of the sensitive/withdrawn character include, "the world is dangerous, unsafe, or overwhelming," "there is something wrong about me (strange, unsociable, distant)," and "I need to suppress my aliveness or emotions."

Working with this strategy goes hand in hand with trauma healing and attachment healing. I need to find a sense of "me" in my body that is safe and stable. The more I practice inhabiting a solid me, the more that place will become a foundation and a resource. My core beliefs are that I'm too fragile and that the world is overwhelming. I want to practice staying present in myself to discover that even though I'm sensitive, I'm also actually strong and resilient. Experiencing my own staying power is how transformation happens. In addition, I want to come into ownership that I have a habit of overwhelming myself. I use other people, my environment, or my big emotions to overwhelm myself because that is my familiar safety. I may even secretly enjoy overwhelming myself. Once I can own that I choose my overwhelm, then I become free to choose something else. With all the immature character strategies, taking ownership that *I do this pattern* is a crucial step in moving into the sovereignty of my adult.

When these character strategies become integrated, they offer tremendous gifts for the Magician. Increased sensitivity gives me access to my talents and genius. I know how to go inside myself, how to listen, and how to attune to other people and my environment. The capacity to perform will open the channel for my genius to express itself to the world. The integrated performer brings a tremendous amount of creativity, fun, and adventure.

Magician

The adult expression of this archetype is the Magician. Here, my focus is on filling out into fullness as an individual adult. The magician opens up realms of knowledge and the capacity to harness the forces of nature for willful creation. He teaches me how to access my soul, the spirit world, and my soul's work in this world.

Alchemist

Moving to the transpersonal level, the Magician becomes the Alchemist. While the ego works for its self-benefit, and the soul self is on its individual path of growth, the Self naturally benefits all because the Self includes the all. The Self includes and encompasses the collective unconscious. As Jung pointed out, this includes the universal God-symbol. Because the integrated whole psyche now accesses collective consciousness, identity broadens in two ways: the collective recognizes the Self, and the Self works on behalf of the collective. Let's take the example of Black Elk. Here is a human in the Magician archetype who fulfilled his mission so fully and completely that he created powerful changes for his people. Moving beyond his personal mission and into the Alchemist, his story has become a gift to all of Western culture. Our collective is benefitting from him and in turn, we recognize and mythologize him. Black Elk has moved from being merely a man who once lived to a mythic figure. This is the transpersonal collective level that individuals rise to through the archetypes. It is immortality by becoming myth, which represents the highest achievement on the archetypal ladder. The Alchemist accomplishes the great work, benefits the world, and in turn is immortalized in myth.

Figure 14.6 Mercury Renewed (1687)[2]

The intellect is the domain of the Magician. Power is gained through knowledge, particularly secret, obscure, or protected knowledge. And that power is wielded by the Magician's will, symbolized by the wand. At the Alchemist, the transcendent qualities that come online are *concentration* and *imagination*. Concentration is the act of densifying or distilling—to make into a concentrate. The alchemist pulls together the forces of nature into the crucible through mental concentration. *Imaginatio*, or imagination, is the alchemical method of creation. Imagination brings something new into reality through the act of visualization.[3] These two qualities bring both more power and greater responsibility to the Alchemist.

Summary

The Magician occupies the intellectual part of the psyche and leads us on the spiritual path. The character strategies of performing and sensitive/withdrawn point to the dysfunctions we are prone to when we do not wield the Magician's power responsibly. As these strategies are integrated, the Magician becomes a source of agency, enchantment, discovery, and play for us. Eventually, the emergence of the Self brings the Alchemist online in the psyche, which becomes a powerful conduit in the creative energies of life itself.

Prompts for Journaling and Discussion

For the Magician's character strategies, *performing* and *sensitive/withdrawn*, share about a time that you experienced yourself in each role.

Where does the Magician show up for you across mind, body, spirit, relationships, work, and nature?

How does your Magician interact with the other archetypes: Monarch, Warrior, and Lover;

Masculine, Feminine, and Androgyne?

Imagine yourself as the Alchemist—what would change from where you are today?

The Archetypal Mandala of the Self

Now let's take an overview of the maturation progression for each of the four archetypes, knowing that you will find a full description in each of the Lore Books in this series. As we just explored, the Magician integrates the character strategies of performing and sensitive/withdrawn. The adult Magician uses intellect and will to harness natural forces. In the transcendent form, the Magician becomes the Alchemist, recreating reality for the benefit of all.

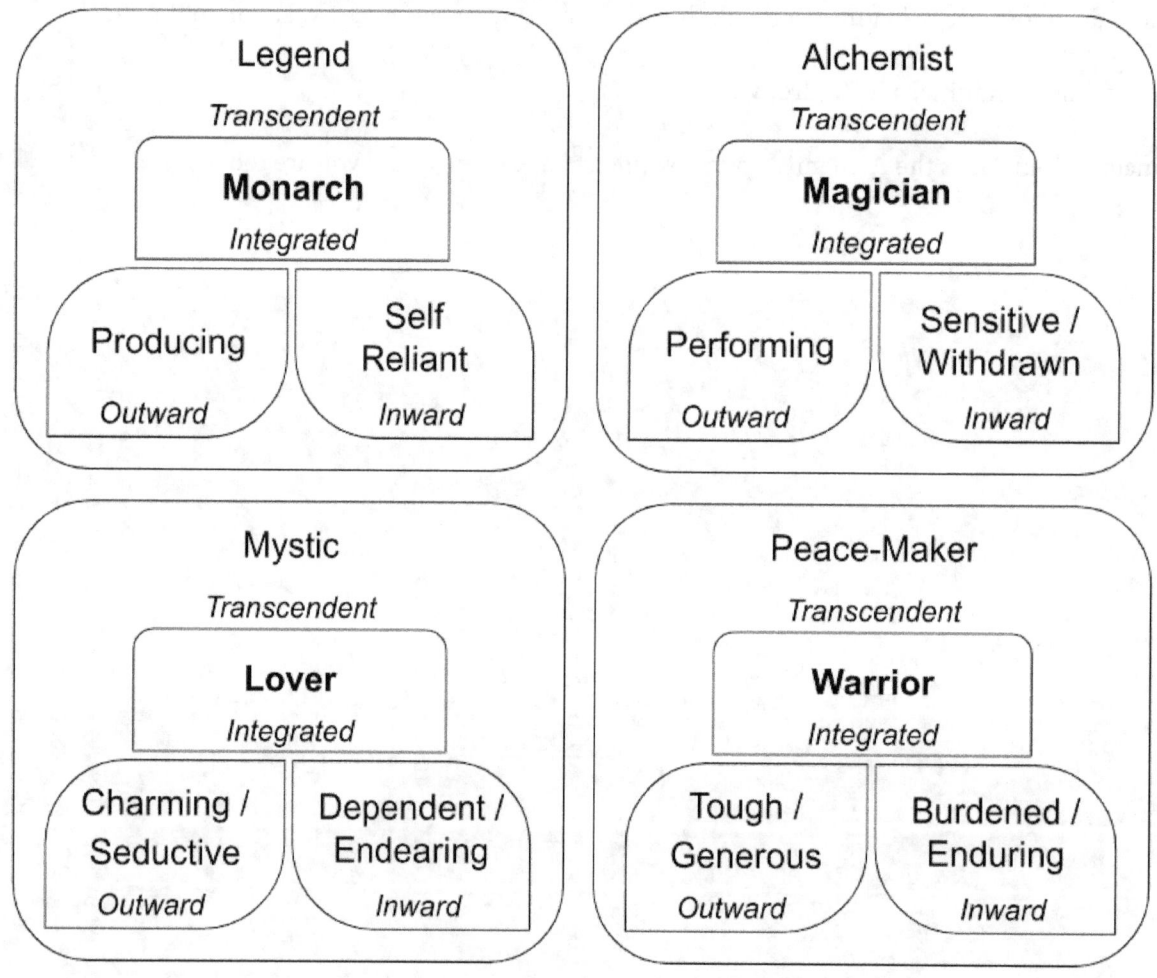

Figure 14.7 Maturation progression through the four archetypes

The immature character strategies for the Warrior are *tough/generous* and *burdened/enduring*. As the tough/generous character I put up a big invulnerable show of power. I push others around and then reward them with my generosity. As the burdened/enduring character, the weight of the world falls on my shoulders and I feel chained by my duties to care for others. In integrated form, the Warrior acts, provides discipline, and enforces my boundaries. In transcendent form, the Warrior becomes the Peacemaker, whose myth brings people together and creates harmony.

The immature character strategies for the Lover are *charming/seductive* and *dependent/endearing*. As a charming/seductive character, I present an attractive facade to be loved. In the dependent/endearing role, I make myself weak, pitiful, or helpless to receive support from others. The dependent/endearing strategy stems from a fear of abandonment, whereas weakness in the Magician's sensitive/withdrawn strategy is about managing overwhelm. In integrated form, the Lover channels desire and passion into a zest for life, and opens to me into deep emotions and love. In transcendent form, the Lover becomes the Mystic. Passion transforms into devotion and the love affair shifts focus onto the divine Beloved.

Finally, the two character strategies for the Monarch are *producing* and *self-reliant*. As a producer, I need to work and achieve in order to receive love. In self-reliance, I believe that only I can take care of my needs. When these integrate into the Monarch (which includes the King and the Queen), I step into service to my realm. In the transcendence of the Self, the Monarch enters the collective and becomes a *Legend*. There have been countless Kings and Queens throughout our history but only a handful we know by name and story—these are the Legends. The Legend offers a new example of the ideal of humanity.

Character Strategy	Overview
Performing	Need for attention through drama and performance
Sensitive/Withdrawn	Retreat from overwhelming emotions and world. Survival response
Tough/Generous	Hides vulnerability. Connection through the illusion of power
Burdened/Enduring	Pleasing and putting others' needs first. Freedom costs connection
Charming/Seductive	Hides authentic desires. Connection through an attractive identity-mask
Dependent/Endearing	Needing others' support. Fear of abandonment
Producing	Achievement and self-criticism to earn approval and belonging
Self-Reliant	Others cannot meet my needs, only I can take care of myself

Figure 14.8 Overview of character strategies[4]

Archetype	Quality	Transcendent	Transcendent Quality	Transcendent Overview
Magician	Thinking	Alchemist	Concentration & Imagination	Channels kosmic powers
Warrior	Acting	Peacemaker	Compassion	Brings peace through compassion
Lover	Feeling	Mystic	Devotion	Devotion toward the Beloved
Monarch	Being	Legend	Blessing	Redefines the ideal human

Figure 14.9 Integrated and transcendent qualities of the archetypes

Each of the four masculine archetypes has his own symbolic power objects: the King reigns with his scepter; the Warrior fights with the sword; the Magician has his wand; and the Lover's instrument is the phallus. The Lover also has a sword, referred to as *the naked blade*, that lies between lovers as they sleep. Beyond these phallic symbols for the masculine archetypes, there are countless other power objects for each, like the Magician's spell book, the Lover's love potion, and the King's throne. The power objects bridge the gap between the personal human realm and the transpersonal archetypal realm.

In addition, each creates a unique type of sacred space: the King's domain is the city; the Warrior is home to the battlefield (i.e., Armageddon or apocalypse); the Magician casts his magical circle; and the Lover inhabits the garden of paradise (i.e., Eden). As we have discussed, it is through sacred space that I am able to touch the life-giving energies at the center of the Self. Each quadrant of the psyche provides its unique access route to the center.

Summary

In summary, the archetypal psyche has four parts that mature through three stages. The first immature stages are called character strategies, of which there are eight. As children in a world that is not perfectly attuned to us, we use these strategies to meet our needs for survival, love, and belonging. As adults, the four archetypal parts are the Magician, Warrior, Lover, and Monarch. Each integrated archetype rests on the foundation of two immature character strategies, one externally focused and the other internal. If one continues to mature to trans-egoic levels, the archetypes take on transcendent and collective qualities as the Alchemist, Peacemaker, Mystic, and Legend. At the center of the adolescent archetypes is the ego. At the center of the integrated adult archetypes is the soul self. At the center of the transpersonal archetypes is the Self. Each of these stages is available (but is by no means guaranteed) for every human. Advancement through stages happens via initiation when a person's age and healthy development of the prior stage form a foundation to advance. All of these archetypes interrelate as the mandala of the psyche (fig. 14.10).

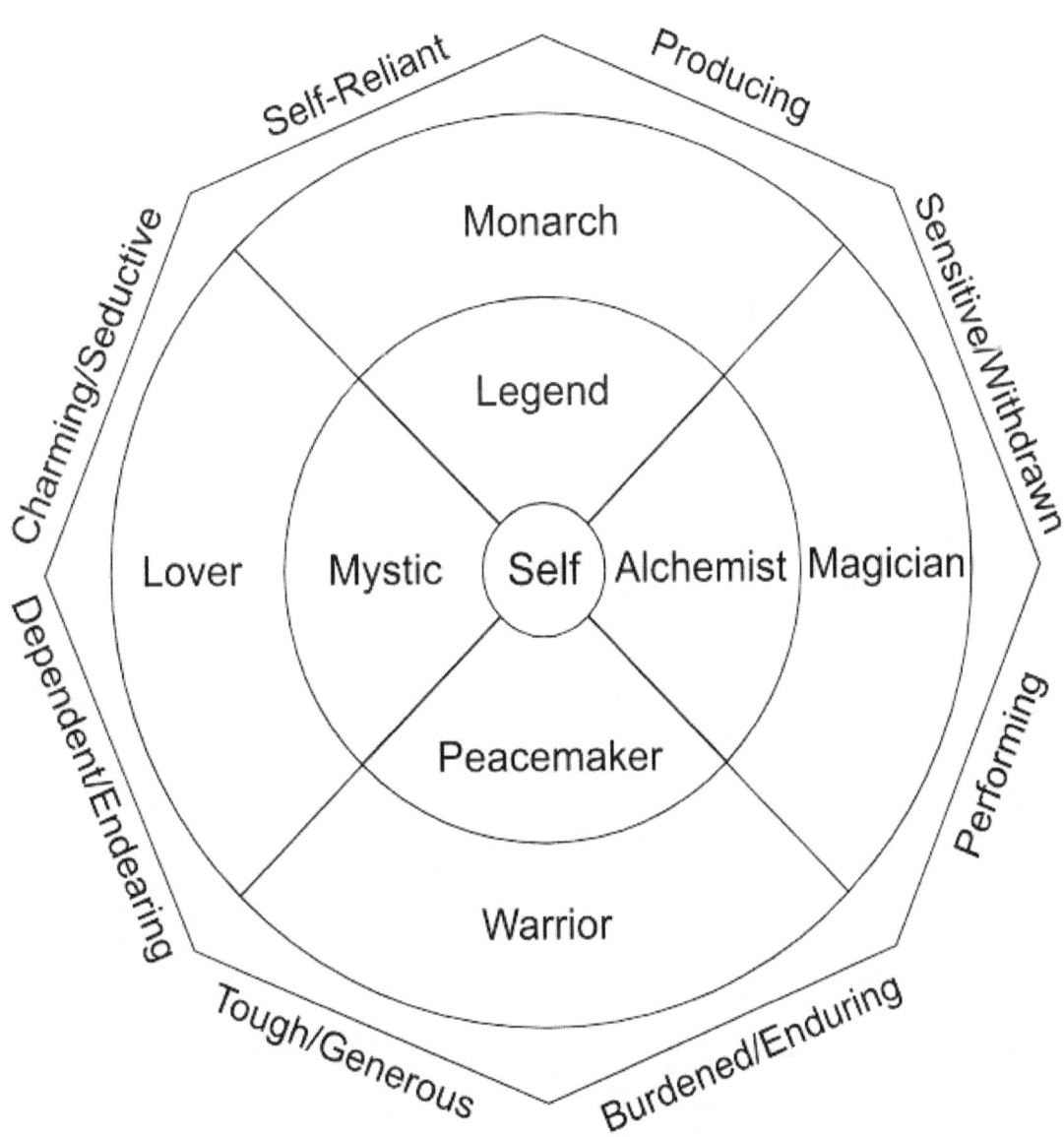

Figure 14.10 Archetypal mandala of the Self

The mandala of the psyche originates at birth and continues to develop until death. This mandala evolves through lifecycle phases from the child, to the adolescent, adult, and elder. The life cycle contains the gendered archetypes of boy and girl; hero, heroine, and maiden; man, father, woman, and mother; and finally the old man, grandfather, crone, and grandmother. Advancement through the gendered high-archetypal phases of life, as well as the maturation of the four quadrants of the psyche happens via initiation.

Prompts for Journaling and Discussion

From the list of character strategies, which one or two are strongest in your personality?

Which transpersonal archetypes feel alive in you today?

Notes

[1] *The King Within.*

[2] *Scrutinium chymicum*, Maier.

[3] "The *imagination*, or the act of imagining, was thus a physical activity that could be fitted into the cycle of material changes, that brought these about and was brought about by them in turn. In this way the alchemist related himself not only to the unconscious but directly to the very substance which he hoped to transform through the power of imagination." *Collected Works of C. G. Jung Volume 12: Psychology and Alchemy*, Jung.

[4] Derived from *Hakomi Mindfulness-Centered Psychotherapy*, Eisman.

| 15 |

Conclusion to Lore Book I

Figure 15.1 Merlin[1]

"Please," said the Wart, *"dear Merlyn, turn me into a hawk. If you don't do that I shall do something. I don't know what."* Merlyn put down his knitting and looked at his pupil over the top of his spectacles. *"My boy,"* he said, *"you shall be everything in the world, animal, vegetable, mineral, protista or virus, for all I care before I have done with you but you will have to trust to my superior backsight. The time is not yet ripe for you to be a hawk, for one thing Hob is still in the mews feeding them so you may as well sit down for the moment and learn to be a human being."*

—T. H. White[2]

I can recall a time when I lost my inner Magician. Stress, work, and routine dominated my life. My work was tedious and unimaginative. My heart wasn't in it. I was bored and I hated how I was spending my time, so I would numb out with food and alcohol. I would blow off steam by partying. And then wake up again on Monday morning and trudge back into my lifeless routine. There was a part of me that wanted to play, to explore, and to learn. But I was afraid. Afraid that without my safe and secure job, I would never make it in the world. Afraid to imagine a life for myself beyond the station that had been handed to me. Afraid to be a naive beginner and make mistakes. I was still following society's script for a successful life and I hadn't yet found my inner genius.

But *the call* was there within me. The Magician whispered in my ear, "You're made for more than this. It's time to learn how to fly." Once I really heard the call, it took me a year before I made the jump. I quit my safe and cushy corporate job. I spent my savings traveling the world and volunteering. I chose to jump. It was the first of many big jumps. By jumping off the cliff without holding anything back, I rediscovered my Magician and he gave me wings. *The time was ripe for me to become a hawk.*

Over the course of that year traveling, I stepped out of ordinary time and into sacred space. I found the inner spark of my true calling, my dharma, and received my soul-initiation into adulthood. Once I was connected to my purpose, everything in my life made sense. In mythic terms, I found *the center* and it has guided me these past ten years. In many ways, the material I'm sharing in this workbook is my harvest from that life-changing initiation.

My Magician is the one who taps me on the shoulder to let me know it's time for a ceremony. He's the one who inspires my voracious intellectual curiosity and who guides my studies in alignment with my path. He's the one who opens sacred space and shepherds my initiations. And he's the one who assimilates my life experiences into offerings for the world. It's not exactly the case that *I am the Magician*, as much as *the Magician lives in me*. He has set up his laboratory in my psyche and my body—these are the *prima materia* for his alchemical work. Just like Merlyn, my Magician is busy in his idiosyncratic process of transforming me into *everything in the world*.

The Magician's Lore Book is a big one. In these pages we have explored who the Magician is and what it means to inhabit his archetype. The quality of the Magician is *thinking*, and this lore book is appropriately the most intellectual in the series. In addition to introducing himself, the Magician has been diligently explaining the nature of the kosmos and the psyche. These are not just topographical maps however, they are spells whose careful reading and study transforms the consciousness of the reader. When consciousness sees itself, it evolves. This is the gift of the Magician.

The structure laid out by the Magician provides the framework for understanding and engaging with all the other archetypes in this series. This is why the Magician came first. His direction is the East, home of the rising sun and the dawning light of consciousness. He has opened the portal into sacred space. With his guidance, we are now ready to encounter the ordering, life-giving energies of the Warrior, Lover, Queen, Androgyne (who is truly a Magician hirself), and the King.

In this Lore Book, I have laid out the core thesis of the Organic Masculine in fullness. In summary: existence is a multilayered tapestry in an ongoing process of becoming. Each layer has the properties of being whole in itself, being composed of parts, and forms a part in a larger whole—it is holonic. This process follows an observable progression toward increasing complexity and wholeness, called *Eros*. Thus, reality is a growing hierarchy of holons—a holarchy. Each entity in existence has an interior, felt, prehended aspect and an exterior, phenomenal, relational aspect. The evolutionary process that blossoms moment to moment across all entities, throughout all interiors and all exteriors is what I call the *kosmos*.

Human consciousness is the most complex interior-space that we know of. Physical processes and living systems are its foundations. Human consciousness constellates throughout the subjective psycho-spiritual arena of the individual, and the inter-subjective cultural arena of the collective. This consciousness has three interrelated but distinct axes of growth: states of consciousness, paradigms (and structure states), and archetypal roles through the life cycle. Across all three axes, human consciousness displays *eleutheropoiesis*—we naturally move toward greater degrees of creative liberation. The higher we move along any single axis, the more fully it begins to embrace the other two and the ultimate telos, end-point, is nondual suchness.

Within the archetypal maturation axis, the organic masculine, feminine, and androgyne are primal morphic fields that provide unbounded sources of vitality, purpose, and order. In its essence, masculinity is life-affirming. Despite all the shadow and pathology seen today, there is a sacred core of masculinity. I access the organic masculine through the process of initiation. The masculine, feminine, and androgyne high-archetypes are available to all humans as morphic fields in consciousness. On my path to wholeness, individuation, and the Self, I will necessarily reckon with the shadows of each, and welcome the love and light of all three within me.

Understanding the wisdom of life's evolutionary processes, I align to my personal evolution. My own growth is the greatest tool I have to address the challenges in my personal life and the crises that the world is facing. Whether I do this through spiritual practice to access higher states of consciousness, shadow work to embrace more comprehensive worldviews, or initiation to mature through the archetypes, growing myself is the most empowering and impactful action I can take. It benefits me as an individual and it benefits all beings everywhere. In equal measure that I am reaching upward to grow, I am opening to receive Spirit's compassionate embrace, and I am sharing the best part of my gifts with all those around me. Engaging in this way aligns me to my inborn eleutheropoietic blessing for life, as life, and through life.

This metaphysical, psycho-spiritual framework is the Magician's finger pointing at the moon. Your task is to digest this framework, make it your own, and use it to step into naked contact with reality—to live it.

I am re-membering myself as an individuated locus of consciousness within the living, breathing kosmos. I am precious, I belong, and I am sacred. My awareness is not separate from the awareness of the kosmos. The kosmos is none other than my body. Through my body, I am experiencing who I am. Through my love, I am embracing who I am. Through my life, I am becoming who I am.

Notes

[1] Image: W. H. Margetson, from *Legends of King Arthur and His Knights*, 1914.

[2] *The Once and Future King.*

WORKS CITED

Adams, Maurianne et al. *Teaching for Diversity and Social Justice 4th ed* (New York: Routledge, 2023).

Adyashanti. *The Way of Liberation: A Practical Guide to Spiritual Enlightenment* (San Jose: Open Gate Sangha, 2012).

Agrawala, Vasudeva Sharana. *SIVA Mahādeva, the Great God; an Exposition of the Symbolism of Siva* (Varnasi: Veda Academy, 1966).

Alpert, Jane. "Mother Right: A New Feminist Theory." *Off Our Backs*, vol. 3, no. 9, 1973, *JSTOR*, http://www.jstor.org/stable/25783650

Aurobindo. *The Life Divine* (Pondicherry: Sri Aurobindo Ashram, 1970).

Aurobindo. "The Teaching of Sri Aurobindo," http://intyoga.online.fr/ttosa2.htm (1934).

Beck, Don Edward, and Christopher Cowan. *Spiral Dynamics: Mastering Values, Leadership and Change* (Malden: Blackwell Publishing, 1996).

Bohm, David. *Wholeness and the Implicate Order* (London:Routledge, 2002).

Butler, E.M. *The Myth of the Magus* (Cambridge: Cambridge University Press, 1993).

Caetano, Kalie. "The Mother-Love Myth: The Effect of the Provider-Nurturer Dichotomy in Custody Cases." *The Macalester Review.* V2 Iss 1, 2011. https://digitalcommons.macalester.edu/ macreview/vol2/iss1/2/.

Campbell, Joseph. *The Hero with a Thousand Faces* (Princeton: Princeton University Press, 2004).

Capra, Fritjof. *The Web of Life: A New Synthesis of Mind and Matter* (London: Flamingo, 1997).

Capra, Fritjof, and Pier Luigi Luisi. *The Systems View of Life: A Unifying Vision*(Cambridge: Cambridge University Press, 2014).

Case, Paul Foster. *The Tarot: A Key to the Wisdom of the Ages: The Classic Guide* (New York: Jeremy P. Tarcher/Penguin, 2006).

Chafetz, Janet Saltzman. *Gender Equity: an Integrated Theory of Stability and Change* (Newberry Park: Sage Publications, 1990).

Chardin, Pierre Teilhard de. *The Phenomenon of Man* (New York: Harper Perennial Modern Thought, 2008).

Collins, James C. *Good to Great* (London: Random House Business, 2001).

Connell, Raewyn. *The Men and the Boys* (Cambridge: Polity Press, 2000).

Cook, Francis Harold. *Hua-Yen Buddhism: The Jewel Net of Indra* (Delhi: Sri Satguru Publications, 1994).

Cook-Greuter, Susanne. "Ego Development: A Full-Spectrum Theory Of Vertical Growth And Meaning Making" (2021) https://www.researchgate.net/publication/356357233.

Cook-Greuter, Susanne. "Ego Development: Nine Levels of Increasing Embrace," (2005). https://integralartlab.com/wp-content/uploads/2020/12/9-levels-of-increasing-embrace-update-1-07. pdf.

Cowan, James. *Mysteries of the Dream-Time* (Bridport: Prism Press, 1992).

Csikszentmihalyi, Mihaly. *Flow: The Psychology of Optimal Experience* (New York: Harper and Row, 2009).

Daily Evolver [Internet] "A Quick Intro to Integral Theory." https://www.dailyevolver.com/theory/.

Dattatreya, translated by Mackay, Rory. *Avadhuta Gita.* https://www.unbrokenself.com/avadhuta-gita-the-song-of-freedom-chapter-3/.

Deida, David. *The Way of the Superior Man: A Spiritual Guide to Mastering the Challenges of Women, Work, and Sexual Desire (20th Anniversary Edition)* (Louisville: Sounds True, 2017).

Diaz, S. et al. "IPBES: Summary for policymakers of the global assessment report on biodiversity and ecosystem services of the Intergovernmental Science-Policy Platform on Biodiversity and Ecosystem Services." IPBES secretariat, Bonn, Germany. (2019) doi:10.5281/zenodo.3553579.

Dierkes, Christopher. "Indistinct Union: An Integral Introduction to Nonduality in Christianity." *Journal of Integral Theory & Practice* (Sept 30, 2022).

DiPerna, Dustin. *Streams of Wisdom: An Advanced Guide to Integral Spiritual Development* (Integral Publishing House, 2014).

Dowman, Keith. *Dzogchen: Sex (Dzogchen Teaching Series)* (Independently published, 2022).

Eakins, Pamela. *Kabbalah and Tarot of the Spirit* (Half Moon Bay: Pacific Center Library, 2014).

Eckhart, Meister, and Maurice O'C Walshe. *The Complete Mystical Works of Meister Eckhart* (New York: Crossroad Publishing Company, 2009).

Eliade, Mircea. *The Sacred and the Profane: The Nature of Religion* (New York: Harvest Book, 1968).

Gebser, Jean. *The Ever-Present Origin* (Athens: Ohio University Press, 1997).

Gelfer, Joseph. *Numen, Old Men: Contemporary Masculine Spiritualities and the Problem of Patriarchy* (London: Routledge, 2009).

Goelet, Dr. Ogden, Jr., et al. *The Egyptian Book of the Dead: The Book of Going Forth by Day: The Complete Papyrus of Ani*, 3rd ed (San Francisco: Chronicle Books, 2015).

Griffiths, R.R., et al. "Psilocybin can occasion mystical-type experiences having substantial and sustained personal meaning and spiritual significance." (2005). doi: 10.1007/s00213-006-0457-5.

Habermas Jürgen. *Communication and the Evolution of Society* (Boston: Beacon Press, 1979).

Hanh Nhat, Thich. *How to Fight* (Berkeley: Parallax Press, 2017).

Hixon, Lex. *Mother of the Buddhas: Meditation on the Prajnaparamita Sutra* (Kolkata: Alchemy, 2004).

Husum, Charmaine, DKATI, RTC, CT. "Default Mode Network: Ego Vs. Mindfulness." https://lindenandarc.com/what-is-your-default-mode-network.

Huxley, Aldous, et al. *Moksha: Aldous Huxley's Classic Writings on Psychedelics and the Visionary Experience* (Rochester: Park Street Press, 1999).

Jackson, Joe. *Black Elk, The Life of an American Visionary* (New York: Farrar, Straus and Giroux, 2016).

Jackson, Roger R., et al. *Tantric Treasures: Three Collections of Mystical Verse from Buddhist India* (Oxford: Oxford University Press, 2004).

James, William, et al. *Essays in Radical Empiricism: A Pluralistic Universe* (New York: Longmans, 1912).

James, William. *The Varieties of Religious Experience: A Study in Human Nature: Being the Gifford Lectures on Natural Religion Delivered at Edinburgh in 1901–1902* (New York: Longmans, 1902).

Johanson, Gregory, and Monda, Lorena. *Hakomi Mindfulness-Centered Somatic Psychotherapy: A Comprehensive Guide to Theory and Practice* (New York: W.W. Norton & Company, 2015).

Jung, C. G. *Collected Works of C.G. Jung, Volume 9 (Part 1): Archetypes and the Collective Unconscious, 2nd ed* (Princeton: Princeton University Press, 1980).

Jung, C. G. *Collected Works of C.G. Jung, Volume 9 (Part 2): Aion: Researches into the Phenomenology of the Self, 2nd ed* (Princeton: Princeton University Press, 1979).

Jung, C. G. *Collected Works of C.G. Jung Volume 12: Psychology and Alchemy.* (Princeton: Princeton University Press, 1980).

Jung, C. G. *On the Nature of the Psyche* (Princeton: Princeton University Press, 1960).

Jung, C. G. *Psychological Types* (New York: Pantheon, 1953).

Jung, C. G. and Sabini, Meredith. *The Earth Has a Soul: The Nature Writings of C.G. Jung* (Berkeley: North Atlantic Books, 2002).

Kegan, Robert. *In over Our Heads: The Mental Demands of Modern Life* (Cambridge: Harvard University Press, 2003).

Krishnamurti, J. *Choiceless Awareness* (Ojai: Krishnamurti Foundation of America, 2000).

Kuhn, Thomas S. *The Structure of Scientific Revolutions, 2nd ed* (Chicago: The University of Chicago Press, 1970).

Laszlo, Ervin. *Evolution: The Grand Synthesis* (Boston: Shambhala, 1987).

Levine, Stephen, and Ondrea Levine. *Embracing the Beloved: Relationship as a Path of Awakening* (Dublin: Gateway, 2002).

Lusthaus, Dan. "Sāṃkhya" (2018). http://www.acmuller.net/yogacara/schools/samkhya.html.

McIntosh, Steve. *Developmental Politics: How America Can Grow into a Better Version of Itself* (St. Paul: Paragon House, 2020).

McIntosh, Steve. *Integral Consciousness and the Future of Evolution* (St. Paul: Paragon House, 2007).

Mansfield, Stephen. *Mansfield's Book of Manly Men* (Nashville: Nelson Books, 2013).

Miller, Earl K et al. "The prefrontal cortex: categories, concepts and cognition." *Philosophical transactions of the Royal Society of London. Series B, Biological sciences* vol. 357,1424 (2002): 1123-36. doi:10.1098/rstb.2002.1099.

McLeod, Sean. "Maslow's Hierarchy of Needs." (2005, updated 2020). https://www.simplypsychology. org/maslow.html.

Masters, Robert Augustus. *Spiritual Bypassing: When Spirituality Disconnects Us from What Really Matters* (Berkeley: North Atlantic Books, 2010).

Matt, Daniel. "Ayin: the concept of nothingness in Jewish mysticism." In L. Fine (ed.), *Essential Papers on Kabbalah* (New York: New York University Press, 1995).

Macy, Joanna, and Molly Young Brown. *Coming Back to Life* (Gabriola Island: New Society Publishers, 2019).

Maslow, A. H. "A theory of human motivation." *Psychological Review*, 50(4), 370–396. (1943) doi:10.1037/h0054346

Maturana, Humberto R., and Francisco J. Varela. *Autopoiesis and Cognition: The Realization of the Living* (Dordrecht: D. Reidel Publishing Company, 1980).

Mayr, Ernst. *Toward a New Philosophy of Biology: Observations of an Evolutionist* (Cambridge: Harvard University Press, 1988).

Metzner, Ralph. *Ecology of Consciousness: The Alchemy of Personal, Collective, and Planetary Transformation* (Oakland: Reveal Press, 2017).

Mickey, Sam, et al. *The Variety of Integral Ecologies: Nature, Culture, and Knowledge in the Planetary Era* (Albany: State University of New York Press, 2017).

Mill, John Stuart. *On Liberty* (Kitchener: Batoche Books, 2001).

Moore, Robert, and Douglas Gillette. *The King within: Accessing the King in the Male Psyche* (New York: William Morrow and Company, 1992).

Moore, Robert, and Douglas Gillette. *The Magician within: Accessing the Shaman in the Male Psyche* (New York: William Morrow and Company, 1993).

Moore, Robert, and Max J. Havlick. *The Archetype of Initiation: Sacred Space, Ritual Process, and Personal Transformation: Lectures and Essays* (Xlibris Corp., 2001).

Mukitbodhananda. *Hatha Yoga Pradipika* (Munger: Yoga Publications Trust, 1998).

Naess, Arne. *The Ecology of Wisdom: Writings by Arne Naess* (New York: Counterpoint, 2010).

Nāgārjuna. *Root Stanzas of the Middle Way: The Mulamadhyamakakarika* (Boulder: Shambhala, 2016).

Nāgārjuna, translated by Gelongma Karma Migme Chödrön. Sarvāstivādin-Sautrāntika Debate on Time. From the *Maha Prajnaparamita Sastra* (Berkeley: University of California Press, 1984).

Neihardt, John, et al. *Black Elk Speaks the Complete Edition* (Lincoln: University of Nebraska Press, 2014)

Nicholson, Sarah E., and Fisher, Vanessa D. *Integral Voices on Sex, Gender, and Sexuality (SUNY series in Integral Theory)* (Albany: State University of New York Press, 2014).

Nielsen, Joyce McCarl. *Sex and Gender in Society: Perspectives on Stratification* (Prospect Heights: Waveland Press, 1990).

Nietzsche, Friedrich. *The Gay Science* (Cambridge: Cambridge University Press, 2001).

Philo, et al. *Philo* (Cambridge: Harvard Univ. Press, 1929).

Pine, Red. *The Lankavatara Sutra: A Zen Text* (Berkeley: Counterpoint, 2013).

Plank, Liz. *For the Love of Men: From toxic to a more mindful masculinity* (New York: St. Martin's Griffin, 2019).

Plato, and Benjamin Jowett. *Dialogues of Plato* (Cambridge: Cambridge University Press, 2010).

Plato, and Benjamin Jowett. *Symposium* (Project Gutenberg, 2013).

Plotkin, Bill. *Nature and the Human Soul: Cultivating Wholeness and Community in a Fragmented World* (Novato:New World Library, 2008).

Pratt-Chadwick, Mara L. *Myths of Old Greece: Volume II* (Boston: Educational Pub. Company, 1896).

Prigogine, Ilya. "Time, Structure, and Fluctuations." Nobel Lecture (December 8, 1977).

de Quincey, Christian. "Consciousness All the Way Down? A Critique of Panexperientialism." *Journal of Consciousness Studies*, 1(2):217–229.

Ray, Reginald A. *Secret of the Vajra World: The Tantric Buddhism of Tibet* (Boulder: Shambhala, 2002).

Rosado, Raúl Quinones, PhD. *Consciousness-in-Action, Toward an Integral Psychology of Liberation & Transformation* (Caguas: ilé Publications, 2007).

Rosenberg, Marshall B. *Nonviolent Communication: A Language of Life* (Encinitas: Puddledancer Press, 2015).

Rudhyar, Dane. *The Planetarization of Consciousness: From the Individual to the Whole 2nd ed* (Santa Fe: Aurora Press, 1977).

Sanday, Peggy Reeves. *Female Power and Male Dominance: On the Origins of Sexual Inequality* (Cambridge: Cambridge University Press, 1981).

Schneider, Michael S. *A Beginner's Guide to Constructing the Universe* (New York: HarperCollins, 1994).

Sheldrake, Rupert. *The Presence of the Past: Morphic Resonance and the Memory of Nature* (Rochester: Park Street Press, 1995).

Stanton, Elizabeth Cady. "Seneca Falls Keynote Address" (1848).

Sullivan, Nikki. *A Critical Introduction to Queer Theory* (New York: NYU Press, 2003).

Swimme, Brian, and Thomas Berry. *The Universe Story* (New York: HarperCollins Publishers, 1994).

Tarnas, Richard. *Cosmos and Psyche: Intimations of a New World View* (Viking Penguin, 2006).

Taylor, Jeremy. *The Wisdom of Your Dreams: Using Dreams to Tap into Your Unconscious and Transform Your Life* (New York: Jeremy P. Tarcher / Penguin, 1992).

Trungpa Chögyam, et al. *Cutting through Spiritual Materialism* (Boulder: Shambhala, 2008).

Trungpa Chögyam, et al. *The Myth of Freedom and the Way of Meditation* (Boulder: Shambhala, 2005).

Turner, Victor W. *The Ritual Process: Structure and Anti-Structure* (Ithica: Cornell Paperbacks, 1977).

Underhill, Evelyn. *Mysticism: The Preeminent Study in the Nature and Development of Spiritual Consciousness* (Grand Rapids: Christian Classics Ethereal Library, 1930).

Van Vugt, Mark, et al. "Gender Differences in Cooperation and Competition: the Male-Warrior Hypothesis." *Psychological Science.* Vol 18 No 1 2007 10.1111/j.1467-9280.2007.01842.x

Wade, Jenny. *Transcendent Sex: When Lovemaking Opens the Veil* (New York: Paraview, 2004).

Walby, Sylvia. *Theorizing Patriarchy* (Oxford: Basil Blackwell Limited, 1991).

Wallis, Christopher. *Tantra Illuminated: The Philosophy, History, and Practice of a Timeless Tradition* (Petaluma: Mattamayura Press, 2013).

Warren, William Fairfield. *The Earliest Cosmologies* (New York: Eaten & Mains, 1909).

Weinberg, Steven. *First Three Minutes: A Modern View of the Origin of the Universe* (New York: Basic Books, 1993).

Westcott, W. W., & Nagy, A. *Sepher Yetzirah, or the Book of Creation: Understanding the Gra Tree and Kabbalah* (Ancient Wisdom Publications, 2010).

White, T. H. *The Once and Future King* (London: Collins, 1959).

Whitehead, Alfred North. *Process and Reality* (New York: Free Press, 1978).

Whitehead, Alfred North. *Science and the Modern World: Lowell Lectures, 1925* (London: Cambridge University Press, 1929).

Wilber, Ken. *The Eye of Spirit* (Boulder: Shambhala, 1997).

Wilber, Ken. *The Religion of Tomorrow: A Vision for the Future of the Great Traditions: More Inclusive, More Comprehensive, More Complete* (Boulder: Shambhala, 2018).

Wilber, Ken. *Sex, Ecology, Spirituality: The Spirit of Evolution* (Boulder: Shambhala, 2000).

Young-Eisendrath, Pauline. "Ego Development: Inferring the Client's Frame of Reference." Social Casework, vol. 63, no. 6, June 1982, pp. 323–332, doi:10.1177/104438948206300601.

Zuckerman, Ben, and Matthew Arnold Malkan. *Origin and Evolution of the Universe: From Big Bang to Exobiology, 2nd ed* (Singapore: World Scientific Publishing, 2020).

ABOUT LIVING KOSMOS

Living Kosmos represents a self-worldview that is

vital, alive, evolving and inter-connected.

This is an invitation to experience living beyond dualism, beyond materialism and beyond secularism. We recognize that the universe isn't simply *out there*, but that it's also *in here*... which is to say, we are an embodiment of the living, breathing, creative, growing universe – the kosmos in its process of becoming.

Living Kosmos is the embodied recognition of our participation in the creative advance of the universe, life, and consciousness. I founded the school, *Living Kosmos*, in 2020 when I powerfully stepped into this self-worldview myself. During the great pandemic pause, I undertook initiation into the Western Mystery Tradition, immersed into Ken Wilber's Integral Theory, and moved to Kaua'i. The interweaving of these three threads catalyzed the birth of Living Kosmos as a vehicle for me to share the path of active co-creation in the evolution of consciousness.

The **foundational tenets** of Living Kosmos are as follows:

1. The entirety of the kosmos is simultaneously diverse and whole. Nonduality, meaning not-two, signifies the essential continuity of reality that unites opposites, embraces paradox, and

welcomes us as individuals into our home here. I am not separate from the kosmos. I not only belong here, but everything that I encounter is essentially *of me*. The kosmos is alive because I am alive. The kosmos is conscious because I am conscious. I am, you are, an intelligent, living, breathing kosmos. We are self-reflective universe!

2. This kosmos contains (at least) four realms of beingness. *(1) Objective exterior* dimensions are measured by the hard sciences; *(2) subjective interior* dimensions are the domains of psychology and mysticism; *(3) collective exteriors* which contain emergent systems, populations, ecosystems, and societies that cannot be described solely by the interactions of individual members; and *(4) collective interiors* of cultures, values, and shared identity. It is possible to be scientific about each of these domains, which unites diverse modes of knowledge production including science and spirituality. This is known as the *Four Quadrant Model* from Integral Theory which incorporates *panexperientialism* (i.e., every entity has both an objective exterior and a subjective interior of experience).

3. Our kosmos is meaningful. We inhabit a *pansemiotic* reality where every phenomena and every experience across all levels fundamentally carries meaning. Physical matter is encoded light. Biological organisms are encoded aliveness. Human communication is encoded reflexive consciousness. The most fundamental and universal patterns of meaning are the archetypes. By studying the archetypes (such as the tarot deck, religious symbolism, and mythology), we not only learn about the workings of the kosmos, but we can use the archetypes as a bridge to experience the power and diversity of our reality.

4. We live in an evolving universe. As Brian Swimme put it, "If you let hydrogen gas alone for 13 billion years it will become giraffes, rose bushes and humans." This evolution spans physical, biological, and psycho-spiritual dimensions. Evolution is a process of creativity that exhibits directionality toward greater degrees of complexity and wholeness. The developmental drive to advance is *Eros:* our innate capacity to learn and grow. The drive to embrace is *Agape:* our integrating compassion. The interaction of Eros and Agape produces an ongoing creativity across every scale: *a kosmogenesis.*

This represents a radical metaphysical framework and self-worldview – one that psychoactively transforms the student by studying it. In order to step into a new reality, I need to inhabit a new me. **The mission of Living Komsos is to shepherd the transformation of human consciousness.** In recognition of the nondual, panexperiential, pansemiotic, evolutionary nature of the kosmos, our mission is to support individuals to align to these processes – to allow life to unfold through us.

In order to support this mission, we hold the following **five principles**:

1. **Nonviolence.** Through our courses and transformational containers, we do not cause harm. This includes physical, emotional, and psycho-spiritual aspects for individuals, and community, cultural, and ecosystemic aspects of the collectives that we inhabit. Nonviolence means supporting individuals and groups to meet their needs.

2. **Sustainability.** Meeting our own needs today – the goal of nonviolence – is one half of the equation for sustainability. The second component is to do so without impairing the capacity of future generations and all beings everywhere to meet their needs.

3. **Organicity.** Life naturally moves toward healing and well-being. Each individual, when engaging in sustainable processes, will innately move toward their own wholeness and growth. This process leads to ever greater degrees of creative liberation, which I call *eleutheropoeisis*. We recognize that each individual knows what is best for them. Our role as practitioners and teachers is to support the unfolding of life's wisdom through each participant.

4. **Inclusion.** Grounded in the awareness of our coextensive nondual nature, we welcome all participants who align with these principles. We celebrate diversity and learn through integrating contrasting perspectives. In addition, we recognize that every mode of knowledge production is at least partially true. Every religion, every science, and every philosophy contains a kernel of truth and therefore holds an inherent dignity for consideration. Simultaneously, we recognize that within a developmental framework, some truths will be *more true* or *more comprehensive* than others. However, no truth is *fully and completely true* – it is always part of the ongoing advance which produces ever-greater truths.

5. **Humanness.** "Being human first" orients us to the path of awakening and development. Human consciousness affords us the opportunity to explore countless realms, planes, and states – and this is our birthright. However, we recognize that we came here to be a human in this 3D reality: ordinary, mundane, and imperfect. By choosing to be human, we embrace the messy, wounded aspects of ourselves and this world. Centering in our embodied humanness, we open to receive the entire kosmos into our hearts without dissociation or bypass. Human first is a commitment to inhabit our lives as both the practice and the path.

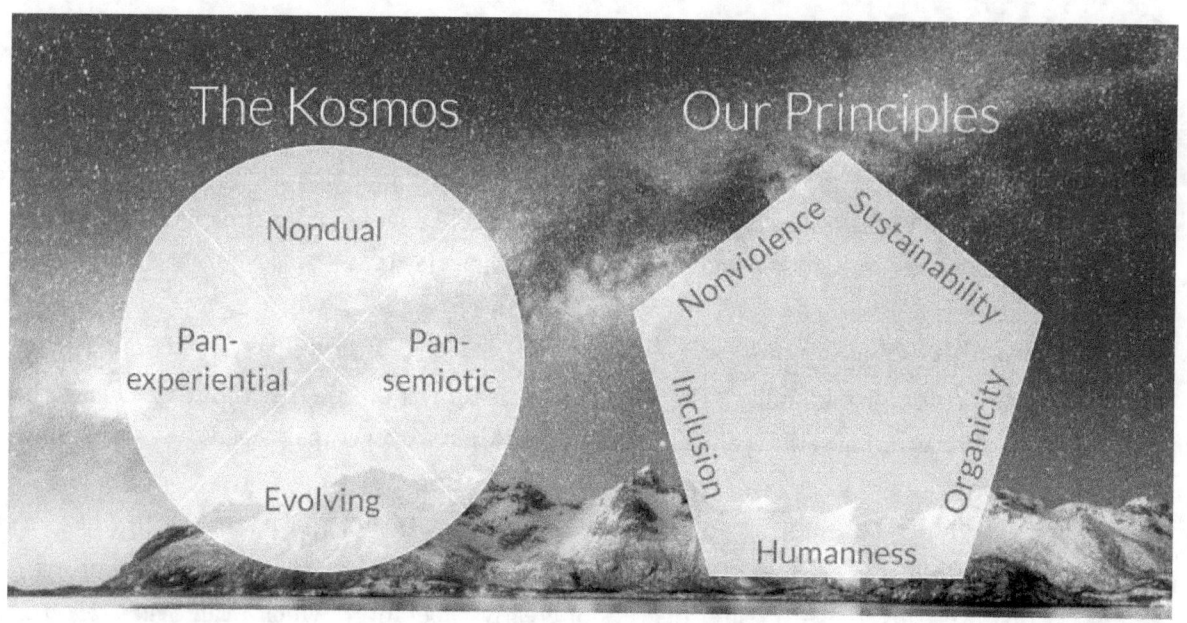

Welcome to Living Kosmos!

livingkosmos.com

ABOUT MATT

Matt Sturm is a guide for transformational experiences. I work with people to slow down, to come into their bodies, and to connect to their innate inner wisdom. I hold a strong, clear container for healing, intimacy, and spiritual awakening within a variety of contexts. These include psychotherapy, psychedelic-assisted therapy, sacred sexuality, breathwork journeys, and men's retreats. I run the Living Kosmos integral mystery school, focusing on the evolution of consciousness at the intersection of science and spirituality. Through the online programs in Living Kosmos, I teach about Integral Theory, the tarot archetypes and the Western Mystery tradition, kundalini awakening, and more.